SECRETS OF SUCCESS

THE SCIENCE

AND SPIRIT OF

REAL PROSPERITY

Also by Sandra Anne Taylor

Quantum Success:
The Astounding Science of Wealth and Happiness*
Secrets of Attraction:
The Universal Laws of Love, Sex, and Romance*

Guided-Visualization Audio Tapes and CDs

Act to Attract (9-CD audio seminar and workbook)
Attracting Love
Attracting Success
Cellular Regression: Timeless Healing
Planting Your Destiny Garden
Relaxation and Memory Release
Successful Weight Loss
Your Sacred Identity
Healing Journeys

Also by Sharon Anne Klingler

Intuition & Beyond
Life with Spirit
The Magic of Gemstones and Colors
GemCast, the Astro-Oracle Kit
(with book, gemstones & casting chart)

Guided Visualizations, Audiotapes, and CD Programs

Speaking to Spirit (8-CD audio seminar with workbook, journal,
and Sharon's book *Life with Spirit*)
Drawing on Your Intuition
(kit with instruction book, CD, and colored pencils)
Divine Connections
Healing Journeys
Higher Realms, Higher Powers
Openings
Speaking to Spirit Meditations
Spirit Comes to Life!
Working with the Masters
Meet Your Angels and Guides
Reading the Signs
Travel into Your Past Lives

*Available from Hay House

Please visit Hay House USA: **www.hayhouse.com**®
Hay House Australia: **www.hayhouse.com.au**
Hay House UK: **www.hayhouse.co.uk**
Hay House South Africa: **www.hayhouse.co.za**
Hay House India: **www.hayhouse.co.in**

SECRETS OF SUCCESS

THE SCIENCE

AND SPIRIT OF

REAL PROSPERITY

SANDRA ANNE TAYLOR
AND
SHARON A. KLINGLER

HAY HOUSE, INC.
Carlsbad, California • New York City
London • Sydney • Johannesburg
Vancouver • Hong Kong • New Delhi

Copyright © 2008 by Sandra Anne Taylor and Sharon A. Klingler

Published and distributed in the United States by: Hay House, Inc.: www.hayhouse.com
Published and distributed in Australia by: Hay House Australia Pty. Ltd.: www.hayhouse.
com.au • **Published and distributed in the United Kingdom by:** Hay House UK, Ltd.:
www.hayhouse.co.uk • **Published and distributed in the Republic of South Africa by:**
Hay House SA (Pty), Ltd.: www.hayhouse.co.za •**Distributed in Canada by:** Rain-
coast: www.raincoast.com • **Published in India by:** Hay House Publishers India: www.
hayhouse.co.in

Editorial supervision: Jill Kramer • *Design:* Riann Bender

All rights reserved. No part of this book may be reproduced by any mechanical,
photographic, or electronic process, or in the form of a phonographic recording; nor
may it be stored in a retrieval system, transmitted, or otherwise be copied for public
or private use—other than for "fair use" as brief quotations embodied in articles and
reviews—without prior written permission of the publisher.

The authors of this book do not dispense medical advice or prescribe the use
of any technique as a form of treatment for physical, emotional, or medical problems without the advice of a physician, either directly or indirectly. The intent of the
authors is only to offer information of a general nature to help you in your quest for
emotional and spiritual well-being. In the event you use any of the information in this
book for yourself, which is your constitutional right, the authors and the publisher
assume no responsibility for your actions.

Library of Congress Cataloging-in-Publication Data

Taylor, Sandra Anne.
  Secrets of success : the science and spirit of real prosperity / Sandra Anne Taylor
and Sharon A. Klingler. -- 1st ed.
    p. cm.
  ISBN-13: 978-1-4019-1911-5 (pbk.)
  1. Success. I. Klingler, Sharon A. II. Title.
  BF637.S8T2845 2008
  131--dc22   2007051381

ISBN: 978-1-4019-1911-5

11 10 09 08   5 4 3 2
1st edition, June 2008
2nd edition, July 2008

Printed in the United States of America

For our incredible mother, Sarah Marie Klingler—
our generous, caring, fun, and fantastic friend!

★★★

CONTENTS

FOREWORD

BY CANDACE PERT, PH.D.

My connection with Sandra Taylor has been filled with one synchronicity after another. Just when I finished my second book, *Everything You Need to Know to Feel Go(o)d,* I was asked to write a sample interview about it for use in publicity. To give me an idea of what she was looking for, my publicist at Hay House sent me the interviews that had been done by other authors, and one of those was the one Sandra Taylor did for her book *Quantum Success.*

The four-page synopsis was so interesting that I carried it around with me for days, reading it over and over again. Finally, it dawned on me—why keep reading just those few pages when I could get the entire book? I soon found myself devouring the whole thing and experiencing many moments of realization. I was struck by the structure and clarity of Sandy's approach, and the facility with which she applied some complex scientific principles to the arena of personal achievement. My son Evan liked the principles, too. He'd come to visit me and had seen Sandy's book on the table. He'd been having problems finding the loving relationship that he wanted, so he started reading. He liked *Quantum Success* so much that he took it with him when he left—even though I hadn't finished it yet!

One of the things that hit home for me the most was the concept of paradoxical intent—something I'd never seen explained anywhere else. This is the phenomenon whereby we block our attraction because we get so desperate to make our goals happen. Our negative, needy energy actually pushes our desires away. When I read that, I realized I was smack dab in the middle of my own paradoxical intent.

My husband, Mike Ruff, and I had been researching a peptide treatment for AIDS. We had also made some significant advances in developing a vaccine and had formed our own company to continue the research and clinical trials. However, we were having trouble getting the funding necessary to continue our work. It had been so frustrating—every time it seemed as though something good was going to happen, some hurdle appeared and the bar was raised higher. I hadn't realized it, but the more things dragged on, the more desperate I was becoming. After all, Mike and I had spent 20 years on this approach, and it was taking too long.

But in reading *Quantum Success*, I realized what kind of resistant energy my desperation was creating. Besides making me (and Mike) miserable, it was actually pushing away the longed-for funding! I decided I wanted to talk to Sandy about it, so I contacted my editor, Jill Kramer, who connected us. After several e-mails, Sandy and I finally spoke in September 2006. I remember that it was a beautiful Saturday morning and I was in my hot tub looking at the fall foliage when she called.

It was great to finally connect voice-to-voice. I found out that Sandy was as excited to meet me as I was to meet her. She told me that after seeing me in the movie *What the Bleep Do We Know!?* she was compelled to buy my first book, *Molecules of Emotion*. This led to her research of neuropeptides, which she included in *Quantum Success*.

We instantly hit it off, talking and laughing like we'd known each other forever. I spoke to her about my concerns and frustrations over not getting the funding, and she encouraged me, giving me some advice about how I could look at things differently and change my energy around that issue.

I also told Sandy about Evan's search for love, and she sent him her *Act to Attract* audio seminar, which he started listening to right away. The ninth CD has a guided visualization called "Attracting Love," in which listeners send the energetic hologram of their higher selves out into the Universe to attract their ideal partners. Believe it or not, after less than a week of doing that process, Evan met the simple love of his life! Of course, he'd been working on changing his energy since he started the book, but even Sandy said it was a high-speed attraction record!

After seeing Evan's success, I was determined to apply the principles myself. Little by little, I noticed some changes taking place. I became far less urgent about the funding, yet even more focused and determined. I had several conversations with Sandy, and we even planned a joint speaking engagement for the following summer.

Six months later, when Sandy called about our event, I had amazing news for her. A private investor came through with all the money needed to set up the research program! After years, the goal that Mike and I had been working toward had finally manifested. When I told Sandy that it was all because of *Quantum Success,* she giggled self-effacingly, but it's true. The principles that she teaches really work and have changed our lives!

I finally met Sandy in person when we spoke together at Lily Dale, New York. It was a wonderful weekend, and Mike and I got to know Sandy; her husband; and her sister, Sharon. In fact, even before we met Sharon, we were able to see her demonstrating her mediumship at an outdoor message service. Without knowing who Mike was, she gave him an amazingly accurate message; she honed right in on exactly what he was dealing with, providing advice that was right on. We were both utterly amazed at how a perfect stranger could give such specific and applicable information.

In addition to having incredible intuitive powers, Sharon has brought her considerable expertise to this book, adding her profoundly spiritual wisdom and many inspiring techniques, showing how to use this power effectively. She explains how the energy of spirit is available to help you have a successful life and open up the unlimited potential all around you!

What I love about this book is that it really gets to the root of that unlimited field of potential—and it all starts within. Through quantum psychology, Sandy investigates how your past is energetically connected to your future. More important, she reveals some very direct ways to dramatically reverse the patterns you've been living with for so long, changing the very structure of your thoughts and emotions, the core of your life force. That's the message here, and it's one that so many books miss. It's your life force, the power of your full energy—not wishful thinking—that really gets the results.

I've experienced those results in my career and my family! After several stagnant and unfulfilling relationships, my son found a wonderful girl, a potential soul mate, through using these techniques. And Mike and I finally got the funding for our research, which not only changed our lives, but (it's my intention) will change the lives of millions.

Perhaps my husband, Mike, a consummate scientist, put it best when he said, "The day Sandra Taylor came into our lives, miracles started to happen." It's true! I encourage you to open your heart to the wisdom in these pages; make the changes—you can do it—and soon you'll be seeing miracles in your own life, too.

INTRODUCTION

MATTERS OF THE MIND

BY SANDRA ANNE TAYLOR

In 1908, a man named William Walker Atkinson wrote a short book called *The Secret of Success,* in which he discussed the Law of Attraction, a natural law driven by desire and mental imagery. Now, a century later, the whole world is talking about this same concept. The difference is that in the past hundred years, we've learned quite a lot about the science of energy and consciousness creation.

It's the science that I find so compelling—more accurately, it's the human application of that science that's so very liberating and empowering. I've been teaching these astounding principles for 25 years. My first book, *Secrets of Attraction,* examined how personal energy determines romantic experience. My second book, *Quantum Success,* explored all of the Laws of Attraction, the magnetic energies, and the powers of consciousness involved in the pursuit of success. But in this book I want to go deeper and broader—to investigate the concepts of attraction and manifestation in a more holistic fashion.

Back in 1985, I read a book called *The Holographic Paradigm and Other Paradoxes,* a compilation of many articles by and about various scientists and leaders in the study of consciousness. It provided me with a wonderful new model for understanding my life and the workings of the world around me. At that time, I was working in a private psychological practice, and I started teaching the principles of quantum physics and the holographic model of consciousness to my clients. I soon discovered that people's psychology is largely responsible for their energetic action in the Universe; and if they could apply these principles, they could change the vibration of their *quantum psychology*—and transform their life results at the same time.

Quantum psychology is the study of how your mental and emotional patterns influence your destiny creation. It reveals the inextricable connection between mind and manifestation. As you'll see throughout this book, the results of your life aren't merely determined by a single desire. They depend on your whole life force, with the workings of your mind smack at the center of your personal vortex of energy.

Your consciousness reaches across time and space and connects with Universal consciousness to influence your destiny and that of the world. As a result, your attraction lies in becoming aware of the very real powers of your mind. I've seen in countless cases—in my life and in my clients'—that when the mental changes are made, personal happiness and many successful results soon follow.

Part I of this book focuses on the three major elements of the manifestation process: consciousness, energy, and intention. Having a more holistic understanding of these dynamic personal powers gives you much greater control where your magnetic vibration is concerned. More important, it promotes a life-driven pursuit of joy rather than a limited, goal-driven hunt for specific outcomes. This vibration of joy is really what success is all about—and it will attract much more of what you desire.

To me, an honest and holistic look at manifestation and attraction must include the presence and assistance of spirit. I'm happy that my twin sister, Sharon A. Klingler, joins me in writing Part II of this book, which covers this subject in depth. Sharon is a world-renowned intuitive who lectures internationally about how to access the spiritual realm for guidance and assistance in every area of life. She's sought after for her amazing accuracy and mediumship skills, and her clients come from across the globe and from all walks of life, including Hollywood stars and international politicians. She has been teaching her techniques for more than 30 years, and they've been life changing for me and countless others.

The spirit is so easily dismissed by so many, yet it's a considerable part of our energetic power! So if you want to speed up your results and create a truly blissful life, practice the exercises that Sharon teaches. I've used many of her intuitive processes to get immediate answers when making important decisions. I myself have received such incredible support from the spirit realm—in both my personal and professional life—that this has become one of my most important priorities. So I sincerely recommend that you make some pursuit of this kind a very real part of your daily life.

There are many self-investigative processes in this book. Several are similar in structure, but focus on different issues. Give yourself time to do them all—and repeat them whenever the goblins of fear or doubt creep in. Keep a journal to record your reactions and to work on these exercises; also use it to vent emotional energy and align your thinking.

Chapter 14 has a section on journal writing—please refer to it when you feel ready to look more deeply into the issues discussed. There are many places throughout the book that recommend using a journal to help sort out the details. The purpose is to do this investigative work in a more analytical way, allowing you to see your responses more clearly and to refer back to the personal information and the thought changes whenever the need may arise. I find this enormously helpful when trying to make real changes in my life.

The daily journal form recommended in Chapter 14 will also help you keep track of your intentions, your consciousness focus, and your energy production. I advise setting up a personal-success journal now to record your impressions and respond to the suggested exercises. It's well worth the effort. In addition, the final chapter has a list of affirmations and intentions. Use them every day to keep your energy high.

In Part III, I've included some of the questions that have been most commonly asked regarding the process of personal manifestation and the Laws of Attraction. It seems that the more this information is spread, the more concerns people have about it. I've tried to answer those queries based on the science, psychology, and prevalent patterns I've seen while working with my clients. It's my hope that throughout these pages, you'll find the answers you're looking for, and that they'll help move you forward in peace and happiness to the real fulfillment of your dreams.

I've attempted to address the key elements that are needed to create a full life force of vitally attractive energy. It's important to turn attraction and manifestation from mere idealistic concepts into viable daily practices—to understand that joy in everyday life is the source of real prosperity. Instead of being just a desperate materialistic pursuit, your entire existence can vibrate with blissful energy and emotional success.

That's what I hope this book will do for you—bring the irresistible power of real happiness into your daily experience. The full spectrum of your life turns upon this very moment. Your present choice to live in joy, courage, and grateful celebration spreads success in every direction. With that as your core vibration, don't be surprised when the blessings of the material world start to magically flow your way.

PART I

LIFE, LAW, FORCE, AND FUTURE

by Sandra Anne Taylor

CHAPTER 1

FORCES OF CONSCIOUSNESS

"Consciousness Creation is about the power of our thoughts to create the life we wish to experience."

— Dr. Wayne W. Dyer

What have you created today? Whether you realize it or not, you've been very busy in the act of creation. Perhaps you've been hard at work or maybe just hanging out "doing nothing," but either way you've actually been forging your future. This ongoing construction of your destiny is taking place every moment of every hour of your life, and the most significant source of your future invention is your own individual consciousness.

The Universe is a sparkling river of unending potential, one that flows with both purpose and serendipity; its seemingly random direction leads to very specific outcomes. In this unending paradox, which is the background of our earthly experience, there's a power that can't be denied—the power of consciousness. Consciousness is a force that exists outside of time and moves freely through the Universe (although there's some discussion about whether it moves from place to place or merely exists—and exerts its influence—in all places at the same time).

It has long been known in the quantum physical world that consciousness creates reality. Fascinating theories that discuss this principle have been applied to the measurement of light, the formation of the cosmos, and even the life (and death) of a cat! I recommend a look through the Suggested Reading section at the end of this book to see a list of works that describe how this incredible line of thinking functions in the physical world. For our purposes here, however, we'll be focusing on how *consciousness-created reality* influences your personal life and career experiences.

> *Your life force reaches beyond this time and space into unknown quadrants of existence. The consciousness that you project in the form of thought, perception, vision, and expectation has a very real impact in the world. While you may be unaware of what your consciousness is doing in distant places, you can—at a glance—become keenly aware of how it's shaping your life. In fact, most of what you see and experience is a result of your own consciousness creation.*

This is the function of the Law of Manifestation, a law that works the same way in the Universe as it does in your daily existence. It reveals a fundamental truth in the cosmos: Consciousness does create reality. This is globally true, and your individual consciousness can't be exempt from its implications. *Consciousness-created reality* governs all types of manifestation —from conjuring up a funny joke to affecting the world economy. Consciousness is always the originating element.

It can be very liberating to finally realize that your consciousness is the primary generator of the situations and people that make up the tapestry of your life. Over time, you can see how each experience follows the patterns of your powerful, yet predictable, consciousness output. And if you don't like the trends you've been experiencing, at least there's something you can do about it. You can shift your consciousness projection so that you can determine for yourself exactly what you want to create.

Hologram of Self

From quantum physics to biomechanics, the hologram has been used as a model for such complex things as the nature of the Universe and the workings of the brain. A hologram is a three-dimensional picture that's created when a laser beam is split in two; the first beam is reflected off an object, and the second beam is directed to collide with the light of the first. The "picture" on the film—or plate—is a record of this light-interference pattern. Unlike a normal negative, the holographic film looks like a mishmash of circles, rings, and wavy lines. However, when another laser light is beamed through that film, a three-dimensional picture is formed, revealing all aspects of the original subject. A hologram isn't limited to two dimensions; the picture shows what's behind and on every side of the object being photographed.

The fascinating properties of this phenomenon don't stop there. If you were to cut the holographic negative into pieces, an entire three-dimensional image would be revealed by directing a laser through any one of those fragments. No matter what scrap you chose, the entire image would be revealed over and over again. No matter how small the piece—or its place on the film—the hologram would reveal the entire picture: front, back, and sides.

This irreducible, three-dimensional element is why the hologram is used to represent the many nuances of consciousness, and why it's an apt representation of how your own individual consciousness works in the world. You're like that wavy, undefinable picture on the film because your full consciousness isn't really visible on the surface. It's only when you shine a light on your own true nature that you see the real and full picture of your consciousness creation. It's not just your individual desires or intentions that get projected out into the world; it's the many dimensions of your personal consciousness that will create your destiny.

This is the undeniable truth of your consciousness-created reality. All of you—everything that you're conscious of—gets projected into the cosmic formation of your future. And what becomes manifest reflects the innermost recesses of your personal worldview.

This holistic nature of the process of attraction and manifestation requires you to look much more deeply than simply focusing on what you want. It's not enough to have a single-minded intention, for that's only part of the process. The pursuit of happiness and success—no matter what the arena—calls for an honest look at the energy of your entire life. Your consciousness is a picture of your whole self. It's not just the surface information that you choose to reveal; it's also the multidimensional representation of who you *really are*—everything from your most deeply held beliefs to idiosyncratic behaviors. All that is *you* broadcasts your truth in waves of thought-forms, perceptions, and expectations.

So your investigation into your destiny creation must start with this question: If you were to project a laser light through the hologram that is your own consciousness, what would that picture hold? What would be revealed in the front, in the middle, in the back, and all the way around? Would there be a confident image on the surface with fear hiding behind it? Would there be an exterior of optimism with an interior of doubt? If so, you need to know that the Universe sees your entire truth—every bit of it—and responds accordingly.

So if you're visualizing meeting your perfect partner, yet a part of you thinks such a person doesn't exist, then that consciousness of limitation overrides your specific intention and actually creates a stronger vision of lack. If you've created the goal to attract a better job but you consistently doubt your ability to make it happen, then that failure-consciousness will move out into the Universe, projecting a dark void where no real value can come to be.

Your entire consciousness needs to be considered. You may send out intentions, treasure maps, and even prayers to make something happen, but all of that will go unanswered if it's the only approach you take. Without a supportive consciousness, your individual desire will just float out in space, and your results will be hit-or-miss at best—or nonexistent at worst.

But if you add an optimistic and focused life force to your individual intentions, they'll be propelled by the irresistible power of consciousness creation. They'll shoot out into time and space, and the abundant Universe will send unexpected blessings in return. It's the power of your whole life—all that you are conscious of—that determines your present.

So what's *your* worldview? How do you perceive yourself and your place in this amazing Universe of ours? Whether you realize it or not, you *are* a powerful manifestor. You may not like what you've brought into being so far, but you have both the ability and the option to change everything. Happiness isn't a future commodity. It exists right now within the hologram of your eternal self, and it can be the accelerant that will ignite a future of endless joy.

Uncertain, Exciting, Unlimited Future

The *uncertainty principle* reveals that the Universe exists in a constant state of flow or flux. Anything can change at any given moment, and even a small shift in consciousness can create long-lasting and real results. The great news is that in spite of the holistic truth of consciousness-created reality, you don't have to feel stuck. By understanding your consciousness options, you can at any moment make an immediate shift that permeates the hologram of your entire life force. In this astounding Universe, time is not only malleable, it's ever present; and your genuine shift in heart-centered mentality can reach backward and forward in time to alter both your causes and your effects.

The word *mentality* may be misleading, however, because it's not merely an academic analysis of life that creates your consciousness. It's the whole mental and emotional filter through which you view the world. Although this may sound like a big thing to change, with some focus and attention in the right direction, it's absolutely doable. Linear time marches on, and since you're going to get from here to the future anyway, you might as well work on the changes that will not only shift your consciousness, but will also accelerate your desired outcomes.

Shifting your consciousness is the only way to get the results you want. The process of achieving success—although this may seem to reverse the order of things—comes from first moving into happiness as your core consciousness right now. You may seek success for the joy it will bring, but why wait? When you choose perceptions of peace, trust, and optimism within your present worldview, the brilliant vibrations of those existing emotions will—in perfect synchronicity—bring about the fulfillment of your specific dreams.

When I speak of your worldview, I don't mean your approach to politics or even to social issues, although those things are, of course, part of your hologram. What's much more important in terms of your destiny creation is your opinion of yourself and your place in the world—especially in how your value and power tend to play out in your experiences. If you see yourself as worthless or ineffectual, it will be very difficult to create the kind of consciousness that will bring about happiness or support your individual intentions. But keep in mind that you're always free to create a new view—to finally let go of the old perceptions that just don't fit with your new intentions.

Tracking Your Consciousness Patterns

There are several different types of consciousness that you could be engaging in at any given moment. The following eight pairs represent very different approaches to life. Each is a polar view of yourself and your power (or lack of it), both within your personal world and in your Universal experience. As you read through the descriptions, identify which type in each pair most accurately describes your attitude toward fundamental issues. You may find that you sometimes shift into the opposite point of view, but try to honestly identify which item in each set reflects your approach the most.

SOMEONE WITH A POVERTY CONSCIOUSNESS	SOMEONE WITH A SUCCESS CONSCIOUSNESS
Focuses on what's going wrong and often can't identify his goals	Focuses on what's going right, even if he's still working on his goals
Doesn't really know how to be happy; views himself as generally incapable	Looks for and creates happiness now; views it as a present pursuit
Sees success only in monetary terms; doesn't feel hopeful about any real success in the future	Acknowledges many kinds of success and expects more success in the future

SOMEONE WITH A LACK CONSCIOUSNESS	SOMEONE WITH A VALUE CONSCIOUSNESS
Focuses on what's missing and how there's never enough—both in his personal experience and in the world at large	Recognizes and acknowledges the value all around—both in his personal life and in the world
Is often self-critical and dismissive of his own value	Acknowledges the many levels of value within himself
Sees himself as cursed with bad luck; envies and is threatened by the success of others, thinking it reduces his chances	Appreciates all that he has and all that he is, and is happy for the success of others, knowing there's plenty to go around

SOMEONE WITH A LIMITATION CONSCIOUSNESS	SOMEONE WITH AN ABUNDANCE CONSCIOUSNESS
Believes the world is an empty, hopeless place	Sees an unlimited source of good available in the Universe
Assumes that the few good things in the world are never going to come to him	Is optimistic about what lies ahead and expects unforeseen blessings
Sees himself, his abilities, and his worthiness as limited and doesn't expect things to change in the future	Acknowledges his own resourcefulness, creativity, and worthiness as being unlimited, also

SOMEONE WITH A FEAR CONSCIOUSNESS	SOMEONE WITH A TRUST CONSCIOUSNESS
Filters much of his experiences through the expectation of problems, and even the likelihood of a catastrophe	Filters his life experience through an attitude of trust, hope, and optimism
Sees the world as threatening and unsafe; believes that he won't be able to handle it	Sees the world as relatively safe, and trusts that he'll be able to manage even the difficult things that may come up
Always tries to anticipate problems out of a need to control the outcome and prevent disaster	Lives in the present; is willing to take risks and move forward no matter what the outcome

SOMEONE WITH AN ANGER CONSCIOUSNESS	SOMEONE WITH A PEACE CONSCIOUSNESS
Looks for hostility and aggression from other people in his life and other groups in the world	Views his life and the world as comfortable and relatively tranquil
Often feels suspicious and feels the need to be defensive	Doesn't analyze others too much; feels peaceful around diverse groups of people
Is critical and controlling of others, yet is often arrogant himself	Is authentically empowered and doesn't have to demean or control others

SOMEONE WITH A HATE CONSCIOUSNESS	SOMEONE WITH A LOVE CONSCIOUSNESS
Always analyzes what's going on around him to ensure his power	Lives from the heart and tries to create harmony instead of competition
Sees others' differences as a problem or threat	Sees people as equals and their differences as safe
Uses personal, political, and social issues to create and promote conflict	Has a high regard for himself and for others, valuing other people and respecting their beliefs
Defines and gets his power through hatred and his need for superiority	Authentically empowers himself, seeing the value in all

SOMEONE WITH A VICTIM CONSCIOUSNESS	SOMEONE WITH A POWER CONSCIOUSNESS
Is submissive and powerless in his own life and in the world	Sees himself as the designer of his own destiny
Rarely takes action for himself; is often withdrawn and unwilling to ask for help	Always takes action on his own behalf; views the world as supportive
Is passive around others, seldom setting boundaries; is usually willing to sacrifice his own needs in order to please the people around him	Sets clear boundaries; is willing to ask for help, accept it graciously, and offer it willingly to others

SOMEONE WITH A COMPETITIVE CONSCIOUSNESS	SOMEONE WITH A CREATIVE CONSCIOUSNESS
Creates an adversarial role for himself and others	Is supportive of others and a team player
Feels that everyone should be out for themselves or be on guard	Sees things through the greater good and the bigger picture
Is ego driven and full of anger and stress	Is spirit driven, tranquil, and productive

Glancing down each of these lists, it's easy to see why embracing a life consciousness from the right column will go far in promoting your individual goals. In fact, the highest consciousness that you could create would be a combination of all of the attitudes on the right. Such genuine and lofty intentions will move you into a powerful—yet consistently peaceful—manifestation. This can only come from having an overarching, ever-present consciousness of joy and optimism as your holographic approach. It's equally easy to see, however, how thoughts from the left column—swirling in the holographic energy of your consciousness—would create conflicting vibrations and greatly reduce your likelihood of success.

A client of mine named Ray experienced this firsthand. His consciousness was filled with negativity, and his career results showed it. He'd struggled his whole life to create a business of his own. He moved from one type of company to another—first lawn care, next a carpet-cleaning service, and then several others—but they never seemed to pan out. He came to me in total frustration, trying figure out why he was never able to make things work.

When we examined his upbringing, the source of his problems became clear. He'd grown up in poverty as an only child, living in a trailer with his father, a laborer, and his mother, who was a cook. They were caring parents, but their fear and negativity had a very strong influence on him. They constantly told him how difficult life was and that people like them could never really succeed. One of his father's favorite sayings was "What's the use in trying? Nothing ever changes anyway."

Ray hadn't known two important things: First, he was living in a poverty consciousness—a self-perception and worldview that kept him stuck. Second, the mental and emotional focus that made up his psychological hologram reached out into the Universe, dictating his results and turning up enough failure to convince him that his fears were right!

Ray realized that he had to restructure his thinking and establish a whole new consciousness of abundance. Once that became clear, he also understood that he'd never really given any of his ventures a chance. His father's voice saying, "What's the use?" kept ringing in his head, causing him to give up long before he'd taken the time to really try. So he figured out which business he liked best, and he gave it another go. This time he saturated himself with attitudes of abundance and authentic power. He worked on transcending his childhood drama, and he released and changed every fear thought that came his way. He also gave himself time to ride out the difficult spots of a start-up business, and his patience and positive attitude paid off. Now he owns a successful carpet-cleaning company, and he has bought his parents their very first home.

If you're like Ray was, your general approach moves you from one toxic attitude to another. Your consciousness throws one negativity after another into the concoction that is your life force—with fear and lack bubbling in the cauldron of your destiny creation. Such a miserable worldview sends out a dark, damning energy that permeates every part of your holographic projection, calling forth deeper unhappiness in your destiny.

But you *do* have the power to change this. Since thought is the source, it's also the solution, so don't despair! You don't have to stay stuck in a black hole of vibration. You can start right now to establish a consciousness of joy, and your intention to do so will *immediately* be noted in the energetic realm.

Holographic Projection

Perhaps the most famous early holographic projection took place in *Star Wars,* back in 1977. In the scene, a moving hologram of Princess Leia is projected into the middle of the room; and a clear, three-dimensional image shows her asking for help. The Universe replies, and the day is saved—only to be threatened again in several more films.

You may not be aware of it—and you don't need an android to deliver it—but *you* project such messages all the time. Your hologram is a clear, vibrating picture of your beliefs and expectations, sending the Universe a very precise depiction of who you are. This transmission is always going on, and it's the way your inner truth connects with the world of manifestation.

When I first realized the full importance of this, I was in my 30s and going through my second divorce. I knew I had to do something different, but I wasn't sure exactly what I needed to fix where my energy was concerned. So I decided to start sending out a conscious projection. I visualized my higher Self in the form of a three-dimensional hologram, adding the energies that I prioritized—and the ones I wanted to attract in a partner. I imagined qualities such as integrity, loving communication, and respect, vibrating within my own higher Self. I put all these great frequencies in my own hologram and then sent it out into the Universe, intending it to connect with my ideal partner. I also created the intention to live with those healthy frequencies in my daily life—in my thoughts, my choices, and my self-talk. It didn't take long! After doing this imagery every day for about six months, I met my present husband—a wonderful man who mirrors all that energy.

I knew that I was always sending out a holographic projection anyway, and I realized that was what created my results. So I designed this exercise to shift my energy, to focus on more positive vibrations, and to project an entirely new picture of myself and my expectations. In the process, I established a healthy self-view—knowing that to attract real love I needed to feel it for myself. For love is a key vibration, and it formulates a most powerful hologram.

Take a moment to envision a hologram of yourself. What does it look like? What does the energy feel like? Now think of all the wonderful feelings and positive qualities you'd possess if you already had every success you wanted. Begin to see all those vibrations filling your holographic image. How is your new self different? Which hologram will be more likely to succeed?

Love at the Core

The primary component of your consciousness is your perception. First, your self-concept defines you, and your awareness of the world connects (or disconnects) you with the flowing tide of synchronicity. Your fundamental views—good or bad—are formulated in your youth and become the predominant filter through which you see your life, make your decisions, and plan your future. You may project visions of success; but if deep inside, you really perceive yourself as a failure, they're likely to fade into the ethers.

So when you send your specific intentions out into the Universe, you have to realize that there are strings attached—and those strings lead directly to the numerous beliefs hidden within your consciousness. Just as you can't snip off a piece of the hologram (each fragment still contains the whole image), you can't separate any specific intent for success from the underlying perceptions of your life. These all-important elements of self-view and worldview determine the ultimate results of your consciousness creation, and at the center and core of your holographic consciousness is your self-valuing.

In a nuclear reactor, the core is the center region, containing the fissionable material that can sustain a nuclear chain reaction. When developing the atomic bomb, scientists first believed that it would take a lot of fissionable substance to create a critical mass. However, they were amazed to find that it took only $6/10$ of a gram of matter to achieve a chain reaction that would change the world. In many ways, your core activity is the same: It doesn't take a lot to create a huge reaction in your life.

> *Since the core of your consciousness creation is your self-valuing, you need to know that all it takes is a small shift—a genuine intention to sense your own worthiness—in order to ignite the major results that you want. A willingness to see your true value—now and always—will initiate a positive chain reaction that can bring dramatic changes to your entire life.*

Unfortunately, feelings of unworthiness and self-lack are a very common part of poverty consciousness. For many of us, these assumptions of inadequacy are layered into our perception, creating a poverty of self that's coded into our consciousness in such a way that it becomes a significant part of our holographic projection. If this is the case, the foundation of our entire psychology rests on a false and corrosive belief—one that insidiously moves out into the cosmos, naturally creating undesirable results. When we ask ourselves why we're not getting what we want, we aren't even aware that this is the underlying answer.

Your Quantum Psychology

Psychology is the study of mind, behavior, and emotion, all of which become very influential forces in the world. Your personal psychology is at the core of your consciousness projection and your energetic vibration. As such, it's the biggest part of what really determines your destiny. So to get to the root of the external results in your life, you need to know what's going on inside. Only then can you understand what's destined to happen outside.

This is your quantum psychology—the inextricable connection between mind and manifestation, between energetic source and reality outcome. Take a look at how this important nexus works:

1. Your personal psychology is created by your mental and emotional makeup, the accumulated information that you've coded into your consciousness throughout your entire life.

2. This coded data—including desires, fears, beliefs, and self-definition—spins a vortex of life-force energy and projects your holographic picture to the world.

3. According to the patterns of attraction and manifestation, the projection connects with like energies and produces specific results that reflect the whole truth of your quantum psychology.

This is why the study of your thoughts and emotions is so important: They activate the energetic patterns of attraction. It's an absolute fact that your mental makeup is a force that moves causally (although not casually) through the Universe. It's a complex connection, but one that you can have great power over—for at the center of your quantum psychology is what you *choose* to believe about yourself and your life.

To get the Law of Manifestation to work the way you desire, you must consider the whole. It's not enough to say, "If I only focus on what I want, then I'll get it." You need to support that intention with a positive multidimensional view of yourself. You must see yourself as capable and worthy of receiving—and perceive the world as abundant and willing to provide. You can visualize buying a winning lottery ticket all you want, but if you look in the mirror with judgment and self-doubt, your outcome will be consistently disappointing.

> *This is the holographic reality of manifestation: Your consciousness can't create something that you're not fully aware of deep within yourself. Your system of thoughts and beliefs is a driving force in the field of Universal intention, so it's important to know that the value you seek in the external world can only come from a pervasive sense of value within.*

If you're always—or even often—focused on worry, lack, and unhappiness, then that is all that your consciousness can create for you. If you're not aware at least on some level of the intrinsic value already within yourself and your life, it will be a constant struggle to create value in your destiny.

This pit of self-negation is one of the biggest problems people face in trying to create a brilliant future. You'll see throughout this book that if you're facing failure, this is usually the first place to start. Even if your self-esteem doesn't seem all that negative, if you're merely self-conscious or experiencing some self-doubt, or you're just confused about your place and your power in the world, it can be enough to darken your energy and move your consciousness and your quantum psychology in a negative direction—and send out a holographic projection that attracts rejection!

You may have been taught in no uncertain terms that you're faulty, unworthy, or fundamentally flawed, but this isn't your truth. Your *real* truth stands apart from the misinformation of others—even when they're your parents or other authority figures. Your truth existed before the difficult experiences of this life, originating in your spiritual core and reflecting the Divine source of your unchanging, eternal value.

Spirit in the Hologram

Your Divine source is a huge part of the solutions you're seeking in your earthly pursuits. Your spiritual identity represents more of your power—and much more of your truth—than anything you may have learned elsewhere. Whatever unhappy situation may be occurring, whatever lack you may have experienced in the past, shifting your focus to this dynamic and very real part of yourself can create a brand-new consciousness—one that will manifest the brilliant destiny that your eternal self so deserves.

Your soul, your higher Self, is the part of you that vibrates most clearly and magnetically in the flow of Universal abundance. As such, it's your most powerful advocate in the energetic realm. Amazingly, most people go from decade to decade never thinking about their spirit or even being aware of its presence. But this kind of dismissal is a serious mistake. Your spiritual identity is a key part of the consciousness that you project to the world, and it can be a hugely helpful and accelerating force in your destiny creation—if you allow it.

The hologram of your identity reveals every dimension of yourself, including the one that both preexists and outlasts your earthly experience. This soul-self is every bit as much a part of your creative consciousness as any negative self-view, but to utilize its power, you must start to see yourself through the crystal lens of eternal truth. You need to realign your personal perception with the unqualified and infinite value of your spiritual identity. When you support yourself with a positive, self-loving perspective, you shift your consciousness from personal limitation and lack to unlimited Universal abundance.

You are an expression of God's love, which is the real foundation of your identity. Although your parents seem to have had the most impact on your feelings about yourself, it's your eternal worth and Divine connection that are your key accelerants to Universal consciousness. Coming from any place other than your source causes you to completely turn off a powerful current of magnetic vibration. More important, your disconnect from Divine experience greatly reduces the synchronicity of support and unending possibilities that resonate near and far in the field of assistance from the Universe. All of life—past, present, and future—vibrates in connection with the energy of your soul, placing you at the confluence of personal and global intention. When this power is denied, it dams up the flow. But when it's acknowledged and embraced in your daily life, it becomes a stimulating force that easily overrides the negative thoughts and difficult experiences that have been blocking your way.

The spiritual truth of your Divine connection is so important, it cannot be overemphasized. Whatever you've been told, however you've been treated—by parents, lovers, bosses, or anyone else— you are an inestimably valuable, eternal being, incandescently brilliant and unlimited in your essential vibration. You are a child of Divine love, one whose worthiness and self-definition can only come from that shining source with whom you co-create all of your life experiences.

When you choose to see—and fully experience—this part of yourself, you address the most fundamental piece of consciousness creation. In fact, embracing this profound inner sense of yourself is one of the most effective things that you can do to shift your consciousness and begin to manifest a wonderful new reality.

In Part II, you'll be examining all the ways that this connection can assist you on your journey. You'll also be exploring several techniques to forge this magnificent union and make it more real. For the time being, though, start to expand the spiritual influence in your life by doing the following:

- Practice turning to your eternal power now—ask for assistance and be open to receiving.

- Contemplate a deeper truth about yourself and your spiritual origin.

- Define yourself with a stronger, surer, purer consciousness of the spirit that pulsates within you and always radiates its strength.

- Affirm—and know—that your real value comes from your eternal spirit and your Divine legacy.

Within your hologram is an invisible intelligence that exists within all things and is capable of helping you understand, achieve, and heal. You're one with all information and have access to every solution. Through your eternal identity, you achieve a profound greatness—an energy that's so powerful, it will transform you, raise you up, and lead you into a destiny you may have never even imagined. The blissful, unencumbered focus of your spirit will help you erase your limited thinking; release your urgency and need; and finally move into the radical self-love, forgiveness, and valuing that will help you redefine yourself forevermore.

Tapping into this unlimited, eternal force is the most empowering part of your consciousness and energy evolution. Although it existed before your present psyche, it's actually the underlying force of your quantum psychology and your conduit to all of creation. Start to open up to this magical connection now. Affirm your intention to align yourself with the Universal hologram and enlist its energies of assistance, purification, and acceleration in your own destiny creation. You're one with the Source and with the entire Universe; real success starts the very moment that you let yourself connect.

CHAPTER 2

SHIFTING CONSCIOUSNESS

*"No problem can be solved from the same level
of consciousness that created it."*

— ALBERT EINSTEIN

The pursuit of success isn't just planning and performing the linear tasks that will technically promote your career. It's a many-faceted approach that moves you toward all-encompassing happiness and victory on many levels. For a profoundly successful life, you need to take a deeper look at the steps for shifting both personal and Universal consciousness. The first important step is to identify the warning signs of toxic consciousness creation. Only then can you move on to the second vital step of changing destiny—that is, making consistent shifts in your own consciousness by charging your perceptions and expectations with deliberate intent.

To achieve positive consciousness creation, it will be absolutely necessary to create a core of confidence, self-valuing, peace, and authentic empowerment in your personal perception. It's also necessary to hold a view of the world as safe, unlimited in abundance, and exciting in its potential.

Unfortunately, many people embrace attitudes and beliefs that are contrary to those healthy and productive perspectives. Their quantum psychology is like sludge in a motor, stopping their attraction cold! For these individuals, consciousness shifting will require consistent intervention on the old, negative, and self-destructive mentalities that keep creating misery. One must first identify toxic thought-forms in order to move them out of the engine of destiny creation.

Spotting Your Consciousness Red Flags

The single most important red flag of toxic consciousness is *self-negation*. This can take many forms—from the severe state of chronic self-condemnation to the unaware dismissal of your own needs and priorities. But why is this such an important issue? As discussed in the last chapter, your self-regard is perhaps the most intrinsic part of your holographic experience. It's the inner light (or darkness) of the vibrational picture that you send out into the world—along with your specific intentions and all other aspects of yourself.

Remember, your hologram can't be reduced. You could no more remove your self-regard from your consciousness creation than you could extract your heart and sustain physical health. If it's happiness you seek, you must start with happiness inside—and that comes from genuine self-love.

> *Consciousness creation is the event where your full consciousness creates your ultimate reality. At the center of all that you're conscious of is your genuine feeling for yourself, so your self-view—good or bad—is a driving force behind your destiny formation.*

Your life is formulated from the inside out. The fullness of your consciousness thoroughly reflects what you feel for yourself in your own mind and heart. You may show confidence to the world, and you may even live with bravado, but the truth of your genuine emotions toward yourself cannot be covered up. A healthy quantum psychology starts with a choice, not a reaction. *Your self-esteem—which forms the core picture of your life projection—needs to be consciously and purposely chosen, not merely accepted from other people's uninformed and unenlightened input.*

Throughout all my years as a counselor, I can say that this issue is by far the biggest source of dysfunction and unhappiness for people in their emotional, personal, and professional lives—no matter what their income or level of material success. There are so many individuals who are hurting and confused—completely stalemated by the fact that, deep inside, they perceive themselves as inadequate and unworthy. They consider their negative view of themselves as absolute truth, dismissing any options for improvement.

There are still many others who, although they're functional and even somewhat successful, experience a smoldering undercurrent of dissatisfaction. They just can't understand why they always seem to feel a nagging unhappiness and sense of something missing. Countless people go through their lives frustrated and empty, never quite figuring out that they're living with an undertone of unknowing self-dismissal.

I often sit across from my clients and think, *If only they could see themselves as I do, they'd see the light and beauty that dances behind the present darkness in their eyes.* That light and beauty is their pure nature—the one that preceded the misinformation that they now call their self-esteem. The truth of their eternal worth shines beneath the falsehoods that they've been taught, revealing the ever-present reality of their value. Like a gold mine waiting to be discovered, limitless worth is right below the surface, under the dirt, silt, and heavy rocks of false beliefs. The same holds true for you, too—and it's time for you to start mining the treasures within.

> *Right there beneath your misinformed history is the gold of your real and eternal value. No matter how fearful or filled with self-doubt you may be, you can always choose to redefine yourself according to this genuine truth and create a new, bright, and honest sense of self-esteem. This is the beauty of our energetic world: Change can happen with intention. Time loops back on itself and choices are engaged. Information shifts, and new realities are born.*

Your self-esteem is the center of your hologram. It's amazing how something so important is so easily formed—and so powerfully influenced. Your self-view usually develops according to a specific pattern. It's important to know each step so that you can make the consciousness shift involved, reversing the influence of the process along with the associated results.

As you look at each of the following steps of psychological indoctrination, try to analyze how the experiences of your past fit into the puzzle.

Write down your impressions, and be honest about your inner voice of self-regard. Each step offers a suggestion for shifting your negative awareness into a positive self-view. Take some time to work though these changes in your journal, returning to this process of analysis and transformation whenever you may feel any glitches of self-doubt. Later, you'll be doing some deeper investigation, but this exercise will help you start to build an awareness of your patterns of self-esteem.

Forming and Shifting Your Self-regard

1. People (usually your parents) who were given misinformation about their own value unwittingly project their toxic assumptions, misguided expectations, and often-unreasonable demands upon you as you're growing up.

Shift: Write down any toxic conclusions you were taught about your own value; follow them with some new, healthy conclusions of self-worth.

2. As a child, you don't have the skills or awareness—or even the emotional power yet—to make clear choices about what you *want* to believe about yourself, so you embrace the negative input as truth.

Shift: Write some affirmations about your present power, your ability to take control, and your conscious choice to create a new self-accepting and self-actualized truth.

3. You project your limited self-expectations out into the Universe, and your negative consciousness yields some disappointing results, perpetuating the problem.

Shift: Write down some new expectations of happiness and success. Repeat your positive intentions and affirm your worthiness to receive.

You may think that your difficult experiences and false conclusions have been irreversibly established in your psyche, but even now—at any point in your process—you can make the choice to change the conclusions that are central to your information field. In fact, your intention for happiness and success absolutely *requires* it. So let go of the past and take back your power. As a thinking adult, you always have the option to make clear and healthy choices regarding what to believe about yourself, your value, and your power in the world.

Remember that even a small shift in consciousness can reverse the course of history. You may have lived your whole life with nagging feelings of doubt and inferiority, but it's time to let them go. Always be aware that you have the power to choose a different way at any moment. You can and must establish an entirely new system of belief, one that redefines you as unlimited, vibrant, empowered, and creative—projecting a force of consciousness that will shift your reality and change the very quality of your life!

What would you do if you could never criticize or judge yourself again? That alone would change everything. You would vibrate a hologram of self-honor and self-acceptance, the very core and heart of brilliant consciousness creation. Once these positive elements become encoded into your consciousness, you'll find yourself moving into accelerated success.

Many successful people have been faced with difficult patterns of low self-esteem, but just one voice of reason helped change everything for them. This voice could have been a friend, a teacher, or their own determination. You can be the voice of reason for yourself right now; you can be the loving adult who always encourages and accepts *you.* Choose to believe in yourself just one thought at a time. You can change your history and your future in one single moment of unqualified self-love.

There are many wonderful books that can help you raise your self-regard and learn how to genuinely love yourself. Two of my favorites are *The Six Pillars of Self-Esteem* by Nathaniel Branden and *Ten Days to Self-Esteem* by David Burns, which is a very thorough workbook offering practical tools for significant cognitive changes. And if you feel that this issue is just too difficult to tackle on your own, try seeing a cognitive therapist for assistance. Your self-esteem is the central issue through which you filter every experience of your life. You're worth taking the time to believe in yourself!

This is the first—and most important—step in the intention to achieve ongoing personal and emotional prosperity. If you really want to succeed, your old patterns of self-dismissal, self-criticism, or even self-condemnation must be a thing of the past. You always have the option to think differently—to focus on a self-valuing truth and arrive at a brand-new conclusion. The very moment that you make this choice, your consciousness hums with joyous appreciation, signaling the Universe that you're ready to receive.

Beware of the Green-Eyed Monster!

Another red flag of unhealthy and self-sabotaging consciousness is *envy*, the habit of focusing on what other people have and longing for it yourself. In my counseling, I've seen almost as much unhappiness emanating from people living in this state as from those who live in self-negation. So many people are miserable, always comparing what *they* have to what *others* have, believing they can never be happy because they consistently come up short. *Envy of others will always turn into lack for yourself!*

There's a status-seeking process that people go through—often without even realizing it. Some long for prestige; others yearn for luxury, leisure, or even the excitement they think other folks are having. I once worked with a man in sales who envied people with fancy cars, second homes, and expensive vacations. When I asked him how much he earned, he said that he had a base of about $100,000, but sometimes was able to double or even triple that with his commission—if he worked hard enough.

As we investigated his life more thoroughly, he found that he'd achieved more than he realized. He had a half-million-dollar home—although he wanted one that cost twice as much. He longed for a second residence, although he realized that he couldn't use it anyway because he was always working in order to maintain his lifestyle. He spent his money eating out a lot and buying expensive clothes and jewelry for himself and his wife. He belonged to a golf-and-tennis club and sent his kids to the most prestigious schools.

In spite of all of this, his most common complaint was "No matter how hard I work, I never seem to make enough money," which was partially true because his striving for status caused him to spend well beyond his income.

He was always comparing himself to people who had more, envying his brother who owned two homes and his business partner who skied in

Europe. He never took time to appreciate—or even really experience—all of the wonderful things he had in his own life. Instead, he lived in bitter longing and envy, and then he compounded that difficult experience when he moved into envy's emotional cousin, *greed.*

This is an attitude of desperation, the aching need to have more, no matter how much you already possess. Like envy, greed focuses on what has yet to be obtained instead of what's already there to be valued. This creates a very toxic vibration of urgency and striving, and its energy does so much to devalue the present circumstances of your life that it actually sabotages the intention to create and attract more.

In our modern culture—where the wealthy and flamboyant lifestyles of others are paraded in front of us every day—greed and envy are always perched on the edge of our consciousness, waiting to gobble us up. It reminds me of two evil characters in Greek mythology, Scylla and Charybdis. In *The Odyssey,* Homer wrote about the long journey Odysseus had to make to return home from the Trojan War—and all of the trials and tribulations he encountered on the way. One of those ordeals was the passage of his ship through the narrow straits between Scylla and Charybdis. Scylla was a six-headed monster sitting on a cliff waiting to devour the men off the ships that went by. On the other side of that very narrow strait was Charybdis, a monster who formed a huge whirlpool, strong enough to suck an entire ship below the surface.

I find this to be a very apt metaphor for greed and envy. Like the many-headed Scylla, greed eats you up. You're so consumed with need that you can never rest, and can never stop striving for more. Like the whirlpool of Charybdis, envy of others sucks you down into a deep depression of emptiness and longing. Your obsession with what's missing totally devalues what you already have, and you always see yourself as falling short in the light of what others may possess.

Living in these treacherous emotional waters only reverses your intention for success! To create a clearer holographic projection, you need to navigate between these two extreme emotional states. And when you find a middle passage of peace and value in the present, you'll project a much brighter consciousness of appreciation.

Envy and greed hide a far deeper problem—a palpable, ongoing sense of lack. This refusal to see the abundance and unlimited potential for joy that's already available to you keeps you stuck in your own whirlpool

27

of discontent, and your longing perpetuates more of the same. Keep in mind that the quality of your present journey is what determines your future results. When a fundamental perception of lack is swirling around in your present hologram, your consciousness can only create more of the same in the time to come.

It's helpful to remember that in the energetic Universe, your consciousness expands. That which you focus on grows and grows. So when you consistently dwell on what others have, you only increase what *they* possess—never what you do! Your energy of lack can only expand the loss in your life, although it brings more gain to those you envy.

> *Instead of envying what others have—or constantly, desperately striving for more—it's time to make a higher choice! Consciously acknowledge all the wonder and beauty in your life—refuse to spend even a minute in lack. Your heartfelt recognition of worth will generate an abundance consciousness that attracts even more blessings to appreciate in the future.*

You may want more, but you don't have to live your life reducing the value of what you already have. A hologram of self-valuing and present appreciation pulsates with joyous expectation. So stop and make a consciousness shift. At any given moment in this fluid and ever-changing world, you have the option to change your focus and produce a different reaction—one that will inevitably lead to a vastly different result.

Your Adjacent Possibilities . . .

The *complexity theory* is a fascinating look into the process of change, examining how our layered lives evolve into what we experience. The theory says that although a system's evolving outcomes should be predictable and relatively simple, they can take an unexpected turn, becoming extremely unpredictable—leading in entirely new and unique directions. The result is always a variable, waiting to be revealed.

This is made clear in the concept of *adjacent possibilities,* an important part of the complexity theory. It reveals that no matter what predictable outcome may be expected, there's always the chance that something different may happen, expanding the opportunity for diversity and creating new outcomes.

In terms of your personal experience, this means that you're never limited by your old patterns or definitions. Your life and your consciousness are evolving all the time. In fact, at any moment there are dozens—even hundreds—of adjacent possibilities, countless options of perception, thought, and reaction that will completely alter your reality. *A purposeful shift in focus—or the choice to create deliberately optimistic interpretations—could result in wonderful, unexpected surprises. Just one moment of moving into an adjacent possibility could lead your life in a far different direction.*

This is the function of another concept of complexity called *sensitive dependence,* which reveals that the world's evolution is sensitive to even the smallest influence. With even the slightest change, a system's entire future (*your* entire future) can change. The more recent term *butterfly effect* is used to indicate the nonlocal nature of influence—implying that a butterfly flapping its wings in one part of the world can have an impact across the globe. In your life, you need to know that a movement of thought, a slight shift of intention, or just the breath of a different vibration can result in long-term, far-reaching, and significant shifts.

This is so beautifully liberating in its implications that it renders the future—and the evolution of all that you experience in it—filled with truly limitless potential. No matter what pattern may have been consistent for you in the past, there's always the potential to slip into an entirely different response. It's right there—right next to the thought or emotion you're in. All you have to do is take control and step into a different view. That momentary shift can move you into some other new adjacent possibility, one that will lead to the ultimate arrival at yet another divergent outcome—unpredictable and excitingly removed from anything you might have expected!

Absolutely anything is achievable in light of this understanding. Whether it's physical healing, financial wealth, intimate connections, or mind-boggling acts of creation, a magnificent future is within your grasp when you consistently choose to move into more purposeful and empowering *adjacent possibilities* of thought.

Road MAP to Success

If you're driving down the street and you realize you're going the wrong way, you can change course and choose a new route that will take you where you want to go. The same holds true for your consciousness, too. If you're proceeding in a negative direction, you don't have to keep going down that same counterproductive path. You just have to realize that your life is heading down a dead-end road. Remind yourself of your options, and then let them redirect you—just like a map to a new destination.

When I'm in need of a consciousness shift, I try to consider **My Adjacent Possibilities**, a MAP of options that I can choose in order to move in a different direction—either in focus or emotion, or both. If I find myself worried about something, I investigate my adjacent possibilities and know that it's safe for me to trust. In fact, in the whole of consciousness, trusting is the peaceful and preferable choice I want to make, and this alternative exists within my grasp. It's not foreign or foolish; it's my right and my responsibility to embrace.

Sometimes I visualize the adjacent possibility—whether it's trust or some other conscious choice—floating like a cloud beside me, and I actually take a step into that intended energy! It helps make the shift more real. If I'm feeling self-doubt, I know that right next to that conclusion is the adjacent possibility of self-encouragement—and I also know that it's the only choice that will move me in the direction I desire.

> Close your eyes and envision yourself stepping into a sparkling, beautiful cloud. Every dewy molecule that alights on your face and arms is a joyous adjacent possibility . . . and the options stretch out for miles. Spin around and feel the refreshing touch of another and another. How exciting it is to always be surrounded by possibilities!

Whatever state of consciousness I may be in, I can reevaluate my decision to stay there. I can examine what I'm thinking, then look at all the thoughts around me. I can always choose to make a higher, purer conclusion about my life. In this way, when I switch my focus, I also shift my consciousness, projecting an entirely different picture of myself and my expectations—and moving in a new direction of manifestation.

This is your choice, too: At any given moment, you have the power to shift into an adjacent possibility of existence—a fresh definition of what's going on, a different conclusion and emotional reaction. It may not be easy at first, but it's a skill that you can definitely master. And every time you decide to activate a new approach, you'll be stimulating a butterfly effect that will in essence change your entire life. Even just the intention to investigate adjacent possibilities is in itself choosing an adjacent possibility!

There's an exquisite elegance in the simplicity of consciously choosing what you want to observe as your reality. Your intention to change immediately loops back into your perception, reversing the vibration of your consciousness. While you may have been in the habit of monitoring what's missing or wrong within yourself and in your world, you always have the power to switch to noticing what's present and enduringly valuable within and around you. This change in attention—even if you only stay there for a moment—is how the observer creates reality.

Four Steps to Shifting Personal Consciousness

There are many things that you can do to transform your personal consciousness and therefore shift your reality. Since your consciousness is the record of your primary feelings, thoughts, and beliefs, any intervention in the pattern of negative expectations or fearful assessments will lead you in the right direction. The two most important levels of personal change, however, are mental and emotional. You'll be dealing more with the process of both these changes throughout the book, but right now it's important to consider—and step into—your healthier consciousness options. Keep in mind that any action you take and any transformation you make will shift the essence of your holographic projection and lead your life in a new direction.

The following four steps represent the basic approach to creating a higher mentality of consciousness. Whatever the issue may be, you can apply this process to understanding and realigning the content of your thinking. It may be helpful to reacquaint yourself with the positive and negative consciousness list in Chapter 1 to see if you can identify some of your most prevalent patterns. Every attitude on the negative list is a red flag of toxic energy, so pay attention!

Any consistent pattern of self-dismissal, limitation, or lack should be recognized and dealt with. You don't need to be convinced that your new choices or perceptions are valid at this time; you just need to remind yourself that there are optional ways of looking at things that don't involve such catastrophic or debilitating views. *When you're in a negative state of mind, no matter what's going on, there's always a more peaceful option—an empowering adjacent possibility that more validly reflects your truth.*

Your quantum psychology starts with your mental and emotional responses and then moves out into the cosmos. By clearly understanding your patterns, you can open yourself to more healthy and self-empowering action. This, in turn, will greatly shift the energy you project. So allow yourself to set this process in motion, knowing that as you do, your bright new hologram of positive expectation will align with the optimism of Universal consciousness and create much more rewarding results. You're already a powerful manifestor; you might as well take steps to consciously direct that manifestation and create the kind of destiny you really want.

Step 1: Develop an awareness of your toxic perceptions as they appear in your daily experience—even if they're subtle and hidden deep within your consciousness. Many of us often live in a state of complacency where we not only fail to resist our negative patterns, we don't even recognize them. This is what *becoming conscious* is all about— choosing to see the truth of your daily habits and arriving at some mastery over them. If you're not aware of how often you criticize yourself, it will be impossible to formulate the high self-regard that the Universe loves to respond to. And if you can't identify the many ways you focus on lack throughout the day, it will be impossible to shift to a value consciousness that will blow lack away.

The first obvious sign that you need to make a shift is uncomfortable feelings. Let that discomfort be an alarm bell to the fact that you're making some conclusions that no longer serve you. It's time to design a higher consciousness—and a clearer, less conflicted holographic projection. So when you notice some difficult feelings coming up, ask yourself: *What are the negative conclusions I may be drawing about the present circumstances?* Be especially aware of any assumption that takes you out of your authentic power, your optimism, your self-acceptance, or your peace. Just by recognizing that you don't want to linger in your discomfort, you'll be initiating a healthy new intention.

Step 2: With each recognition of fearful or worrisome thoughts, consider all your options and adjacent possibilities. Even if you're in the moment of worry or negative self-talk, stop and remind yourself: *I have an option here!* Right next to the thought you're having is a moment that's worry free; right next to the fear is a choice that embraces trust and peace. There are Universes of options and energetic shifts, and through your new awareness there's a whole new world to be experienced. No matter where you are mentally, there's an adjacent possibility that can take you to dramatically different realities—both immediately and in the long span of your life.

So don't just accept your habitual conclusions as truth. It's time to let go of the shackles of false living and move into brand-new thought-forms that—although they may seem strange to you at first—represent your eternal reality. Always ask yourself: *What are my positive adjacent possibilities?* Entertain those options and then move on to Step 3 with full determination.

Step 3: Consciously *choose* to change your focus and step into the adjacent possibility of optimistic thought. Create a positive, self-empowering approach. Change is the present process—not the future goal. You can't just hope for some miraculous transformation to descend upon your life without any of your own conscious participation. The fact is, the only opportunity for change is in the present moment, and each and every instant holds a choice for you. Once you've recognized an old, unhealthy pattern—and considered the healthy adjacent possibilities that surround you—you must muster up the courage to make a clear choice about what you want to focus on.

Reinforce your new options by writing these affirmative approaches in your journal and reading them often:

- For self-deprecation, assert: *I deserve to accept myself. I know that a self-accepting option exists for me now. I open my mind to a more loving opinion of myself.*

- If worried, affirm: *I can let this go. It is entirely possible that things will work out fine.*

- If thinking along the old lines of limiting thoughts, remind yourself: *The Universe is abundant. I choose to focus on the value already present within my life, and I open myself to receiving more. As I choose to see value, I create more value all around me.*

The multidimensional Universe responds to every level of your personal perception, from the emotional core to the cognitive content of your consciousness. With every present choice constructing a more enlightened thought, you build a new vibration, aligning your personal hologram with the Universal expectation of optimism and love. Even the smallest change in these areas can create a cascading effect in your future reality, so be sure to make clear, optimistic conclusions—in both your personal outlook and your worldview.

Step 4: Bring your new positive assumption of the present moment into a whole-life intention! As you've chosen an adjacent possibility and formed a new conclusion around it, make sure you activate that fresh choice into life intention. Capture the shift in the energy of the moment by taking a deep breath, and as you inhale, drop your consciousness (or your point of awareness) into your heart center. Resting your focus there, repeat your new thought—or even just the feeling you desire—until the emotional state that you've chosen becomes a gentle sensation in your present reality. Affirm: *I shift my consciousness now. This moment I choose the vibration of peace* (or *self-love, trust, tranquility, optimism, joy,* and so on). *I consciously move my life in this peace-filled direction.* As you go through your day, affirm this new intention often.

Each and every moment, you have the option to slip into another vibrational truth. Do so now and lock into it as your future intention. Don't dismiss this exercise—it's one of the most empowering and life-changing things you can do. Choosing the adjacent possibility doesn't have to be complicated or full of effort, so try not to make it harder than it is. All it takes is a gentle reminder that you don't have to stay negative when there's a positive view at hand.

I find it helps to have some of these reminders in my environment. I carry an angel coin with me, and when I put my hand in my pocket, feeling the token reminds me that I can choose peace. I also wear bracelets that have words such as *serenity, courage, action,* and *love* inscribed on them. I call these my "adjacent-possibility bracelets," and whenever I look down, I'm reminded that I always have the choice to take the trusting, peaceful, honoring path.

It's good to remember that, no matter what, there are always many adjacent possibilities of thought. Practice looking for and stepping into them often; I do so many times a day. It actually becomes fun to think of all the different ways to look at something and then choose one of them. It's like living in your own board game, where each roll of the dice gets you one step closer to the winner's corner. Besides, you never know when your new intentions will achieve a critical magnitude, creating a chain reaction that will transform your whole life!

> *Your consciousness exists outside of time, and even just a momentary shift can change every moment forever. All of time converges at this present moment, bringing history into the future, enfolding your will into what will be. Time is on your side; the very next positive, loving thought in your life can produce a butterfly effect in your own destiny . . . and in the world.*

Your consciousness is always moving into the mix of when and where, connecting with the consciousness of others and creating a shared destiny that you have—until now—only passively approved of. It's time to be an active participant in the evolution of your own destiny—and that of all humankind. This is no small feat! The power of the world is at your disposal, and the choice you make at this very moment can open your heart and give you access to the realm of your most powerful potential. It may seem insignificant, but the power of your *every* thought is incontrovertible.

What do you want your next thought to be? Choose it consciously!

CHAPTER 3

ECHOES OF ENERGY

"The energy of the mind is the essence of life."

— **ARISTOTLE**

Just as consciousness is an invisible force in the Universe, the vibrations of energy—also invisible—are equally significant in our lives. The truth is, most of the power in the Universe is unseen, including the phenomenal force of our own individual energy. Each of us—and everything of substance in this world—is actually made up of vibrating strings resonating with activity. It's a frequency that defines us and largely determines what we attract.

Unfortunately, much of the time when we can't see something, we don't believe in it, we don't value it, and we don't put much effort into controlling it. But this unseen power is an amazing source of resolution, creativity, and magnetism—and it's accessible to us every moment of our lives. In order to learn how to direct it in more positive, creative, and fulfilling ways, however, we must be able to identify and consciously choose the vibrations that express who we are and how we experience the world.

Hologram of Energy

You're a bundle of energetic activity. You vibrate when you breathe, you resonate when you speak, you produce energy when you walk, and you even create electrical impulses when you think. Every moment that you are alive—even when you're asleep—you're projecting some kind of energy. Like a radio station, you're always broadcasting very specific signals about your life and your expectations.

As with your consciousness, it's important to look at your energy production more holistically and not just limit it to what you project concerning your goals. The quality of your journey isn't determined by your arrival at a destination. Energetically, it's your whole life force—the vibration of your inner and outer resonance—that directs your destiny. It's crucial to understand this if you really want to change the direction of your earthly experience.

> It only takes one second for light to travel 186,000 miles. Your light—your life force—is just as far-reaching and every bit as rapid in its projection. There's no limit in terms of time or distance. Your vibrations move out from you and get echoed back, returning the exact same resonance of thought, emotion, and experience—the resonance of your whole life.

This is a function of the second Law of Attraction, the Law of Magnetism, which states that the Universe can only return the same energy that you send out. This isn't intended to be punitive, merely a statement of truth about the natural patterns of cause and effect. Similar to the impartiality of gravity, the Law of Magnetism is clear. Just as you can't miss a step on a staircase and expect to float instead of fall, you can't consistently project a life force of negative vibration and expect to get back positive results. When you know about gravity, you're careful walking down stairs; when you're aware of resonance, you're conscious about the energy you send out.

Your life force is a bundle of vibrating messages, sending signals about your entire energetic self out into the Universe. Those signals entrain (or match) with similar frequencies, and the people and situations at the same levels are then drawn into your experience. Your broadcast never ends, and your basic energy is always being created in three significant ways—movement, sound, and emotion. It's important to know how you experience each of these energetic factors in your daily life.

Your Energy of Movement

Your first and most basic vibration is mechanical energy or that of movement. It's clearly an important part of your physical resonance, but it also has a profound impact on your mental and emotional frequency as well. In fact, in all areas of your life, regular exercise or major-muscle movement will enhance the quality of your magnetic vibration. This is especially true if you feel stuck in an unhealthy habit; a toxic mind-set; or chronic, uncomfortable emotions.

Studies show that people who have anxiety conditions experience greatly reduced symptoms when they start to engage in a regular exercise program. In my work with phobic individuals, I've found that along with deep breathing and daily relaxation, this helped my clients either significantly reduce or completely eliminate the use of their antianxiety medication.

This triple combination of movement, deep breathing, and regular relaxation purifies your energy. It can also help with depression and self-esteem problems (two big energy depleters), as well as increase physical vitality, optimism, and enthusiasm—all highly magnetic vibrations in your life force.

Most people aren't accustomed to deep breathing, but you need to know that this is a very important element in your mechanical resonance. It helps provide relaxation and increase serotonin levels, but even more important, it creates a clear channel for your life force or *chi.* This opening of chi movement through your body enhances your vibration and creates a greater synchronistic flow. If you remember to stop and take a few diaphragmatic breaths every half hour or so, you'll notice a significantly more tranquil—and therefore more receptive—energy level throughout your day.

Steps for Enhancing Mechanical Energy

The following tips for creating healthy mechanical energy may seem simple, but they'll go a long way toward clearing old, unwanted frequencies from your holographic life force, opening the way for clearer, more productive vibrations that will get better results.

1. Try to get at least 20 minutes of major muscle movement or regular exercise on a daily basis.

2. Even if you don't have an opportunity to work out, take a few breaks during your day to walk or even just stretch for about five minutes.

3. Move with intention. As you walk, stretch, or do any form of exercise, affirm that you're moving old toxic energy out of your cells, bringing in healthy, vital energy.

4. Do some deep breathing every hour or so—as you do, hold the intention to cleanse your energy and create peace in your body and your mind.

Your Sound Energy

The second type of physical energy is that of sound—your acoustic energy. This is a very important part of your resonance because your voice amplifies the intention of your words, creating a doubly forceful impact in the energetic realm. To align the force of your thoughts with the magnetic vibration of sound, you must be conscious of what you say and how you say it.

Your voice is an instrument, and like all musical instruments, it can produce sounds that are either harmonic or discordant. Your harmonic resonance includes both the music of your voice itself and the lyrics of your words. Real harmony—the type that moves out in the world in beautiful vibration—creates wonderful and magical results. The music of your voice amplifies the meaning of your words, doubling your power to change your life direction.

There are many ways in which you can use your voice to lift your vibra-tion and connect with the harmonic flow of the Universe. You can sing, pray, and affirm your positive intentions out loud. You can do a self-loving dialogue while looking in the mirror. You can also chant, either by using one of the many mantras from Eastern religions, or simply by repeating the word *One, om,* or *God* . . . or any word or mantra of your own choosing.

Unfortunately, chanting "om" has become a classic joke in modern comedies where someone sits cross-legged on the floor, hands resting palm-up on their knees, chanting a monotone "om." Every part of that stance has meaning, but since we're talking about acoustics here, let's look at the word. *Om* is said to mean "the thought from which the Universe is manifested." To me, this is a beautiful and accurate representation of the power of thought in the world and in our individual lives. The thought from which the Universe is manifested—just *think* about that!

In my pursuit of meaning and understanding, I've studied numerous mantras and explored a variety of the world's religions. During that process, I came across one of the many forms of Buddhist practices, called *Mahayana Buddhism.* This form was based on the Lotus Sutra and took its mantra from that profound and beautiful teaching. The words chanted—*nam myoho renge kyo*—are adapted from the sutra's title; they mean: "I fuse my life with the mystic law of cause and effect through my vibrations."

When I was introduced to this nearly 30 years ago, little did I know how profoundly real that statement about vibrations would become for me. (And it's no coincidence that the person who introduced me to quantum physics was also the one who told me about this mantra.) It's a simple but all-encompassing truth when you look at the meaning behind it: *I fuse my life—or become one with—the mysterious Universal patterns of attraction through my resonance.*

This mantra may be talking about the vibrations of the voice while chanting, but to me it clearly has a much broader meaning. My own frequency, my signature resonance made up of thought, word, deed, motion, and emotion—in other words, the energy of my whole life force— becomes one with the never-ending flow of cause and effect, uniting me with the entire Universe.

I live with the essential truth of that sentiment in every area of my life. It's wonderful to consider the ongoing fusion of my life force with the eternal current of Universal cause and effect! I consider this to be a guiding principle, one that I now know is based in science, in spite of the fact that it was written in the Lotus Sutra more than 2,000 years ago. The mantra still resonates with me, so I'll occasionally use it—along with several others—as a gentle beginning to my meditations, which are important catalysts to energetic change.

The still and silent time of meditation is another significant element in both your acoustic and electromagnetic energy. Whenever you can rest your body, quiet your mind, and achieve a tranquil sensation in your heart, you do more to initiate an attractive vibration than you can in just about any other activity. People yearn for peace; they move toward it and applaud it in others. Through the process of *phase entanglement*—where your energy mixes with and influences others, and vice versa—a tranquil essence is the most magnetic. Others feel better when they're with a peaceful person, and in their appreciation they long to promote that individual's intentions in any way they can. So meditation not only makes you feel better, it has an expanding effect of well-being that will return to you tenfold.

The final piece of the acoustic puzzle is laughter. It's the only activity that stimulates every quadrant of your brain—even sex doesn't do that. Studies show that people who laugh a lot tend to live longer, recover more quickly from colds and other infectious illnesses, have better memories, and experience fewer chronic or catastrophic diseases. They also have more friends and a wider network of support, and—no surprise here—they tend to be happier.

When you enjoy your life, have fun, and laugh, you create a vortex of expanding energy that vibrates at a highly magnetic rate. Your peals of laughter resonate outward in a blissful frequency that makes the whole Universe smile. On the other hand, if you're always moaning, groaning, and complaining, you create a negative vortex that sucks the life out of you and everyone around you—and the Universe can only respond by sending you more to complain about.

As you'll see in the next section, it's healthy to let yourself vent your negative feelings. It's equally important, however, not to stay stuck there, only expressing how bad things are. Instead, turn your acoustic energy around, affirm yourself and your life, and let yourself be playful and laugh.

Steps for Enhancing Acoustic Energy

The following tips for creating vibrant acoustic energy can be integrated into a healthy lifestyle. Notice how your happiness increases as you implement these techniques into your daily routine.

1. Let yourself be still and meditate each day. Start with a few minutes in the morning and evening, but try to increase it to 20 minutes per day. (There are many meditation CDs available now, or you can use one of the many processes in this book.)

2. The power of prayer is undisputed. Let yourself pray in the way that's most comfortable for you. You can use classic devotions or make it up as you go along—just remember to dialogue with the Divine!

3. Use your voice to affirm your life. Read your affirmations and intentions out loud. Express your love, honoring, and value to yourself as you gaze at your image in the mirror. Make as many optimistic statements as you can, and let them become your truth.

4. Sing, chant, and laugh. Listen to happy or soothing music and let yourself sing along. Chant your affirmations or any mantra you resonate with. Laugh at yourself; smile and think of things that tickle you. Let yourself speak joy, feel peace, and sing life!

Your Emotional Energy

The frequency of feelings is the most dynamic part of your electromagnetic resonance. While this—your light energy—also includes your thoughts and beliefs, it's your emotional energy that drives you. Remember, if you want a specific intention to succeed, it must have the power of your life force behind it. In other words, your emotional broadcast must align with your specific goals if you want to achieve real results.

For most of us, our ultimate intention is happiness. Sure, we may want money, nice homes, better health, and romance, but underneath the desire for all of these things is the desire to be happy. Yet this positive emotional state doesn't require an external source, just an ongoing internal choice.

The irony is that attaching our joy to something in the future actually sabotages our ability to be content now. And according to the laws of intention, it greatly reduces our potential to attract the very things we're pinning our hopes on. *The solution comes from choosing to live now in the happy energy that we want to create.* Real happiness in the future requires us to open ourselves to the things and experiences we have to enjoy now. If we want to feel a sense of accomplishment in the future, we must acknowledge with a genuine heart all that we've accomplished so far.

> *The energy of your life force is largely defined by the emotional quality of your day-to-day existence. In order to support your dreams and desires, you must charge your present emotions with feelings of joy, peace, and appreciation. Live now in the emotions you want to create, because that energetic tide will turn inward, and your destiny will overflow with wave after wave of the very same feelings flooding into your future.*

This is a key—and often misunderstood—principle of attraction. People ask how they can create happy emotions if they don't have the things they want. They don't understand that it's always their choice to create vibrations of love and peaceful appreciation no matter what their circumstances are. This moves them into alignment with the Universal flow. In fact, it's one of the most empowering choices a person can make.

So you must ask yourself: *What are the predominant emotional vibrations of my life? Do I tend to resonate at the agitated frequencies of fear and anxiety, or do I resonate with the fluid energy of trust and peace? Do I align with the heavy, dark, and dense frequencies of depression; or do I live in gentle feelings of present contentment?* As you look at the emotional tendencies of your daily life, what do you think your signature resonance would be? If you're not spending at least half of your time in the higher vibrations of peace, happiness, love, and appreciation, you're projecting a life force that will actually interfere with your desire for success.

Fear and negativity broadcast repulsive vibrations and generate an energetic hologram of doubt. This dims your life force and agitates the pure and positive vibrations that would be more likely to get the results you long for. In terms of attraction, the echoes of your energy resonate with your emotional truth. The world reflects—or echoes back—the quality of feelings you live in most.

I once had a client named Nate who'd been the victim of some rather shady business partners. He lost a considerable amount of money, as well as control of his company. As a result of that experience, he lived in constant fear of being deceived—as well as the terror of losing command. He was suspicious of everyone he met and anxious about always maintaining his grip on things. He was brutal about second-guessing his decisions, and he held on tight to the money he had, always afraid that any action would inspire another loss. He was in an emotional tailspin of fear and suspicion, and his anxiety was only getting worse. He had to pull himself out of this and calm down in order to establish a new, powerful, and positive life force. He realized that he was at a turning point—he could either go deeper into despair, or he could step out of himself and take a good look at what his emotional options were.

The first thing Nate had to do was to rein in his reactions. Instead of seeing himself as a victim, he had to redefine his difficult experience as merely an unfortunate but informative lesson. He then had to work on letting go of his immobilizing fear of future mistakes. He ventilated both his anger and his fear, and then he established new conclusions of self-trust and optimism that helped him shape more positive emotions.

We all have the power to choose our feelings instead of being victimized by them. Some situations may be more difficult than others, but when we learn to define our experiences by the lessons, opportunities, and potential power they bring, we shift their vibration and redirect our life force. This is what Nate did, and although it took him a while, he used the energy-shifting steps that follow to make the changes necessary to bring a higher-quality vibration to his daily life. In time he was able to rid himself of his old attitude and fearful emotions. His energy lifted, creating a truly magnetic life force that got him back on top of his game.

Shifting Your Emotional Energy

In order to create a more positive and optimistic vibration, Nate had to follow several steps that felt a bit unfamiliar—and for a time, even uncomfortable. He had to stop trying to govern external factors and start taking charge of his emotional state instead. As he developed a more intentional and less reactionary approach to his feelings, he became increasingly empowered. He was actually quite surprised by how much internal control he was able to establish.

So many people believe that they're stuck with the emotions they have. The common assumption is that feelings are merely responses to outer occurrences—these sensations just happen, and all they can do is either deny or endure them. But this is simply not the case!

We're always free to choose—either to remain embroiled in the drama of being victimized or to move into a self-actualized and intentional emotional state. It's a choice to shift from spontaneous reaction to understanding and clear action. We need to realize that we never have to stay stuck in an emotional pattern—even if we've been through very difficult times. The process is important, however; and if we race through our emotional changes, we may find ourselves living in denial or unconsciously carrying clouds of unresolved negative energy with us, contaminating our potential projections even if we aren't aware of it.

So let's look at the process for *shifting emotional vibrations.* As you explore these steps, jot down some impressions about how to apply them to your own lingering negativity. Think about what still bothers you, and find out which feelings you may still need to clear out of your personal energy field.

Step 1: Express Your Emotions

The first thing Nate had to do was express his anger and the other emotions concerning his betrayal. In order to stop brooding, he had to get them out. Only then could he have a clear picture of the negative and fearful conclusions he was making about himself and his future. Once he released his feelings, he felt more focused, and it was easier to change his pessimistic and false assumptions.

Expression and ventilation of emotion is absolutely necessary if you're going to project a pure and magnetic personal vibration. Just as you need to get toxins out of your physical body in order to be healthy, you need to remove the toxic energy from your emotional body, too. Unexpressed feelings can make it very difficult to shift your resonance because they accumulate in your energy field, becoming a significant part of your broadcast—whether or not you are consciously thinking about them. Even unresolved emotions from long ago can stay with you, attracting the same old pain, hurt, and doubt that you may have thought you left behind.

This doesn't mean you have to obsess about every past hurt; it just means that you have to know what negative emotions may still be a part of your energetic makeup, so you can get them out and let them all go. And if you're experiencing difficult feelings regarding present situations, it will also be vitally important to deal with and express them so that you can move on.

This has become a widely misunderstood concept lately. Some proponents of the Law of Attraction have indicated that you should never have a negative thought or even express a difficult emotion. It's an off-balance view that has actually created a lot of fear and self-blame for people working on their energy production. Unfortunately, the mandate to never express your worries and pains denies your humanity and actually disempowers you! Where do you go with your real-life responses when you've had something difficult to deal with but don't feel allowed to speak about it or get anything out?

I recently heard from a woman named Karen who had questions about this issue in her own life. She was in a difficult relationship with a critical man, and she felt that she needed to express her feelings about the situation. However, a friend of hers told her that she'd only be directing more negativity to the situation if she did so. She took her friend's advice and suppressed her feelings, but her boyfriend's criticism only got worse.

That's when she called me for a consultation. It was clear that she'd actually become fearful of her own difficult emotions, but I told her that pushing down her feelings wasn't a successful way to keep her energy pure and positive. In fact, it had the opposite effect, sabotaging her relationship and reversing her intention for attractive energy—in at least four ways!

First, her unvented response was tacit approval of his behavior, encouraging him to continue. Second, this choice to not take action on her own behalf—to not establish clear boundaries and promote reasonable expectations in her relationship—created an unmistakable energetic resonance, broadcasting the frequency that she was willing to be treated in a dishonoring way. This created an open invitation for the Universe to send more of the same in this and other relationships yet to come. Third, pushing down her feelings forced her to internalize the negative energy she would have been able to release had she expressed herself in an appro- priate way. This then became a part of her ongoing vibration, sending out unresolved, agitated signals. Finally, her lack of expression turned into depression, and she became sulky and moody, negating her frequency even more and immobilizing her with inactivity and hopelessness.

Internalized and unexpressed feelings are one of the biggest sources of depression. This heavy emotional vibration is not only challenging to live with, but its self-perpetuating energy makes it almost impossible to attract something better. In addition, it's extremely difficult to change the conclusions that come out of that lingering negativity, and the resulting consciousness of lack and powerlessness manifests a destiny of more of the same. So no matter what you may have heard, never be afraid to express a difficult emotion.

> *For a clear and attractive vibration, negative feelings from the past must be expressed, and the emotions of the present must be acknowledged, honored, and released. Then you're free to make new, empowered, and optimistic conclusions. Your choice of self-actualization not only creates a powerful consciousness of positive manifestation, it also projects a dynamic energetic resonance that tells the world you're strong enough to take care of yourself and willing to make that a priority.*

Like Nate, Karen realized that her silence was digging her into the problem more deeply. She had to take action to get out of the energetic hole. She told her boyfriend that his treatment had been hurting her, and he needed to stop the criticism if he wanted their relationship to last. Through the process of getting all of her feelings out, however, she real- ized that she deserved a lot better, and she finally had the clarity and the courage to end the relationship herself. As is often the case, once Karen expressed herself, she was able to see the entire situation more clearly and turn her thoughts around. This effectively redirected her emotional energy and created a newly empowered consciousness for her.

Step 2: Reverse Your Thinking

Throughout this book you'll find references to the need for changing your thinking. In terms of your quantum psychology, the power of this one activity can't be overstated. Underneath it all, thought is the key to consciousness creation. It's also the source of your emotional responses, and as such, it's at the center of your energetic vibration. So if you want to alter your destiny, you must be willing to become the master—rather than the victim—of your own thought patterns.

This isn't a mere Pollyanna approach—it's not just some idealistic but unachievable suggestion. It's a powerful intention that's based in the science of consciousness and personal energy. For this reason, changing your thinking needs to be one of your highest priorities. I guarantee that the effort you put into this will influence the quality of your life in ways you could never imagine!

The power of thought switching is something you can prove to yourself right now. Read the next two paragraphs and then try the exercise described in them. You'll be amazed by what you experience.

First, think about a person or situation you find upsetting. Close your eyes and remember all of the details involved. Think of what you'd like to say about it and how it makes you feel—let yourself really get into it. Now, in that negative emotional state, notice what your energy feels like. Does the situation make you feel angry, hurt, or both? How does it make you view yourself and your place in the world? Notice what you're most conscious of. Do you experience a comfortable or uncomfortable vibration? Take a moment to consider all of these things and be aware of how this unhappy line of thinking makes you feel.

Now stop and let all of those thoughts go. See the entire situation floating up and away like a cloud in the distance. Take a deep breath and switch your thoughts to something pleasant—perhaps a fond memory, a lovely vacation spot, or even a funny event or joke that makes you laugh. Smile as you recall all of the details. Let yourself really get into the happy experience, and then notice the different feelings you're having. Be aware of your energy and your body sensations. What kind of vibration do you have when you switch to this more positive line of thinking? Take a few moments to notice how very different it makes you feel.

This exercise doesn't take long, but it's certainly revealing! If you're like most people, you'll notice a huge difference in the sensations of the two mental experiences. It quickly becomes clear how your thought choices have the power to change your emotional energy, and therefore the quality of your life.

Remember the concept of adjacent possibilities? It's a viable tool for shifting consciousness, and it can be equally helpful when applied to the thinking that generates emotions. Right next to the thought that tells you to fear is the alternative thought that says it's safe to trust; adjacent to the memories of past hurts are options to let them go and choose thoughts that empower you again. Alongside a moment of depression is a happy memory—you just need to remember it's there. You never have to be a victim of your thinking habits, even if they seem more like thinking addictions. No matter what pattern you may be following, if you really desire to change it, you can.

Over the years, I've had many clients who were extremely negative thinkers, but one individual stands out above the rest. Raised by a fearful mother and a very critical dad, Debby could hardly go five minutes without worrying about something. She had very strongly developed thought patterns of negativity, and her fear response was so deeply indoctrinated that it became her spontaneous and life-defining emotional reaction.

I taught her about adjacent possibilities, and she was surprised that she had the option to think something different. It had never even occurred to her that she could choose to focus on something new! In order to assist her process, we made a list of her ten biggest fear thoughts. We then reversed each one, replacing it with a more optimistic and more empowering possibility.

This was difficult for Debby because she'd become so deeply convinced of the truth of her worries. So at first all she could do was remind herself, *I can think something different. There are other ways of looking at this. It's possible that my worries are wrong.*

Amazingly, even this minor concession helped reduce her negative thinking immensely! She could feel the difference even these statements made in her emotions and in her energy. So she continued to entertain her adjacent possibilities, adding more significant thought reversals as she went along. It did take a long time, but eventually she was able to completely replace her catastrophic thinking with peaceful and trusting conclusions. This changed the very quality of her life. She was able to genuinely feel peace and happiness on a consistent basis. And although Debby has achieved many personal goals since, she considers her efforts to free herself from fear to be the greatest success of her life.

If you really want to get to the root of your "feeling bad" sensations, take a close look at your thinking! You'll find that almost all uncomfortable emotions can be traced back to one of three things: thoughts of self-negation, worry about what people think, or fear of the future. Yet each of these types of cognition has an opposite yet adjacent possibility of self-encouragement, peaceful release, or optimistic trust. Take the adjacent path and you'll feel a great shift in your emotions and vibrations.

Everyone has negative thoughts. It's a part of the human experience—but you don't have to let it be a way of life. As I get older, I look back and ask myself, *Why did I spend so much time worrying? Why did I let myself stay in that state?* It all seemed so important then, but now I know that I missed many opportunities to just let go and live in joy. It was when I started teaching these principles to others that I really made these cognitive and emotional choices myself. And it was then that I started to see major changes in the quality of my life and in the results I was attracting.

So when you have an uncomfortable or anxious feeling, let that be a sign that it's time to switch your thoughts and your energy to a higher vibration. Don't fault yourself; just calmly investigate. Identify the situation that's causing the emotional discomfort, and ask yourself the following questions:

1. *What are my negative assumptions? What am I making this mean?*

2. *What other possible conclusions can I draw about this situation that are more positive and empowering? What conclusions would lead to healthier and happier emotional vibrations?*

Constantly engaging in negative and fearful thinking is like taking poison every day. It makes your energy toxic and sends out wave after wave of agitating resonance. In the pursuit of success—or any kind of happiness—it's your thinking that matters most. *Your consciousness, your energy, and your intentions revolve around this important personal power. Take control of your thoughts and you control everything!*

An important word of caution about this, however: Please don't condemn yourself for falling back into your old, toxic patterns! If you judge yourself for negative thinking, your condemnation only makes it worse. As I tell all my clients, this kind of self-blame only adds negation to negation—actually increasing the abrasive vibrations instead of decreasing them! It's utterly crucial that you don't multiply your problems by falling into this fearful, self-critical reaction.

So when you catch yourself thinking negatively, just let it go. Laugh and identify that as merely a visit from your old self. Bless the situation, release the thought, and simply remind yourself that there's always an adjacent possibility. *Forgive yourself and smile every time it happens.* This immediately reverses the negative energy and creates a much more positive process.

Step 3: Practice Emotional Association

When you work on changing your thinking, you'll find that your daily emotions will become more and more comfortable, peaceful, and pleasant. But you'll have days when your feelings may be off and you just can't identify why. At those times—and in fact, anytime you desire—you can bypass your thoughts and change your emotions by *association,* an extension of the earlier process you practiced in Step 2. By letting the worry go and just shifting into a good-feeling memory, you can learn to switch your emotions without a long analysis about what's going on.

Here's how it's done:

1. Take a few deep breaths and quiet your mind. Let any thought go—even if it's a pesky worry that you feel the need to focus on.

2. Repeat the name of the emotion you want to feel. (Use the adjective, not the noun. For example, choose *happy* instead of *happiness* or *excited* instead of *excitement.* This is important because it turns the intention into a present description instead of a vague, future condition.)

3. As you're repeating the word, remember a time when you've been in that state. Let yourself feel the joy and picture all the details. Smile and put yourself in the center of that experience.

4. Continue to peacefully repeat the word and visualize the experience, and as you do, notice that the positive emotional state you're naming is a vibrating cloud all around you. You feel its energy moving toward you until it fills you with the wonderful vibrations you summoned. Continue to smile, breathe deeply, and let your awareness drop into your heart, feeling the gentle sensations grow.

This process may seem difficult at first, and you may actually resist letting your worries go, but if you just surrender to the new, peaceful state, you'll be surprised by how easy it will become in time. When you've practiced this a lot, all you'll have to do is a few repetitions of the desired state along with one or two deep breaths. You may not even have to do the visualization because your body becomes accustomed to the expectation of positive change. It longs for the peace and pleasure you're offering, so it will respond rather rapidly.

At the beginning, though, be sure to pick your positive picture appropriately. There are subtle nuances that the brain is aware of that are important in the process of association. For example, when I use the word *happy,* I picture myself at my favorite lakeside hotel, in a rocking chair on the porch, feeling the gentle breeze. But when I want the *excited* state, I picture myself skiing down my favorite run, fast and free in the crisp, cold air. This doesn't mean I'm not happy when I'm skiing; it's just a different kind of happiness, and the brain is precise. It wants to associate appropriately, so it will be much more effective—and more rapid—if you give it what it wants.

About Your Brain

In the early 1900s, William James, father of American psychology, used the term *plasticity* to describe the flexible nature of the brain. It's now known to be true that the brain is quite adaptable, and the word used to indicate that is *neuroplasticity.* Even if a trauma were to injure a part of the brain assigned to a certain activity, it's often the case that another area can be developed to take over. This flexibility can also be applied to changes in your thought patterns. In terms of your cognitions, the activity of the brain—no matter how deeply indoctrinated—can absolutely be changed.

There are two significant ways in which you can have greater control over the way your thought patterns function. Believe it or not, the first and most dramatic avenue is through meditation. Studies consistently show that people who meditate a lot have the greatest ability and ease in changing their brain functions. So this practice is not only good for your physical vibration, it's one of the best things you can do for your mental and emotional vibes as well. Many people dismiss this, but I can't recommend it enough: Meditate to radiate—a brilliant life force, that is!

The second way to develop a higher thought vibration is by establishing new neural pathways. These are the routes and connections that your thoughts follow in the brain. The more repeated a certain type of thought, the more deeply established its neural pathway is. But you can develop new ones that become stronger than the old. This is done in a three-step process that's as simple and direct as A, B, C:

A. Introduce new, optimistic conclusions, definitions, and perceptions

B. Support the new ideas with enthusiasm and emotional conviction

C. Repeat the new conclusions often—saturating yourself with positive options

This is the fundamental process of cognitive restructuring, and you'll find many variations of these steps applied to specific issues throughout this book. Studies show that this cognitive process can be as effective as medication when treating conditions such as anxiety and depression. And when you can reverse such harsh emotional vibrations, you'll definitely see a difference in what you attract.

Whether you're talking about neuroplasticity, quantum psychology, holographic consciousness, or emotional energy, it all comes down to this: *Change your thoughts!* I've seen it over and over again in my life and the lives of my clients, and I've found that there's no greater or more effective action you can take in the direction of your dreams than this cognitive process of A, B, C!

I've used this process myself to address several important issues in my life. It's hard to believe as I look back on it now, but I used to be terribly afraid of public speaking. I didn't actually realize it until I was thrown into it as a part of my work helping people with phobias. I began lecturing on the topic, and every time I was going to give a presentation, I'd have both an asthma attack and an anxiety attack. Some of my psychologist friends found this amusing since I was speaking about anxiety treatments, but I didn't find it funny at all. It was debilitating and uncomfortable, and I knew I had to do something to change it—or stop my public speaking altogether.

I investigated my thinking and couldn't find any specific fears that resonated with me. I didn't really worry about what people thought, so I wasn't afraid of rejection. I couldn't identify where the trouble was coming from, except that it was performance anxiety—and it was big! So whatever may have been going on subconsciously, I knew I had to create a new picture, a new definition of the experience.

I took some time to write out all the things I enjoyed about the activity, and I redefined my speaking as a positive experience. I affirmed over and over again that I was letting go of whatever worry might be under the surface. Instead, I was comfortable, happy, and completely at ease. I added a visualization of myself having fun in all sorts of speaking situations. Then at the beginning of each engagement, I told myself: *I am going to enjoy this. I give it all to the Universe with love and joy.*

Over time, my attitude and emotional reaction to public speaking completely reversed itself. Now it's my favorite item out of all of my various job descriptions! I travel the world, seeing wonderful places and meeting incredible people at every lecture, gathering, or conference. Now I can get up in front of hundreds or even thousands of people and feel only joy and excitement. And every single engagement fills me with such deep appreciation for the loving energy and the many beautiful individuals who have become such a treasure to me. I love the camaraderie and sharing, and I just can't imagine my life without this. I hate to think of the friendships and fun I would have sacrificed if I'd given in to that dread.

As You Feel, So Shall You Vibrate

I could have stayed in my fear—I could have limited my life based on that one emotion. It seemed strange and difficult at the time, but now I know that that problem held a very important gift for me. It showed me that I, too, could choose my emotions, that I could redefine my experiences and transform the very quality of my life. What I didn't know then was what quantum changes that effort would bring! Because I faced down that negative distortion and made a very specific intention in a more positive direction, public speaking became a very valuable part of my life, both personally and professionally. *That's often how quantum psychology works—you turn your psyche around and the energetic world follows suit, blessing your efforts in unexpected ways.*

Everyone has their own psychology, the mental patterns that create their emotional vibrations. It's important to know, however, that all human beings have the tendency to feel good sometimes and bad at other times. Faulting or blaming yourself for not feeling great is a completely counterproductive endeavor. That only makes you feel worse, perpetuating a vicious circle of fear and self-condemnation.

If you notice a pattern that you want to change, give yourself time to process it. Be patient with yourself as you work on creating your new quantum psychology. It took me quite a long time to get over my fears of public speaking, but it was important to me, so I didn't give up. Find out what matters to you—then let yourself gently move toward it without doubt or hesitation, choosing courage instead.

It helps to see this as something that will evolve over time. All of life is a process, and your self-forgiveness and encouragement—in spite of the difficult patches—will go a long way in moving you forward on your path. Don't worry about mistakes; just gently remind yourself that another possibility awaits. All is in Divine order, and the greatest destiny comes from a peaceful and loving present pursuit.

No matter what may be going on in your life, there's nothing that a second look, another day, and a little help can't fix. So renew your intention for self-support and joyous appreciation each morning. As you move through your varied experiences, be aware that you *always* have cognitive and emotional options. Let the past go and start each moment anew. Open up to your emotional adjacent possibilities and you'll be amazed by what you may find around the corner.

Don't be afraid to let yourself vent your darker reactions either. Come to some new conclusions and then let the old, unhealthy ones go. Visualize, and associate with, the happier feelings and experiences of your life. However long it may take, you're moving toward the future anyway—so practice living in the process of present change. With each intention to do so, your emotional energy will become brighter and more inviting. Choose peace and joy today . . . and your consistantly brilliant life force will attract wonderful feelings and many happy and unexpected returns.

CHAPTER 4

❖　✶　☯

YOUR ENERGETIC BODY

---

*"The more willing you are to surrender to the energy within you,
the more power can flow through you."*

— SHAKTI GAWAIN

We carry and transmit much more power than most of us realize—in fact, our bodies are like miniature power plants. Every moment of every day, we're filled with bioelectrical energy. Our nervous system sends electrical signals to our brain, which transmits messages to our organs. New thoughts are constantly forming, based on memories and environmental information being processed by our five senses (and believe it or not, our sixth sense, too).

Would you like to experience what your own personal energy feels like? Try this: Put the palms of your hands, close together and feel the heat that your physical body generates. You can increase this by first taking a few moments to relax. Then close your eyes and imagine two small spheres of energy flowing from your heart. One travels down through your left arm, the other down your right arm. Both energy spheres meet in the palms of your hands. As you focus on this current moving from your heart into the palms of your hands, feel the heat gently increasing. The energy connects your palms together. Now, move your hands about an inch apart. Can you still feel the link?

Cup your hands slightly so that they almost touch. As you do so, you'll feel an energetic vibration increasing between your palms. And if you focus your consciousness on that energy, you can create an even stronger vibration.

People who do hands-on healing call this "collecting energy." This exercise involving the palms is often performed before the healers are ready to send their power out. Why? Because they want to direct this focused energy *with intention*. I once saw an Eastern mystic "throw" someone across the room merely by doing this exercise and then casting his right hand out toward the person's chest—even though the mystic remained several feet away and never physically touched the other individual.

Wouldn't it be great if we could harness this raw power that courses through our bodies? Well, it can be done, although I hope your goal isn't to fling troublesome people across the room! Instead, learning how to use your body's natural energy system will help you live in balance; heal yourself; become more creative; and efficiently manage your personal energy resources so that you can take better control of your thoughts, your resonance, and your life.

The Chakra System

Let's go back to the exercise where you felt the energy in your palms. Those points in your hands are two of the energy centers in your body that are called *chakras*. This is a Sanskrit word that means "wheel," and refers to the system of energy centers, discovered about 4,000 years ago, that maps and balances the body's energy. Chakras are points where our power vibrates most strongly. Both physical and personal issues can be healed through them. Indian holy men considered the chakras to be psychic centers of consciousness, and believed that when these wheels of energy were spinning in equilibrium, then one could easily live a healthy and dynamic life.

It may seem unusual to refer to an ancient concept like chakras in a book about achieving success in the modern world. But in order to open the door to creativity and consciousness, where the real power of the Universe lies, it's often necessary to examine new—and old—ways of thinking. Never dismiss an idea merely because it may seem foreign at first; these are sometimes the most helpful tools you can find.

Understanding and utilizing this system can help you in so many ways. The seven primary chakras are located in a line that runs up the center of your body from the base of the spine to the top of the head. In addition, there are several secondary chakras, such as those in the palms of your hands, on the soles of your feet, and at your fingertips.

The Universe is alive with energy that pulses through every living thing, and one way we're connected to that flow is through our chakras. They also link us to others; and when they're in harmony, they open a fluid channel of supportive transmission. More than that, they allow us to draw on our own innate power to comfort, heal, and direct a valuable destiny creation. Therefore, it's important to know at least a little bit more about where in the body your chakras are located; what they do; and how you can use them to generate greater joy, health, and abundance in your life.

The Root Chakra

The first wheel in this system is the root chakra, and it's located at the base of the spine. When you visualize this energy center, try to imagine a glowing red sphere. This is the source of your personal power in your energetic field, and meditating on it will help you stay grounded when things in your life get crazy.

The first chakra is associated with physical stamina, harnessing Earth energy, and connecting with the community at large. So if you're working on a project that demands a lot of energy—or if you want to stay grounded while connecting with others—try the following meditation:

Visualize a beautiful white stream of light coming in through the top of your head, and see that illumination flowing down your spine to your red root chakra. Feel the radiance energize your head, neck, chest, and abdomen. Next, visualize the light creating a figure eight through your body. The light crosses over the heart center and circles down to your root chakra, then it loops upward again through your heart, turning back at the top of your head. Around and around, this circuit of brightness whirls gently through your body as it makes figure-eight patterns. Allow yourself to relax as you see the energy flow through you. It revitalizes you. It grounds you, yet helps you connect to the world.

Let yourself be aware of any thoughts or ideas that come to you when you do this process. Since this visualization and other chakra meditations will be very helpful in accelerating your progress as a vibrant, whole-brain thinker, you may want to have your journal and pen handy to record your thoughts and reactions. Many of my clients have found that these visualizations have created "aha!" moments that led to great breakthroughs in thought, emotion, and inspiration.

Doing these exercises will help open your mind to new ideas and your heart to amazing new connections. Try them if you want to fully employ all of the power available to help you draw on the Laws of Attraction and Manifestation.

The Sacral Chakra

The second or sacral chakra is located a few inches below your navel. It's associated with creativity, power, control, and sexuality. Most people visualize this sphere as the color orange. This chakra is one of the vortexes of inspiration, so if you wish to be creative, meditating on this energy center will help you stay focused—especially when it seems as though millions of distractions are getting in your way. If you need some new ideas, if you're working on a project that demands a lot of wisdom and awareness, or even if you're dealing with some sexual issues, try the following meditation:

Close your eyes and take a few deep breaths. With each inhalation and exhalation, imagine the glowing orange sphere of your second chakra, located below your navel. You have the power to make it glow as brightly as you want. The brighter it shines, the more your power and creativity grow. Remember this whenever you need a moment's insight: You have all the strength of the Universe within.

Now, visualize your red root chakra, which is located beneath your orange sacral chakra, and feel the energy flow upward from the first to the second. This bright current feeds your creativity and gives you powerful direction in your desire for success. Let yourself become inspired as you see and feel this energy pulsate within. Open yourself to the solutions and inspirations it will bring.

Try this visualization anytime you feel uninspired or stuck in thought. Be aware of any thoughts or ideas that come to you—perhaps you'll want to make note of them. I know a writer who performs this quick exercise every time he feels blocked, and he's often quite surprised by the words that are released whenever he works with the creative power of his sacral chakra. If you don't get the surge of creativity you're looking for at first, let yourself repeat the process. As you go through your day, be open to receiving ideas from unexpected sources.

The Solar-Plexus Chakra

The third chakra is the chakra of the solar plexus, and it's located midway between your waist and your heart. It's a very important center of your chi, or life force. Indian mystics visualize this life-giving chakra as a yellow orb—like a small, radiant sun. This energy sphere is associated with your view of yourself and the information you receive and send out about you. As such, it's a center of personal power and individual strength.

Focusing on this chakra is helpful when you're feeling isolated or full of self-doubt—or even when you just need a shot of self-confidence. Keep your solar-plexus energy center open and refreshed, because this is the fountain from which your eternal vibration moves through your body and radiates outward.

It's natural for your life force to flow and ebb. Sometimes you may feel very powerful—even unstoppable—while at other times, thoughts about giving up may seem overwhelming. This is normal, but you *can* learn to smooth out the peaks and valleys, and pull yourself out of the mental slumps of self-doubt. When you need to find the energy to move forward, meditating on your solar-plexus chakra can bring you back to center and renew your confident energies in just a small amount of time.

To enhance your power, focus your awareness on your solar plexus and visualize a ball of rotating yellow energy. Feel a vibration growing in the center of your body as this current spins in a circle, then begins to open like a blossom. The bloom emits beautiful colors that radiate light and feelings of confidence throughout your body. With every rotation, the self-loving, self-confident glow expands

*farther and farther—spreading waves of vitality down to your toes,
along your arms to your fingertips, and up to the top of your head.*

As the expanding yellow light energizes and refreshes your physical self, you find yourself feeling more balanced, more centered, more worthy, and much more confident to deal with the ups and downs of pursuing your dreams. As the healing, empowering radiance fills your entire body and pulsates outward, affirm that your power is ever present and your worth is unlimited and eternal. Know that your energy vibrates with confidence and self-love.

The Heart Chakra

The fourth chakra is the heart chakra, and it's located in the center of your chest. Some people see it as a vibrant green; others view it as pink; and some visualize a two-toned sphere, with green on the circumference and pink in the center. With this and all the chakras, go with whatever color feels right for you.

This is the place where you make heart-to-heart connections with yourself, the Divine, and all others. It's the source of unconditional love and all of the peaceful emotions that go with that—forgiveness, compassion, understanding, and contentment. When you focus on this energy center, open your heart to receiving, experiencing, and expressing love.

The link from your sacral chakra to your solar-plexus and heart chakra is energetically crucial if you really want to make your dreams come true. It connects your emotional activity to your creativity and your true desires to your self-love. This is important because if you can't unite your life force with what's in your heart, you'll never be able to fully draw on your innate power to fulfill your deepest longings.

One of the most common maladies that I see in the people I work with is a disconnect between life force and loving source, and this schism manifests as deep unhappiness. In my private consultations, I often do energy readings, which focus on a person's thoughts, emotions, history, and other information that expresses itself in the energetic body. I often see two distinct pools of energy with a clear break between them—one that cuts across the body right at the heart. The lower pool, devoted to movement and task completion, is thick, dense, and slow-moving in the light of this energetic schism. The upper pool, the current that vibrates from the heart through the head, represents the cognitive and emotional experience and often appears cloudy and fragmented. When I encounter this type of split energy in a person, I see someone who is trudging through life without feeling much emotional worth, heartlessly moving from one task to another, lacking peace or joyous fulfillment.

If this sounds like you or someone you know, then it's very important to keep this in mind: It's never too late to align your energy, reconnect your heart and solar plexus, and get unstuck from your vibrational and emotional rut. You can do this by working to unite your life force with your emotional self in one of the following ways:

— **Align your energy centers.** Starting at the base of the spine, visualize the red sphere of your root chakra empowering your sacral chakra; then see and feel both energies ascending your spine. Your yellow solar-plexus chakra is glowing like a golden sun. Let it warm and empower your effervescent green heart chakra, which spins in the center of your chest. Each sphere whirls brightly: red, orange, yellow, green. Feel the healing power of each chakra, and the sense of connection this alignment brings.

— **Write down the answer to this question:** *What is my life's purpose?* Spend some time considering the options and try to find the answer in your heart. Begin to take steps to pursue that path—even if it's just to be happy. When you're doing what you love, you feel a strong sense of personal purpose, and your life force automatically moves into your heart. You'll find that joy replaces drudgery in your life, and even if you still have many tasks to perform—and many steps until you reach your goal—you'll feel focused and motivated by your purposeful pursuit.

— **Pay attention to the higher emotional quality of your life.** Find time for peace in your day. No matter how busy you are, take a few minutes here and there to turn off your phone, close your eyes, take a few deep breaths, and do nothing. Do *nothing* . . . relax . . . and if you *must* think of something, remind yourself of all there is to value in your life. Creating happiness and creating success go hand in hand.

The Throat Chakra

It's not only important to live your purpose, it's also crucial to speak your truth. This is a function of the fifth chakra, which is located at the throat. The flow of this turquoise blue energy sphere is often blocked for people who have a hard time expressing or identifying their feelings. It can also be a problem area for those who have difficulty speaking out for themselves or taking action on their own behalf. The fifth chakra contains the energy of communication—both with ourselves and others.

In the pursuit of success, it's obviously important to be able to interact with other people in a way that clearly honors them and encourages their worth. But something that's equally important is how we connect with and honor ourselves. The way we see and express ourselves is one of the biggest influences on our energetic frequency. The way we think of and speak to ourselves—our "self-talk"—creates a powerful vibration that indicates the extent of our self-approval.

If you're constantly saying negative things to or about yourself, the energy of your throat center will constrict and you'll communicate a very dark vibration to others—and of course, that will be the energy that you get back. If you're self-critical, self-loathing, or even self-dismissive in your inner dialogue, these thoughts will generate powerful, destructive messages, even if they're never spoken aloud. This closes down your communication center, a vital connection in life. So, if your intention is to succeed, your inner dialogue must sparkle with optimism and self-approval. *In terms of consciousness creation, those who find success are those who speak to themselves as if they believe they're worthy of success.*

By strengthening the bonds between your throat and your heart chakra, which is the seat of unconditional love, acceptance, and contentment, you can bring caring energy to all your communication—both to yourself and others. Your heart wants to live in love, and that intention must start with the self and move outward. Someone who condemns others can't dwell in tender emotions, and words of self-loathing block the connection to the gentle vibrations of others' loving hearts. It's going to be very important, therefore, to consciously and consistently silence your judgment and negative self-talk.

When you need to have healthier words of communication, visualize a bright blue orb at your throat's energy center sending out rays of beautiful, loving vibration. Your throat energy pulsates with positive thoughts and encouraging words for yourself and others, projecting confidence and attracting people who are receptive to your ideas.

See yourself sitting before a small group of supportive people. Perhaps they're family members or a group of friends. Whoever they are, they're happy and relaxed as they listen to you talk. Your throat chakra is a sky blue sphere, and you speak in a clear, even tone. Your voice makes others smile. People enjoy listening to you, because you speak a clear and loving truth.

Your peaceful words begin in your green heart chakra, but appear blue as you speak them. The brilliant blue energy surrounds you all, bringing peaceful and supportive connections that then move out into the Universe beyond.

Bringing healthy energy to your throat chakra will enable you to let go of self-criticism and negativity. It will help you learn how to express yourself without doubt or fear of rejection. In addition, it will open you to receiving information as well as expressing it.

The Brow Chakra

The sixth or brow chakra is often called "the third eye" because it's located between the eyes at the brow. This energy center is usually seen as an indigo-colored sphere. It's the center of vision, perception, and intuition; it's also used by many to sharpen their concentration and fire up their imagination.

Igniting the brow chakra helps clear your perception of yourself and your world. This is important, because as one of the three significant pieces of consciousness creation, your perception needs to be positive and creative, and your view of yourself must be unclouded by misinformation. So whenever you find fault with yourself, send that judgment out of this center by creating a clear, light-filled, indigo orb that sweeps those unneeded thoughts away.

The sixth chakra also expands and clarifies your intuitive experiences. Many people believe this energy center is where to connect with the wisdom and information of the Universe. It's also the chakra of clairvoyance.

When you meditate on this energetic sphere, affirm: *I am opening myself to receiving valuable information from unseen sources in just the right time and in just the right way—for the greater good of all concerned.* Even if you do this exercise for just a few moments each day, you'll find yourself receiving messages of personal guidance, inspirational ideas, and unexpected solutions just when you need the information most. Focus on this chakra if you want to develop stronger, more spontaneous intuitive abilities.

This a powerful center for directing your intention. Have you ever felt a strange sensation and then turned around to find that someone was staring at you? Most people have experienced this phenomenon at some time or another—in fact, most folks have been on both the receiving and the sending end.

This isn't just a coincidence; it's an energetic process. The person isn't simply looking at you; he or she is directing the powerful energy of the third eye, probably without even knowing it. This is a simple and quite common example of what some people call *funneling your intention.* In more significant applications, processes like this enable you to visualize your goals more easily and achieve more accelerated and dramatic results. The following meditation is a short, easy way to funnel your goal intention directly into Universal response:

> *Open the meditation by visualizing a deep blue sphere at the center of your brow. See it opening and pulsating with a beautiful light. Then create a detailed, exact visualization of what you want to achieve. Fill it with color and excitement, and put yourself right in the middle of that picture, playing the wonderful scenario on the movie screen of your imagination.*
>
> *Next, keep your eyes closed and raise them slightly, as if you're looking up at that movie on the inner screen of your mind's eye. Hold the image of your dream there, feeling the joy it brings, and then after a moment, release it through the energetic vortex of your brow center. Recall this scene just before you fall asleep, repeating*

this process—even if only for a few moments. Imagine that this is all so real that you can touch it. Let yourself feel the excitement and enthusiasm that it creates. Then release the picture, sending it to the Universe with grateful expectation.

Studies have shown that raising your eyes will instantaneously put your brain frequency in the alpha state, the most creative form of consciousness. When you do this during visualization, you create your vision in the brain-wave condition of your most powerful manifestation. This simple technique of visualizing your desired end result can be done during any meditation, but using this sixth chakra approach will also initiate your highest connection with support from the Universe.

The Crown Chakra

The seventh chakra is the crown chakra, and it's located at the top of your head. Some people envision it as being a white disc, while others see it as royal violet. This energy center is the seat of thought, consciousness, and eternal life. It's also considered by most to be the point where one connects with Divine source. As such, meditating on this point can help bring the perfect love, healing, and peace from the Universal source of all blessings. It can also energize all of the centers of your chakra system, so it's worth spending a little extra time to do the following process.

Close your eyes and take a few deep breaths. Relax and let any tension you may have flow out of you. Every time you exhale, your body feels lighter and lighter because you're letting go of all your stress. Now imagine a pure and powerful white light streaming down from the Universal Source. It warms the top of your head and flows down your spine. Slowly, the diamond-white radiance will touch each of your chakras, healing the resonance there and making those spheres of energy glow brightly and spin vigorously. The colors of your chakras are so beautiful, and their energy is strong. Visualize each one in brilliant, healthy vibration now.

First the Divine light spins your crown chakra, increasing your intuition and your sense of sacred love—sending its illumination throughout your head, healing all your thoughts and beliefs. Now see the rays entering your brow center and healing your vision—both your sight and insight—and especially mending how you see yourself. The bright white energy glows strongly and fills every part of your mind, face, and head.

Now the Divine light slowly moves down into your bright blue throat chakra, healing your words and all your communication, causing you to honor yourself and always speak your truth.

Slowly, the glow moves down into your green heart center, filling your heart with unlimited and unconditional sacred love. You feel the embrace of Divine acceptance. The light fills your chest, flowing into your solar plexus and making it a brilliant, radiant yellow. The radiance is giving you strength and letting you know that you're a powerful being. Your solar plexus spins with healing energy, sending purifying golden vibrations throughout your body.

Direct the sparkling Divine light down into your second chakra and see it glowing a beautiful orange. It brings you creativity, power, and greater control, healing your sexuality and life force. Finally, see the beautiful bright light fill your red root chakra, located at the base of your spine. It also fills your legs and your whole body with vital energy and enduring stamina.

Your body is pulsating with light and radiating Divine life force. The light moves out into every cell, filling you up to the edges of your being. It brings peace, healing, and gentle, loving vibration to all that you are and all that you need.

And now it slowly flows upward again—all the way up your body and out through your crown center, spreading your own light and truth back to the Universe, creating a unified connection between you and all life. The Divine source feels your intention and continues to send its loving, supportive white radiance back down through your energetic body and deep into your soul. This circuit of Universal light continually streams up and down—soul to Divine soul. Its ever-present vibration energizes and revitalizes you and makes you one with the Eternal Source.

This meditation will open your crown chakra and activate all of the energy centers of the body. In aligning your chakras, it will bring balance, healing, and a powerful focus to your life. In addition, it will cause you to feel loved, connected, and supported by the gentle energy of the Divine. Open yourself to this magical union!

The Energy of Success

You may be wondering why it's important to know about these chakras. After all, what do they have to do with success? The answer to this question lies in the chemistry and power of your physical and eternal life forces. The vibrations of your body and the energy centers that pulsate through it contribute to the light and image of your hologram. Changing these frequencies can significantly help you shift your consciousness. In addition, understanding these centers in your physical self can help you direct healing to the specific issues that may be holding you back.

For example, a meditation focusing on the fourth chakra can create heart-centered thoughts and actions, which vibrate a loving and peaceful approach. *Living from the heart increases your authentic power and reduces your worry because the heart lives in trust in the here-and-now.* The brain, on the other hand, has the tendency to dwell in the past or worry about the future, creating a schism in your energetic focus because the heart is present while the mind is busy traveling time!

Studies have shown that the energy measured at the heart center is more powerful and farther reaching than that of any other point in the human chakra system. And while the function of the brain (or mind) and that of the heart can't really be separated in any truly holographic view of the self, you'll find that heart energy is the real source of all that's valuable. *Increasing value—from the most personal to the Universal—is what true success is all about.*

It may be helpful to put these meditations on tape and listen to them as you fall asleep. In time, you'll find that you can do them easily and with increasing effect—and you can utilize these processes in any situation. For example, if I find myself in a negative thought pattern, I just spin the top three chakras—the throat, the brow, and the top of my head (crown). I whirl out all the negative thoughts, then drop my consciousness into my heart and let it rest in the gentle vibrations there. If I have a speaking engagement and find that my energy level is low, I take a few deep breaths and visualize myself bringing energy up from the earth to activate my lower chakras for vitality and stamina. I also connect my heart center to my throat so that my words will come from love. Finally, I often open the crown chakra to access and receive Divine guidance. I feel the light flowing within, and I open myself to receiving inspiration.

This all may seem foreign to you now, but spend just a few minutes each day meditating on the energy center of your choice. See it spinning and colorful, bringing you exactly what you need. You don't even have to think about it too much—just let your intuition be your guide. Your spirit will show you the way, so close your eyes and let yourself focus on whatever chakra you're directed to first. Spend a few moments of peaceful contemplation there; spin the center and then let it all go. When you notice how good this makes you feel, you'll find yourself wanting to do it more and more.

Devoting time to igniting each of your energy centers will bring you wonderful gifts that accelerate many forms of personal success. From physical healing to creating a clear perception of your goals, from increasing your energy to strengthening your harmonic connections—working on your chakras can bring value to every facet of your daily life. Your energetic body is a powerful force. Directing its vibrations will bring you happiness and balance—important core elements of a peaceful yet vibrant life force that magnetizes joyous success.

CHAPTER 5

SUCCESSFUL INTENTIONS

"Choose your intention carefully and then practice holding your consciousness to it, so that it becomes the guiding light in your life."

— **JOHN-ROGER**

The Universe itself is a hologram of time, space, energy, and consciousness. Within the all-encompassing picture of life lies the past, present, and future of human experience. Your intentions are a part of that, and so are the results that flow from them. Since your desires follow a chain of cause and effect through various conscious and unconscious connections in multidimensional reality, it's important to know how your intentions entangle you with the field of manifestation.

To make the right connections on all levels, it's helpful to have a holographic understanding of your desires. This holistic view will help you align your intentions with the vibration of synchronicity in the world. Any number of potential links—both within and outside of your awareness—could move you forward, so you need to know exactly what your intentions are and how they resonate in your process of manifestation.

Like all aspects of your life, your desires aren't merely one-directional, straightforward projections that lead you directly from point A to point B. Instead, your desires—as part of your quantum psychology—are multilayered and complex, and they can actually lead you in many directions at once. Just like a hologram, the picture on the surface of your desires may indicate one thing, but below that, behind the obvious, something entirely different may be going on. It may seem surprising, but it's true. In the hologram—the whole picture—of your motivation, your intentions don't always reflect your real desires.

This may be hard to believe, but there are a lot of ways in which your inner intentions don't match your desires. For example, you may yearn to lose weight, and you may even verbalize a decision to eat less and exercise more. However, you may know in your heart of hearts—deep within the center of your true motivation—that you really don't want to do all that's necessary to reach your weight-loss goal. Whatever it is you long for, you may have the desire to achieve it, yet not have the real intention to carry through.

In fact, it's even possible that you could be projecting an *unconscious will* that's the polar opposite of what your conscious mind intends. And if it's powered by your deeper expectations, it's very likely to have a stronger influence on your destiny creation than your active and aware desires may have. For example, in the forefront of your mind, you may want a loving and supportive relationship—you can even long for it with great zeal, but if you've had a history of abusive romantic experiences, you may be fearful and even anticipate more of the same in the future. It's entirely possible, then, that your fears and inner expectations—being so emotionally charged—could attract yet another difficult partner, rather than the loving one represented in the open desires of your heart and mind.

This is no less an act of consciousness creation even though your fearful intentions may not be conscious at all. Your underlying assumptions join your surface intentions to spearhead your attraction. This is the directional force of your power of manifestation, so you must take control of it by becoming keenly aware of all the levels of your intentions.

Thought Forms!

An intention is a thought-form of expectation. As you've seen, your thought-forms are quite literally thoughts that form, and your expectations are no less influential than any other type of cognitive pattern. In fact, what you expect in your life is far more forceful than what you desire! This is because it has the power of belief and experience behind it, while what you want may be driven only by uncertain hope. In the context of destiny creation, your beliefs and expectations will hold sway over your hopes and desires any day.

Getting clarity here requires a two-step investigation. First, you must ask yourself what your specific intentions are; then you must find out if they match your genuine expectations. For example, you may say, "I intend my future to be happy," yet in your heart of hearts, you may really expect the days and months to come to be dull or even burdensome. This coexistence of contradictory future thought-forms creates a phenomenon called *conflicting intentions*, a process whereby your positive intentions are actually cancelled out by your negative expectations.

It's the old cliché of "one step forward, two steps back," where your optimistic desires lead you in the right direction, yet your doubtful expectations turn you right around again. For this reason, understanding exactly how you may be conflicting your intentions can provide an important clue to the secret of what might be holding you back.

Your expectations are usually based in personal experience. The problem with that is that if your path has been difficult, you may be basing important assumptions about the future on negative past events. You might have had a hard time getting a good-paying job, so you simply assume that this trend will continue. You could have a history of being treated unkindly by your romantic partners, so you expect that a truly kind lover just doesn't exist. Whether your intention is to find that great-paying job or to attract a healthy and loving relationship, your expectations *must* be amended to match your high intentions.

Expectation Investigation

There are several main issues that may be conflicted where your *intentions* and *expectations* are concerned. In order to find out if and how these two important elements may be canceling each other out, consider each of the following life issues and add any that may be important to you.

- Career
- Money
- Love
- Creativity
- Other

Ask yourself the following questions:

1. *What are my desires in each of these areas of my life?*

2. *What have my life experiences caused me to conclude about each of these issues?* (Be honest.)

3. *Deep down, what have I* really *been* expecting *concerning these things?*

If your answers to Question 1 don't match your answers to Question 3, then you're sending out conflicting intentions. And even if 1 and 3 match but Question 2 is strongly divergent, there could be unknown, buried histories that are very much alive. The second question also gives you an indication about where any problems may have come from. You may not have been conscious of it, but your deeper, negative expectations, based on those difficult life experiences, could represent your more emotionally charged intentions. When this kind of conflict exists, the Universe will always follow that stronger feeling—or it will respond with nothing at all.

You don't have to stay conflicted, however. You can open yourself to believing in the potential of your desired intentions more and more strongly every day. First, look at any negative conclusions from Question 2 and consider more positive possibilities. Write some new, healthy options that you'll consciously choose from now on—in spite of past experience. Then rewrite any doubtful or stalemated expectations revealed in Question 3 so that they match the positive vibrations of your desired intentions and your new, healthier conclusions.

Finally, you must reread your optimistic expectations repeatedly and affirm your readiness to see them as your truth. Visualize each successful outcome and charge it with excitement and positive expectation. This will switch the emotional charge from negative to positive and give that optimistic visual image much more power.

Consider each new assumption and successful outcome and affirm the following:

- *I open myself to seeing the real potential of this successful outcome in my life.*

- *I am open to receiving wonderful results. No matter what has happened in the past, I am completely deserving of unlimited happiness in my life.*

- *I am ready, willing, clear, and receptive. I expect my highest intentions, and I always anticipate the best. This is my truth!*

Law and Orders

The laws of desire and intent are very clear. Your quantum psychology moves into every longing, so you *must* support your specific intentions with your beliefs, emotions, expectations, and actions. It's not enough to say, "I want a lot of money" if your desire is fraught with fear. Specific desires must be positively motivated to have your whole life force behind them.

The Law of Pure Desire says that you *can* create with deliberate intent, but you'll only be successful if your motivation is genuine and aligns with your deeper life expectations. You know that your intentions are your order forms to the Universe—you don't want to cancel out your orders with expectations of self-doubt or fear of failure and lack.

A pure desire is never motivated by fear, urgency, or desperation. The center of deliberate intent is an attitude of self-responsibility, a determination to accept full ownership for creating the results you want by engendering an expectation of value and happiness in the present—not merely lamenting the past and longing for some external occurrence in the future. Your intention for the future—at least emotionally speaking—must be activated today.

Remember, it's a backward process to seek a positive emotion only through a particular achievement. You want to *live* in the emotion that you long to create, and then your specific outcomes will come your way.

But if you dwell in worry, anxiety, and desperation about your goals, then those negative expectations will become the core activity of your vibration, creating a toxic resonance that the Universe resists. There's no getting around it—as soon as fear and urgency enter into the mix, you move out of the attractive energies of pure and deliberate intention into the repulsive energies of *paradoxical intent.*

Paradox or Paradise—the Choice Is Yours

In nearly 30 years of teaching this information, I've found that there are two principles that elicit more emotional response than any other—that create that "aha!" moment of recognition and self-awareness that transforms understanding. The first is the principle of self-honoring and the fundamental truth that until you consistently come from a place of respect for yourself, you'll never be able to attract what you desire. Your energy of self-dismissal will inevitably cause you to be dismissed by others—and by the Universe itself.

I always say that if you can only make one change in your life, let it be this: Start to investigate your life, asking yourself, *Does this honor me?* Let yourself evaluate every single aspect of your life in terms of this question—from what you think to what you say and all the decisions you make. When you have the courage to change your dishonoring choices, you'll see—as so many others have—that the very fabric and quality of your life will also be transformed.

The second principle that people respond to with alarming recognition is the Law of Paradoxical Intent. *This law says that the more desperate you are about achieving your goal, the more you'll push it away, actually creating the opposite—or the paradox—of your desire.*

So many people never even realize that it's the negative energy associated with their own needy attachment that's sabotaging the results they're looking for. This is a very common phenomenon, though. Most people find themselves in the grip of paradoxical intent at some time or another.

When your desire becomes a large part of your life, it's a natural emotional response to become hopeful about the outcome. It's very important, though, to reel in any fear, urgency, or neediness because those vibrations are both resistant and repulsive, causing you to move out of the synchronistic flow of Universal manifestation. *You become attached to the result when you value the future over the present.* This creates vibrations of desperation, jagged waves of energy that push against the current of abundance, sending away that which you desire most. Remember, the natural flow of the Universe is love and peace, but when you move in the direction of frantic worry, you counter that intention, magnetizing more effort and disappointment in the process.

A Melody of Love

I once had a client named Melody who, like so many others, was looking for love. She called me in frustration, asking why she wasn't getting the results she wanted with a particular young man she was interested in. She said, "I don't understand it. I've been practicing the Law of Attraction, which says to focus only on what you want, not on what you don't want." She felt that was exactly what she'd been doing, focusing on him and picturing the two of them together.

When I asked her how often she did this, she told me that she thought about him all the time—when she got ready in the morning, when she was driving to and from work, and when she went to bed. From morning till night, she zeroed in on him dozens, perhaps hundreds, of times per day. Unfortunately, that was precisely the problem. Melody hadn't realized it, but she'd moved from focus into obsession, and she'd done what so many people do—ignite the energies of paradoxical intent.

It's healthy to concentrate—even determinedly so—upon your goal, but you actually lose your focus when you become overattached. Your unhealthy investment reduces your positive creativity and poisons the harmonic energy of attraction, completely reversing the direction of your desire.

Obsessing about something you don't have makes you unconsciously brood about what you lack, totally dismissing the present value in your life. Your urgency about getting what you want shouts at the Universe that you don't care about—or appreciate—anything else. This act of dismissal creates a dark vacuum of energy, one that nobody wants to support or even be around, and the Universe has the same response. Instead of generating the results you long for, your paradoxical intent becomes a black hole of obsessive longing, destroying any positive outcomes that may come your way.

When I pointed this out to Melody, she could see how the patterns of her relationships had always gone the same way—and how she'd accelerated her own disappointment! Her palpable longing was energetically picked up by every man she became interested in, sending them running. In order to change this, Melody knew she had to get to the bottom of things. It was necessary to look into her quantum psychology to find out where this desperation was coming from.

When we investigated her history and beliefs, we were able to discover the source. Her father had been distant and unavailable, a capable breadwinner, but totally uninterested in being a loving father. Melody sought his affection and approval throughout her childhood, and when she became an adult, she projected that need onto the men in her life. She hadn't realized it, but a part of her even embraced the belief that until she had male approval, she wouldn't be happy and could never really approve of herself.

Of course, this only made her go after love more aggressively. Every man she met became a potential partner, instantly causing her to become clingy and obsessed. And whenever someone didn't call, she went further into obsession and bitter urgency, digging herself deeper into her paradox. Not only was this attitude dishonoring to her, it was absolutely poison to her desire for romance.

In order for Melody to find love—and even more important, real happiness—she needed to build a new hologram of self-love and self-approval. So we created a multilayered approach, one that would deal with her present emotions and conclusions as well as her history. She was willing to work through it because like most people, when she learned that the Universal laws could only return her own energy and consciousness to her, she was finally motivated to understand and change.

Taking the Paradox Out of Your Intention

Here's a list of things that Melody did to change her quantum psychology in order to shift her energy and get better results. Although this process is similar to the technique of changing emotional energy, this one needs to be applied to the potential sources of your paradoxical intent. Think of the things you feel urgent about achieving, and use these steps to turn your desperation around.

1. Attack false, conflicting beliefs. Melody realized that she had to change her self-view. Although she'd never considered her self-description before, she needed to write a new definition that included the truth about her eternal self and her worthiness of unconditional love. She affirmed that in spite of her father's misinformation and skewed priorities, she'd always been deserving of affection. And she decided to give it to herself now in the form of her own love and encouragement—something she'd never done before.

2. Meditate on releasing the past and creating peace and self-approval. In this approach, Melody sat quietly and saw herself letting go of the hurt and frustration of the past. She visualized these emotions lifting up and out of her, floating away on the wind. She then imagined the golden light of the Divine radiating in her own heart center, causing her to connect with her real and eternal loving Source. This meditation brought Melody a profound peace and satisfaction, the depth of which surprised her. She saw it as a cleansing intention, making her new again and bringing her the love she had always deserved.

3. Ventilate any unfinished negativity and influential feelings from the past. Melody had to grieve the loss of her father's love. She never received what every child deserves, and she had an innate sense that something was missing. That sense of lack caused her to self-sabotage throughout her adult life. She had to let go of the past and become her own loving parent. In her journal, she wrote letters to her father, venting her anger and pain. Even though her dad had long since passed away, she needed to move the toxic energy of her past out of her emotional vibration and fill in what was missing with forgiveness, self-care, self-love, and trust. (You'll find a healing process you can do with loved ones who have passed over in Chapter 9.)

4. Change unhealthy behaviors and attitudes. Melody had established very aggressive and clingy approaches to men, but she needed to reverse that now. She actually had to learn how to meet and get to know members of the opposite sex without making it mean anything. She had to breathe, relax, and let go of urgency and immediate longing. She talked to herself, changed her attitude, and stopped looking at men as the solution to life's problems. Instead she started seeing them merely as other people—without any future investment. Later, when she began to date more, she needed to learn that she didn't have to accept just any kind of treatment in order to keep male attention. These adjustments were all foreign to her at first, but with conscious intention, she was able to incorporate them into her lifestyle over time.

5. Take responsibility for creating a life full of happiness and self-fulfillment—even before the outcome is achieved. Melody had to let go of the expectation that something outside of her, somewhere in the future, was the only thing that could provide what she desired. Instead, she had to figure out how to create happiness, enthusiasm, and fulfillment for herself. It seemed frightening, but she actually had to get to the point where her own life was so peaceful and filled with self-love that it would actually be okay to be alone. *This is the ultimate reversal of paradoxical intent: When you've finally arrived at the place where you don't need your specific desire in order to be happy, that's when it will come to you.*

It took a while, but Melody did learn the unyielding power and truth of this law as she worked diligently on her new intentions. Little by little, she started to feel a genuine sense of self-activated happiness, and she finally released the urgent need for love that she'd been living with for nearly 30 years. She was able to create an active, happy, and fulfilling life—one in which she had no need to glom on to every man she met. She established a new belief in herself, a perception of worthiness, value, and self-approval that was genuine and heartfelt . . . and she was happy to live in this peaceful state alone.

In time, Melody did meet someone who mirrored her newfound self-respect. Interestingly enough, she didn't even notice him at first, but as is true with every paradox, once she became happy with herself, he certainly noticed her! They've been together for 12 years now and have two wonderful children. And every time Melody begins to worry or feel urgent about anything—whether it's work, money, or the kids—she reminds herself that that type of energy will never get her where she wants to go. Instead, she releases it and chooses the adjacent possibility of peace in the present and trust in the future—whatever that may bring.

Leaving the Paradox and Sailing into Trust

Everyone can think of an experience similar to Melody's. In fact, you may have dealt with paradoxical intent several times. When you think about your life, I'll bet there's at least one issue that has kept you confused about why things aren't going your way—wondering how you can stop getting the same old disappointing results.

Don't be discouraged—everybody's been there. In fact, this pattern is so common that many people spend their entire lives in the misery of paradoxical intent. They yearn for something to happen, and the longer it takes to manifest, the more frustrated they become. This ongoing failure creates an increasing desperation that continues to grow in agitating vibration, repeatedly pushing their desired outcome away. It's a vicious circle where the negative emotion generates devastating results, and those awful consequences stimulate even more urgency and toxic energy.

You also may recognize a variation in the process that occurs when you actually get what you want—or something close to it—and you're so afraid of losing it that you become overly desperate to hold on. Eventually, you're likely to find that your energy of striving and your need for control will actually create the results you fear, causing you to lose the very thing you thought you'd finally received. Even if you don't have to relinquish your dream, your ongoing desperation and fear create such constant misery that you're guaranteed to lose the happiness you attached to it in the first place.

This scenario can take place in any arena of achievement, whether it's career, money, or any other kind of acquisition. But it's especially prevalent in the pursuit of romantic relationships, and it's easy to see why. Not only does the Universe pick up on your repulsive, agitated vibration, but the other person—the object of your interest—does, too.

In the quantum physical world, the phenomenon called *phase entanglement* (which I mentioned briefly in Chapter 3) indicates how two entities come together and pick up on each other's essential nature. When they part, each one carries a portion of the other's energy and essence with them. This is true in the natural world and in the human experience, too. When people come together, profound communication happens on an energetic level—an exchange of life force that may not be noticeable in the five-sensory realm, but is very real and influential just the same. Two people may be attracted upon meeting, or at the beginning of a relationship, but when one person crosses the line into fear and urgency, the other picks up on that vibration and is repulsed.

This phenomenon is common in—but not limited to—romance. In the workings of the energetic world, we're all connected in every way. Supportive and creative energies surround us, but when we live in worry, lack, and fear of failure, we contradict our higher intentions and create a very fragmented vibration in our personal energy field. When this becomes our primary frequency, we move through our life broadcasting a very agitating and unsettling resonance that breaks our connections and drives away the many sources of support. The Universe may be trying to get through this energetic storm, but we're completely incapable of receiving its assistance. Such is the sabotaging power of paradoxical intent—to push everything you desire out of reach.

But there is a way to reverse these energies and move out of their resistence and into synchronistic flow. You must release any emotional desperation for the goal and live your life in the here-and-now—with a sense of value and peace in your present circumstances. Even if you feel that there isn't much to value in your life at the moment, you must find something of worth in it—and in yourself—right now. You must define yourself and your existence in a positive perception at this point—not in some distant future hope.

If this is the first time you're hearing about the emotions involved in paradoxical intent, you're probably asking what everyone does: *How can I really want something without becoming emotionally attached to it?* The reality is, you can certainly become emotional about your desire—in fact, you should get excited, enthusiastic, and joyous about its potential. But you don't have to become *attached* to it. Attachment to an outcome not yet achieved means that you've invested an important and even necessary part of your present experience in an unknown future event. In essence, you're saying that some external circumstance is going to bring you the happiness, security, or love that you should already be providing for yourself. This paradoxical intent has two important effects: First, it implies that you're incapable of creating these things for yourself. Second, it shifts your intention from appreciation to worry and lack.

In this way, your attachment or investment reveals a holographic picture of doubt and need vibrating deep within. Your surface intention for success may shine, but it's your inner consciousness of limitation that will determine your destiny creation. In addition, desperate attachment projects at a very low resonance of depression and fear, the energetic echoes of which can only bring more of the same. There's no getting around it—your single-minded focus on urgency about the future only removes the happiness from your present reality, creating a reversal of cause and effect that will undoubtedly make your future unhappy as well.

The solution to paradoxical intent is clear: Want whatever it is you want, but *never* pin your happiness upon receiving it. Move with peace, purpose, and determination (not desperation) in the direction of your dreams. Then instead of channeling the agitating vibration of fear into your desires, you'll be projecting a hopeful and optimistic intention about your very life, one that other people and situations—and especially the Universe—will find impossible to resist.

The Happiness Chain Reaction

What would happen if you could want something without ever needing it to be happy? It's a big question. *Can* you do that? How would you approach your desires in that frame of mind? In fact, how would you approach your *life* if you no longer chose to put your joy on hold? Would you decide to expect happiness each day? Would you let go of fear? How would you change your attitude to ensure that heartfelt peace and appreciation were your primary emotions—and the energies of your whole life force? It will be an extremely valuable tool for you to answer *each* of these questions in your journal. Don't put it off—this is a life-changing issue!

Your genuine expectation for present happiness is a vital part of a truly magnetic life force. If you're incapable of being content now, you can't possibly generate the positive vibration that will attract the joy you seek in the future. So if you take a look at your life and realize that a peace-filled happiness isn't in your daily experience, it needs to be of primary importance. Look for joy in the mundane. Live each day with heartfelt appreciation and blissful intention, and the energy of your life will shine!

Your self-imposed anxiety over focusing on what you lack must be released so that you can choose a higher emotional vibration and a more dynamic consciousness. Your ability to find life rewarding can't be a rare occurrence, usually allocated to some vague but hoped-for future outcome. That's a severely limited view that will only limit your results and stop your dream in its tracks.

Expecting real joy in your day-to-day life creates readiness to experience it at every opportunity. Affirm: *I expect to be happy today! I choose to love myself today! I create joy in all that I do and think!* Widen your gladness options and you'll increase the likelihood of finding wonderful surprises, even in unusual places and experiences. Bring playfulness to the mundane—the next time you wash the dishes, try making the event fun and see what happens. Bring love and cheer to everything you do and see it coming back to you!

Living in joy and leaving the worry of the future behind will accelerate your desires into more rapid success. So allow real happiness to become an ever-present intention, and your exciting life force in the here-and-now will move powerfully out into the Universe. These pure and unconflicted intentions will fill your heart with present wonder and clearly direct an unrestricted flow of continued contentment your way.

CHAPTER 6

THE THREE COSMIC PARADOXES

"Life begets energy. Energy creates energy.
It is by spending oneself that one becomes rich."

— SARAH BERNHARDT

Getting a handle on the complexities of your paradoxical intent will give you a quantifiable advantage in terms of your personal achievement, in large part because your successful escape from urgency and need allows you—without any conditions—to achieve peace in the present, wherever that present may be.

But paradoxical intent isn't the only interesting and influential dichotomy in this "fun house" we call life. There are actually several paradoxes that seem to toy with our senses and oddly impact our emotional experiences. The three most important of these are the *Paradox of Time,* the *Paradox of Experience,* and the *Divine Paradox.* Each of these is an active participant in destiny creation, employing subtle truths and astounding contradictions.

The Paradox of Time

When I was a little girl, I used to imagine that I could slip through a slit in the air and step out of this world into another place and time—one that was filled with fantastical people and sparkling things for me to explore.

I imagined that if I put my arms out and ran my hands through the open spaces around me, I'd be able to find just the right place where a narrow, invisible, vertical line would provide a sort of elastic portal to that other reality. I always looked forward to the moment when my fingers would slip into nothingness, and I'd know that I had finally found that secret—and perhaps even sacred—slice of space that would magically open into unknown realms.

Strangely enough, I was never disappointed not to have found it. If I couldn't locate it in one place, I always knew it would be somewhere else. In fact, I could always feel the presence of these other worlds just beyond the reach of my personal experience. Something deep inside told me that there were many of these mysterious apertures, just waiting for me to discover them when the time was right. I suppose even then that I'd been feeling—or daydreaming about—the presence of *parallel universes,* although I had no idea that's what they were called.

The popularity of the concept of parallel universes has waxed and waned over the years, but there has recently been a resurgence of interest due to the current excitement over a relatively new item on the quantum physics menu: *M theory.* It explores the possibility of an 11-dimensional Universe made up of membranes or sheets that ripple with energy; vary in form; are cylindrical, flat, or doughnut shaped; and possibly loop back on themselves or intersect with other sheets. It would take volumes to explain the science of M theory and to discuss the complexities of the dimensions numbered five through ten. (These are promoted in several string theories and are described more through mathematical formulations than the physical or temporal characteristics a layperson might expect. If you want those details, there are several books in the Suggested Reading section that can lead you in the right direction.)

For our purposes here, however, the most intriguing element is the 11th dimension, which carries within it an infinite number of parallel universes. This dimension and the universes in it may be very close—as close to us as the ends of our eyelashes—yet we aren't aware of their existence because of the vastly differing vibratory rates. These parallel universes may have an infinite number of civilizations—some just like ours, and others that may have entirely different laws of physics.

While this may sound more like science fiction than scientific theory, it offers important implications that can be applied to some of the stranger phenomena of the human experience, one of which is the nature of time. Some people have found the existence of membranes, extra dimensions, and parallel universes to be very helpful in explaining the space-time continuum.

The Paradox of Time says that we just seem to move from past to present to future—in separate and sequential moments. The reality is that all time exists at the same time, each passing moment merely shifting into another vibration.

This may be hard to wrap your mind around, but it's actually very empowering, especially where your intentions are concerned. To create an intention right now is to plant the seeds of what you want firmly in fertile ground of the future. That's why it's so very important to live in the emotion you want to create. Your vibration of peace, happiness, or appreciation passes the boundaries of time, moving at this very moment into future manifestation.

Time and Intention

No matter what the human experience of it may be, time is actually a vast illusion. Linear time, the passage of hour to hour and year to year, is a format of perception that allows us to compartmentalize our experiences in easy, quantifiable segments. This experiential view lets us structure and label the periods of our life, marking time accordingly. We say things like "When I was in college . . ." or "After the baby was born . . ." or "When I retire . . ." in an attempt to catalog the significant moments in our earthly journey.

Yet this isn't the true nature of time, and such labels can keep us stuck in a limited perception. We think our life is relegated to long sequences of perceived mediocrity suspended between a few major events that define us. In this view, our present moments quietly and tediously build upon each other to evolve into some vaguely predictable future where a few more of those special events are hoped for. Unfortunately, this attitude lulls us into inactive complacency about both our present and our future experiences. *It shifts us from a creation intention to a waiting intention, which is a very narrow perspective. This causes us to lose time rather than use it.* We then miss the opportunity to grasp the very real value and joy that exists within the present moment.

But when we understand that chronology doesn't exist as we know it—that all time exists simultaneously—we're free to experience the spontaneous and instantaneous nature of consciousness creation. We can open ourselves to the vast potential of uncertainty, knowing that anything can happen at any time, that this very moment is brimming with opportunity, and that our present intention can manifest immediate results.

One of the great teachings of Mahayana Buddhism is *Ichinen Sanzen,* which is the concept of "3,000 worlds in a single thought moment." To me, this is a beautifully poetic expression of some of the most important truths of modern physics. It seems to roll uncertainty, complexity, and M theories all into one, reminding us of the power we have in every single second of thought. There are thousands of realities open to us right now, and we're free to choose which one we want to be in. We move through time like it's an invisible, unchangeable environment, but time is actually our tool—and like all tools, it's what we do with it that counts.

Fly-fishing in the River of Time

Time is considered to be the fourth dimension of our Universe. It follows the first three physical dimensions of length, breadth, and width, adding the element of duration—for anything of physical substance can't take up space before it's manifested or after it ceases to exist. But consciousness is a field that transcends time and space, a realm of information that exists now and always, unlimited in its intrinsic power and its ability to influence the past, present, and future. Your individual consciousness is no less powerful, and your present choice of intention directs it. Right now is the doorway to every moment—"now" is yesterday, tomorrow, and next year!

Whether you know it or not, you're always sending your unconscious intentions out into the Universe. Like a fly-fisher who repeatedly casts the line into the water, each new moment casts a new intention into the cosmic stream. "Now" is just one drop of liquid life flowing in the sea of yesterday, tomorrow, and always. Use the right energetic bait and the golden gifts of the Universe will bite!

Time-Tool Techniques

Time is a bizarre and beautiful paradox. In order to use it to your advantage, there are some things you need to remember when casting out your moment-to-moment intentions:

1. The present is your most powerful tool for creating dynamic destiny. Establish emotional and spiritual prosperity now, and every other kind will follow.

2. You have the power to instantaneously change your future at this moment. You don't have to go through elaborate machinations for years to come in order to force a future of joy. Take a breath of happiness now, and feel that choice reaching out into time.

3. The emotional, cognitive, and perceptual quality of this instant not only shifts your consciousness and energy, it sets the tone for your future moments, which are already taking place at a different vibration. Shift your vibration to a higher level of consciousness now.

4. Your goals must be oriented toward the present as well as the future. Make clear and conscious plans about the present—this moment, this hour, this day—in order to accelerate your specific goals for the future.

5. The most dynamic present intentions revolve around self-honoring choices, optimistic and appreciative thoughts, and emotional expectations for happiness in the here-and-now. Think something that values and respects you *right now.*

6. Always remember that it's *never* too late. In terms of consciousness creation, there's no such thing as late or early—only now. This moment is the connection to everywhere and every time. What do you want this moment to create?

The Paradox of Experience

The next interesting dichotomy is related to the events that you experience and how you respond to them. The fundamentals of this particular paradox are extreme, and its concept is a tough one for most people to accept.

The Paradox of Experience says that nothing really matters—yet in terms of your interpretation and response, everything is absolutely important.

Now, at first glance, this just doesn't seem to make any sense at all, but when you look into the deeper meaning of it, there's a truth that can't be denied. It simply means that in terms of the minor and even major events of your life, the experience is *not* what's significant. What really matters is *how you respond to it*. Whatever may happen to you—however good or bad it may be—it's not the event that defines you. *What defines you and determines your future and your influence in this world is how you choose to react.*

Since the Paradox of Experience is intrinsically tied to your consciousness and intention, it means that the quality of your life is up to you—even though the circumstances may not be. Bridging this polarity requires a movement from external experience to internal understanding, a leap from unconsidered emotional reaction to a conscious and considered multidimensional response. In this way, the meaning of every experience comes not from the event itself, but from your energetic reaction to it.

This isn't to say that you should be cavalier about what happens to you! It merely means that whatever may be going on, it doesn't have to cause you to lose sight of your ability to create personal peace and authentic power. Good or bad, grief or joy, the quality of each experience is up to you.

You may undergo something difficult, and of course you need to vent and honor the emotions that go along with that, but instead of becoming a victim and ranting and raving about how unfair life is, you can choose to step back and view the situation as an opportunity to create value. On the other end of the spectrum, you may achieve great success and immediately jump into arrogant attitudes and behaviors of self-indulgence.

You may view your victories as making you better or more worthy than others, but that response takes the merit out of the positive experience altogether. Your personal frequency broadcasts a failure of integrity no matter what seemingly successful things may be going on in the external world.

If you understand the energetic implications, the truth about this paradox becomes clear. In essence, your losses aren't really losses if you can respond with grace, nobility, and courage. And no matter how it may appear on the surface, your successes aren't really successes if you choose to respond with arrogance, greed, and selfishness.

> *In the depth of difficulty or the height of achievement, the real significance of any experience can be measured in the consciousness and intention of your response. When you intend value—no matter what—your life is filled with choices and cognitions that reflect that. And your energy vibrates with courage and profound integrity, a truly brilliant magnetism.*

The Paradox of Experience may sound weird, but it's extremely liberating. It means that you no longer have to strive to control the external circumstances of your life. All you need to take charge of is yourself! Your power comes not from forcing anything in the outside world—but from simply mastering the reactions of your mind and heart.

This may require some significant awareness on your part, however. It can be very easy to lose yourself in a highly charged situation, getting sucked into a vortex of spontaneous, unthinking reactions. But the Paradox of Experience requires you to stop, think, and see things from a different angle—with an objectivity that comes from deep within and expands to the far-off reaches of time and space.

This cosmic approach takes your *eternal* process into consideration, offering a much more comprehensive view of things. The choices and interpretations you make from this perspective are well-considered, honoring, and authentically empowering, and they vibrate with the energy of harmony and flow. This is the focal point of the Paradox of Experience—an eternal view of the journey that we call this earthly life. Your spirit knows that it doesn't matter whether you're financially rich or poor; real wealth is personal peace, and true achievement is spiritual connection. In the light of your soul's identity, these are the measures of success.

Experience with Intention

There are three levels of intention included in every experience. The first is the most obvious—the *technical motivation* for doing what you're doing. For example, when you're driving to work, your primary intention is to get to your job so that you can make some money. That's the technical side of intention, but it's important to know that there's a feeling aspect as well.

The second level is the intention relating to the *emotional quality* of what you're experiencing. Most people never think about it, but this is a significant element of the Paradox of Experience: *You're actually able to choose the emotions that you engage in!* For example, you're perfectly free to spend your morning going to work with feelings of resentment over not having the kind of job you want. This is the emotional intention of the experience, and if that's what's going on for you, your uncomfortable sensations are sending you signals that it's time to find another occupation; and your energy is broadcasting miserable and unhappy vibrations out to the world.

Whether or not you choose to get a new job, however, you definitely need to change the emotional intention—and therefore the vibration—that you're perpetuating in this daily experience. If you don't, the negative emotional charge that's attached to your work will only cause you to endure more career difficulties whether you stay in your present position or move on to another.

To change your emotional intention, you need to shift your focus off of what's wrong with the situation and try to find something more positive to acknowledge. Concentrate on whatever may be worthwhile or pleasurable in your job (even if it's simple or small). Expect something good as you're waking up in the morning and as you're going through your day at work. Cultivate a sense of appreciation for your life and each day in it, and try to see and feel the value all around you. This will show you that you have the power to shift the energy of your feelings, and it will demonstrate to the Universe that you have the intention to be happy in your career—a very important message if you want to find something better, or even if you just want to make your present situation more comfortable.

This example represents a relatively common and routine experience—getting ready and going to work every day. *The fact is that everything you go through, whether it's mundane or extraordinary, carries some kind of emotional content that can be directed by intention—yes, everything! Every moment of your life is charged with some kind of feeling vibration.* Many periods may seem uneventful, but there's always an undercurrent of emotion, and you can choose to direct where that current takes you.

The more negatively charged the situation is, the more difficult it may be to shift and choose the feelings around it. Extremely traumatic occurrences, such as serious illness or the loss of a loved one, are a much more complicated process and require a very systematic and self-compassionate approach. You'll never be able to shift into new feelings if you don't identify, express, and honor the original emotions attached to these types of situations.

Emotional Recovery

No matter what feelings you're dealing with, the following steps will help you shift the experience and eventually arrive at a healthier, more comfortable emotional intention:

1. Identify your feelings about the situation and express them, either by talking about them or writing them down. It's often helpful to write a narrative—or a description of what has happened—in order to stimulate your true feelings about it.

2. Give yourself time to process your initial reactions. In terms of hurtful or traumatic events, it may take longer than you think to move into a different emotional understanding of things.

3. Look for something more positive upon which to focus in your life. Get support from your friends and plan activities that you'd enjoy—even if you have to force yourself to do so at first.

4. Let yourself move back and forth between the old spontaneous, negative feelings and the new, more positive emotional intentions. If you've been feeling down about something for a while, it may take repeated reminders that you do have the option to think and feel

differently about it. Creating clear intentional conclusions—as described in the next section—will help you make this shift.

Your emotions are valid. Don't condemn yourself for having negative feelings! They're actually gifts to you—signals that something is going on that you need to deal with. Whether it's grief, anger, or anxiety, your reactions must be acknowledged and expressed in order to move on. Honor them, and as you let them go, investigate some happier options. Little by little—or maybe even overnight—you'll start to notice that you're feeling better, and your emotional intentions will start to clear. To support these changes, it will also be helpful to work on the third level of intentional experience—your mental conclusions.

Intentional Conclusions

The third level of intentional experience is choosing your cognitive reaction. Your feelings are a natural and spontaneous part of human experience, and it may sometimes be very difficult—at least initially—to take control of them. But if you stop and let yourself think things through, you'll realize that you always have an option to consciously choose how you want to interpret the circumstances of your life. This informed and controlled decision includes both your cognition and your behavior—how you think about something and what you intend to do about it.

Again, you find yourself investigating thought—the basis of your quantum psychology and the magical connection between your mind and what you manifest. Thought is at the center of every emotion and vibration in your life, two powerful influences of energetic attraction. You may not be able to control your spontaneous thoughts or knee-jerk reactions, but you can definitely determine whether you want to stay with your initial impulses or change them to a higher, brighter vibration.

Remember, the Paradox of Experience says that nothing external matters—even the seemingly big events—yet every experience is absolutely important in terms of how you interpret and respond to it. It may seem hard to swallow, but more important than getting a divorce is what you make the divorce mean; more significant than getting fired is how you choose to live your life from that point on. And no matter what someone has done to hurt you, it's far more important that you decide to deal with that in a self-honoring, authentically empowered, and purposeful way.

Experience-Altering Techniques

The following steps will help you stay out of paradoxical intent regarding the difficult experiences of your life. It may be helpful to write about these approaches in your journal so that you can apply them more thoroughly and choose your interpretations more consciously.

1. Redefine the situation you're experiencing. Ask yourself, *What am I making this mean?* Be careful not to give it catastrophic power. Even significant issues can be redefined to bring a clearer understanding. For example, a negative cognitive intention might be: *He wants a divorce. It's the end of the world—I'll never make it through this!* But a healthy, restructured cognitive and behavioral intent would be: *Yes, it hurts that he wants a divorce, but I will get over it in time. I'm resourceful and resilient, and I'm determined to create a happy new life for myself.*

2. Instead of striving for or against something, allow yourself to keep moving forward with the aim of peaceful action. The energy and intent of striving—either to make something happen or to forcefully prevent it from occurring—moves you into a fearful and agitating vibration, sabotaging your ultimate desire for happiness no matter what's going on.

3. Choose actions and behaviors that resonate with integrity and self-honoring. Even when dealing with difficult people, you can choose to be assertive instead of being either passive or aggressive. Ask yourself what the most honoring way to deal with the situation is, and then muster up the courage to approach things in this healthy manner.

4. Always remember to put intention behind every action. Try to be conscious of why you're doing things and how you can make the energy around them better. For example:

- Pay your bills with a sense of gratitude for what you've purchased or the services rendered. Be careful not to obsess about the money you feel you lack while engaging in this activity. Consciously choose gratitude.

- Do your housework with playful appreciation. Try not to look at every task in your life as a burden. Intend to have fun—it brightens your energy immensely!

- Work on your goals with joy and enthusiasm. Release any doubts about yourself or the results you're creating.

- Whatever you may be doing, intend to live with a pervasive attitude of peace, appreciation, and value; and intend to bring more worth to yourself, others, and the world.

Whatever life may hand you, let yourself be true to your highest intention, the honoring of yourself and your eternal spirit. Acknowledge your joys and redefine your woes. In all that you experience, find a core of peace. Within your heart lies the truth of your ultimate wealth—your gentle connection with the source of every blessing.

The Divine Paradox

The energy of earthly acquisition can project a needy vibration by its very nature. While it's never wrong or unhealthy to want nice things, you need to think clearly about what's really important in your life. It's often the desperate need for more that takes you further away from the very emotion you want to achieve. This is what the third cosmic paradox is all about.

The Divine Paradox says that when you truly connect with the Universal Source, you'll find a profoundly fulfilling happiness that actually renders your external desires unnecessary. Paradoxically, when you do arrive at that deeply blissful state of Divine connection, that's precisely the time when your sublime vibration of peace will attract all that you long for.

This heartfelt unity with Source is such a genuinely powerful state of happiness that it can't be resisted by the Universe. It's so attuned with loving intention that it automatically moves you into the receptive current of abundant blessings and synchronistic flow. There's no greater power than Divine peace and no greater intention than heavenly love.

This isn't just an idealistic concept; it's an experiential truth. When you're in that blissful state of union with the Divine, you truly feel that you don't need all the material stuff to make you happy. Yet it's also a paradox that it's perfectly okay to want things!

While this may sound too spiritual or just too far out to be realistically applied to modern life, it's a fundamental truth and a dynamic force in the energetic world. Connecting with the peace and consciousness of the Divine can totally eliminate all of the fuss, effort, and anxiety that we put ourselves through on an almost daily basis—and dismissing that sacred connection rejects one of the single most powerful tools for success at our disposal.

The Divine/Human Duality

One of the most fundamental and fascinating principles of quantum physics is the *wave/particle duality.* Scientists were surprised when they first found that light was more than just a wave of energy—it could also be measured as a particle. Not only that, when a technician sets about to measure the light, it seems to "know" whether the person is using a machine that measures particles or one that measures waves. In this stunning example of *observer-created reality,* the technician projects an expectation (or intention) that the light will manifest as one or the other. Since light can't be measured as both particle and wave at the same time, it seems to obediently respond to the human request, appearing in exactly the form required by the person using the machine at the time.

When I first read about this phenomenon many years ago, I was speechless. It seemed as though light itself had consciousness, and it was responding directly to the conscious intention of the individual in the room! This has amazingly elegant applications to our own experience. First, it reveals that our expectations move out as very clear intentions that get real results from the Universe. Second, it shows that energy is both active and responsive to the human will. Finally, it's a metaphor for an important duality within our own earthly experience—the coexistence of the Divine and human nature within each and every one of us.

It's easy to see our humanity. It expresses itself in our emotions, creativity, and abundant weaknesses and strengths. It's much more difficult, however, to feel and identify our own Divine spirit, which—although it seems distant—is as much a part of our identity as our human nature is. Yet we won't find any deficiency there—only power, peace, and inspiration.

Although many of us may choose to dismiss it, this duality is an ever-present truth. Just as light is both particle and wave, we're both human and Divine spirit; and it's time that we stop ignoring our truth. It's such a sad fact that not only do we fail to recognize and acknowledge this powerful part of ourselves, we all too often find our dual voices at war. The human within tells us to strive, worry, and somehow prove that we're special. Yet our Divine side is saying, *Relax, have faith, and know that you're special just as you are.*

Ironically, it's often the need to be special that creates our desperation to acquire more, taking us further and further away from that which makes us truly exceptional—the Divine. This source of real bliss and eternal peace actually releases our material need. The paradox is clear: *When we're connected to the Divine spirit within, we no longer need to constantly strive for external, material things—yet when we're in this blissful state, we're so magnetically peaceful that we can rest assured that we will easily manifest them.*

Developing Divine Connection

This issue is explored more thoroughly in Part II, but it's valuable to make your union with the Divine an ongoing intention. In order to achieve this high-powered peace of body, mind, and soul, practice the following:

1. Make a choice to let go of need. Look around at all you have, bless it with appreciation, and then acknowledge that it's all just *stuff.* Remind yourself that this isn't what really brings you happiness, that there's something deeper

and more true, and you're living in that beautiful truth more and more each day.

2. Meditate on your own heart center and feel your connection to the Divine there—bringing you loving peace. Allow yourself to feel unconditional eternal love deepening with each breath.

3. As you go through your day, stop and take a deep breath. Affirm: *I am open to receiving and feeling the unwavering love of God. I live in the eternal peace and unending wealth of Universal Source. Divine light guides me, and Divine love embraces me. Now and always, I am blessed.*

Connecting with Universal Source causes us to detach from future outcomes because of our enduring present peace. It allows us to be in the pure and open state of receiving, and it creates the intention and the experience of being happy first. When this is our reality, all of our intentions vibrate at a much higher, more magnetic resonance, placing us the center of a swirling vortex of Universal flow. Our peaceful aim to live in the grace and love of the Divine *right now* moves our other goals into accelerated time—what I call *spirit time*. And as we travel from minute to minute and day to day, our unity with spirit brings us blissful serenity now and quickens our future manifestation, enhancing every moment and every result.

CHAPTER 7

HOLOGRAM OF SUCCESS

"Life is a long journey, but busy people make it too short;
The world is a very broad place,
But narrow minded people make it narrow—more than it should be;
Flowers dancing in the wind and moonlight in the snow
are beautiful relaxing sceneries,
but worried people move too hectic
and miss the magic right before their eyes."

— from *Tending the Roots of Wisdom,* BY HONG YING MING

I recently heard someone define success as "something that can't be bought and can't be taken away." I like this approach because it removes all material considerations from the prosperity equation.

Instead of relying on big houses and lots of money to be the measure of your achievement, this definition would force you to adopt a more thoughtful perspective—and it would allow you to be aware of what wonderful things you've already got going for you.

There's a big difference between being rich and being prosperous. Nearly every day, headlines shout about young, rich people who have been driving drunk or embarrassing themselves in some way. These folks may have a lot of money, but they aren't what I call prosperous. You can also read about politicians caught in illegal activities—or millionaire CEOs undercutting prices and increasing profits while they sacrifice quality or the well-being of their own workers. All of these individuals have achieved monetary wealth—and even a certain kind of status—but no real prosperity.

When I think of what real success means, I can't rule out things like integrity, grace, and compassion. To me these are of greater value than fancy cars and mansions, which are merely surface representations of success. But you can't buy things like dignity and honesty, and they can never be taken away. Of course, you need money to live, but it should never be the measure of your worth or success. Your life is far more valuable than that!

The Many Dimensions of Success

When you understand that the Universe—and everything in it—is holographic in nature, you realize that success has several deeper levels than most people ever think about. But there are many ways to be successful, and the really important ones don't involve money at all. Acknowledging and working on these other areas of your life will help increase your success consciousness and redirect your focus, reducing the urgency that could be pushing your buttons of paradoxical intent. This multilayered approach shifts your awareness from lack to value, and your energy from desperation to appreciation. For these reasons and more, you'll find that there's expanding value in acknowledging all the present successes in your life.

The following six areas represent the holistic view of real prosperity. The holographic nature of your life requires that you examine how you can (and do) experience each of these elements. Acknowledge what may already be going well and that observation will expand the well-being in your life. Also consider which of these areas could use some work; then let yourself take the steps needed to bring these parts of your life into alignment with your intention to be successful and happy now.

Mental and Emotional Success

The most important achievement in your life is mental and emotional success. If you don't establish this first, no other victory will ever make you happy. Wealth and happiness are an experience of attitude. If you have a troubled mind and difficult emotions, all the money in the world won't calm your fears. But if you can get up in the morning and look forward to the day—if you can gaze into the mirror and smile lovingly at yourself—

you'll be able to create happiness and experience wealth, no matter how much money you have.

You might wonder how creating a good attitude can even be possible if you're having trouble paying your bills. Perhaps you believe that, at least in this case, having money will make you happier. But that's not how the process goes. A big bank balance makes it easier to change your thinking, and it's the *different thinking* that makes you feel better.

No matter what financial state you may be in, you can still change your thinking. Instead of desperation, you can relax about money while you're working on making more. Worry will never make you richer, but your decision to take fear out of the equation will yield better results. In fact, where most problems are concerned, reducing anxiety is part of the solution—a very important experiential and energetic part.

> There's an old saying that goes: "Be careful not to suffer over your suffering." This means that no matter what's going on that may be difficult, you'll only make it worse by fearing it or obsessing over it. A healthy and successful mental attitude doesn't get embroiled in the drama, doesn't take things personally, and doesn't "catastrophize" or expect horrific results. Your state of mind creates the vibrational quality of your life right now, as well as the energy you program into your future. So bless the problem and trust in a resolution. The answer will actually arrive faster that way.

The desire for success is the desire for happiness. Your choice to restructure your thinking and let go of fear makes that absolutely attainable in the present moment. Releasing worry is the way to choose joy despite external conditions. This may be a brand-new paradigm for you, but you still need to make a conscious choice to relinquish your worrisome and fearful tendencies.

In fact, this choice is an opportunity to succeed at something truly important right this very moment. It's not merely trying to convince yourself that you are—or can be—happy; it's arriving at the positive conclusions that actually make it so. Your new conclusions are firm and clear assumptions of trust, hope, optimism, courage, determination, and peace. The success of those present conclusions comes in the form of the great emotions you feel as a result—wonderful ones such as joy, purpose, love, and real happiness. Consciously living in present peace is where real mental and emotional prosperity begins and ends.

Physical Well-being

Closely connected to this type of self-empowerment is your physical well-being. It can be very difficult to enjoy financial abundance without having health and stamina. While there are certainly some things you can't control in this area, there are steps that you can take to promote your body's well-being.

If you recall the section on mechanical energy, you'll remember that movement and deep breathing are very important parts of your energetic production. This holds true for your physical success as well. In order to have a healthy body, a peaceful heart, and a clear mind, daily exercise and regular diaphragmatic breathing are key. A sedentary life leads to inactivity of attraction. It also increases the likelihood of obesity, heart problems, diabetes, and other long-term diseases.

A successful physical life also encompasses a healthy diet. Today, people are eating more food but getting less nutrition; studies show that most folks eat less than half of the daily servings of fruits and vegetables they consumed 30 years ago. And the produce we eat now is more contaminated with pesticides, preservatives, and other processing chemicals than ever before.

This combination of bad eating habits and less-nutritious food is increasing the occurrence of conditions such as diabetes at almost epidemic rates. And while diabetes itself is controllable, complications at a later date can be deadly. So your physical well-being not only requires exercise and deep breathing, it means that you must take an honest look at what and how much you eat.

For this reason, healing your addictive behaviors should be included in your considerations about physical success. Alcoholism, overeating, bingeing, and purging are such destructive patterns that they have the power to negate success in every area of your life.

Many of us—myself included—are tempted to overindulge. When we're young, we feel that we're indestructible and can enjoy any lifestyle that we want; yet as we grow older, we find that we may have to pay for the indiscretions of our youth. But it's never too late to start making healthy choices in the ways we eat, move, and conduct our physical lives. It's an important part of our hologram, so we need to take a more conscious and purposeful direction regarding it.

One way in which I try to increase my focus in this area is to ask myself each evening: *Was I physically successful today?* As I look back on my day, I investigate whether I did something for my health, first in the way of exercise, such as taking a walk or working out. I also try to remember to do regular deep breathing, sometimes just taking two or three minutes to close my eyes, relax, and enjoy a few cleansing breaths. And when I recognize that I've tried to eat healthy foods in moderate amounts, I feel good about my choices.

It can be very helpful to do energy work that balances and aligns your energetic body. There's a lot of material available on this topic, but my favorite resource is *Energy Medicine* by Donna Eden. In this book, Eden explains the energy meridians of the body and how they influence your physical health. She also recommends a simple daily exercise that only takes a few minutes. I find when I complete it even just once a day, I have more energy, more stamina, and a far greater sense of well-being.

Whatever steps you take to make your physical energy and health a priority, doing so will benefit you beyond measure. In our fast-paced world, so often this is neglected, but it's too important to be dismissed. Take care of your body and prioritize your health, and your intentions to do so will send an important positive message out into the Universe. Your self-care will engender more nurturing from the world, and your own bright vitality will attract sparkling results.

Spiritual Success

In my mind, the spiritual side of life is the sweetest, most endearing part of the human experience. It brings about tranquility and repose, support in times of darkness, exhilaration in periods of achievement, and blissful and inspiring connections. When I speak of spiritual success, I'm referring to a sense of unity with the Divine, an awareness of our own spirit soul, and an openness to inspiration from other sources.

But if the physical side of life is often dismissed, the spiritual side can be totally denied. I had a client once who acted with great resistance when I suggested that he cultivate a spiritual life. He said, "I don't have time for that now; I'll think about it when I'm older. In fact, when we're dead, we'll all find out about it."

He felt it was an utter waste of time, a total distraction from his pursuit of career and financial success. What he didn't realize, however, was that he was cutting off an avenue for creating peaceful, magnetic vibrations. He was also separating himself from valuable connections and sources of inspiration that could have increased his productivity, creativity, and magnetism.

The fact is that untold happiness can be gained by pursuing spiritual success. This has become such a valuable part of my life that I just can't imagine how I could be happy, peaceful, or at all successful without it. I'm not just talking about going to church; I mean connecting with spirit in a meaningful way every single day. The door to countless dimensions can be opened through the daily practice of contemplation, prayer, and many different types of meditation.

I believe that all of life is about the spirit. Everything that we go through is leading us forward to our eternal truth and back to our Divine Source. Ultimately, all else will fade away, but this core identity can't be destroyed. It's so essential to all of our earthly pursuits that Part II of this book is entirely devoted to the pursuit of spiritual success. In the meantime, allow yourself to move your consciousness into your soul center. Breathe your awareness into your heart, and feel the eternal peace that's waiting for you there.

A Wealth of Relationships

A crucial element to a happy and fulfilling life is the experience of truly loving, mutually nurturing relationships. This isn't limited to the experience of romance; it includes all of your connections, from family to friends to co-workers. But the central relationship of your life, of course, is the one you have with yourself. In terms of your energetic influence, your other connections will always reflect this one.

With this as your starting point, it's important to remember that respect must drive your self-treatment and self-talk. The intention to honor yourself must guide your decisions and increase your compassion for yourself. Live with balance—with an equal measure of prioritizing yourself as well as others.

For mutually honoring relationships with others, you must be unafraid to speak your truth. There should be no fear of judgment, just as you should never condemn yourself. Successful partnerships offer support and allow you to set boundaries. They're forgiving, comfortable, understanding, and encouraging—and hopefully they're fun.

Love for a friend or a romantic partner is as nurturing to the spirit as food is to the body. The more caring connections you have in your life, the more opportunities there are for joyful moments. The intention to love—starting with yourself and moving out to others—is the goal to accept and be accepted, to honor and be honored, to enjoy, acknowledge, appreciate, and respect. Bring these energies to a caring view of yourself and you'll soon be experiencing them in all your relationships.

Love is a Universal force that guides and gives in great measure. For you individually, it's the most powerful intention and the purest consciousness. It also creates the most magnetic and vibrantly attractive energy. It's a mental, emotional, and physical presence; it's the gentle caring that connects us with others in the most subtle yet profoundly life-altering ways.

So choose love. Decide to expand its energy in all your relationships, starting with yourself. And remember, in this interconnected world, you're in a relationship with every other person on the planet. Bring affection to your life and the lives of others—even strangers—and your most dynamic energy will expand. It doesn't matter what size house you live in or what kind of car you drive—if you have a life full of love, you are successful indeed.

Personal Prosperity

There are a lot of things that you can do that will bring you value but not financial wealth. They make you personally prosperous, increasing your joy without growing your bank account a single cent. Perhaps you have a hobby or an avocation that interests you; maybe you enjoy a particular sport or spending time outside. As long as you can find the time to engage in the activities that bring you honest pleasure, then you're leading a personally prosperous life.

It's important that you *not* make your entire existence about earning money. There's value in your time, your leisure, and your social and cultural activities. Someone who's too singularly focused on career or money vibrates with urgency and obsession, even if that person doesn't recognize those energies within himself. But a well-rounded life—one that easily shifts focus from work to other activities—resonates with diversity and interest. Your decision to pursue other interests for their own sake resonates with the Universe on many levels and opens you up to endlessly joyous options.

But your personal prosperity doesn't stop there. It also reflects your success as a part of humankind, and it's seen in how you handle the situations of your life. When you respond to difficulty with grace and to hostility with civility, you demonstrate that you're a truly prosperous human being. Living with integrity, refusing to judge or cast blame, and showing compassion for others—all of this makes you wealthy beyond compare.

It may sound saccharine, but there's a wealth of the heart that far exceeds that of the pocketbook. One of the greatest indicators of your personal prosperity is when you increase the value in other people's lives. Your actions spread throughout the world and expand the energy of real worth in your own life. There are any number of ways that you can be of service—from merely creating the intention to be more loving to all of the people around you, to donating your precious time in helpful volunteer work. In the tapestry that is your Universal connection, giving to others can be a very important part of your holographic vibration.

You don't have to turn into someone like Mother Teresa to increase the love and value in the world. Send prayers to all of the hurt, lonely, and disenfranchised souls. Spend some time helping out at schools, soup kitchens, hospitals, or places of worship. Find a cause that touches your heart. Whether it's animals, children, or the environment, when you work on something you're passionate about, you'll find that it's easy to give of yourself.

There's a profound sense of gratification that comes from knowing you're doing something good for someone else. Furthermore, every intention you have to bring more value to the planet—in thought, word, or deed—will inevitably create more prosperity in your own life. The nonlocal nature of the Universe dictates that the action you take for just one person spreads across the globe and assists everyone, eventually reaching back to your own life. So consider the things that make you truly prosperous, and never forget that in this energetic world, the loving gifts you bring to others will return to you a thousandfold.

Financial Abundance

Finally, we arrive at the aspect of success that most people want to focus on first. Monetary wealth is a wonderful thing, and in this day and age, it's widely available. While it's clear that this shouldn't be the only thing that defines success, the pursuit of financial gain is both valid and valuable.

Any amount of money that you desire is fine, but you need to be careful not to sacrifice the other arenas of success in that single-minded pursuit. This happened to a friend of mine who now lives in Vail, Colorado. Mike worked for an international-development company, and he was always on the road, making presentations and creating proposals. He earned a lot of money, and his income increased with every proposal that he sold. One day, after he'd been away from home for several weeks, his wife called him and told him how fast his children were growing and how very much they missed him. When expressing his concern about this to someone who was traveling with him, his colleague responded, "Don't worry—they'll get used to you being gone."

That's when Mike had an epiphany. He didn't *want* his kids to get used to his absences. He wanted to see them grow up, and he thought they should be able to get to know their father. He realized that he wasn't living the life he desired, no matter how much money he was making—nor was he allowing his family to have what they longed for.

When Mike got home, he talked with his wife and kids, and they all decided it was time for him to quit that job. More important than the paycheck was their time together, so they decided to move to a place they loved—Vail, Colorado—where he became the manager of a hotel. He and his wife made plenty to live on, and they had ample time to spend with the kids, including skiing together, a sport they all enjoyed.

Mike has never once regretted the decision he made. Although he stood to make a lot of money in his former career, he would have had to sacrifice his family in the process. Now, 20 years later, he has a very close relationship with his wife and each of his kids; and they live in a wonderful house in one of the most stunningly beautiful locations in the world.

Today's Success

Every single day you have the choice to decide exactly what kind of success you want to experience. It can be found in the little things, such as a kiss from a loved one, the scent of a flower, a moment of self-mastery, or a smile of appreciation. Success isn't a future event; it's a holographic state of mind, a condition of being free—free from fear and want—no matter how much or how little you may have.

If you look at the quantum psychology of it, real success is in the quality of your thoughts, the health and stability of your beliefs, and the peace and joy of your everyday emotions. These are all things that you can choose to experience on a moment-to-moment basis. Bring your consciousness to it and you'll create a pervasive and genuine sensation of inner happiness and success, the very core and resonance of the future you want to create.

To make your whole life a success, you need to stop and transform this instant. An important question to ask yourself is: *What is my intention for this very moment?* With every nick of time, you have a choice. Do you intend to judge or have compassion? Do you decide to worry or engage in trust, to give in to an addictive urge or take control, to criticize yourself or just let go and love yourself instead?

This is your life you're talking about here! The simplest and most profound success is held in your heart—a moment's pause where all the striving stops and the soul takes over. In the bliss of total trust and the sweet silence of letting go, you'll find the peace of just being. That moment of non-effort is the greatest achievement of all, successfully spanning time and trials—living in the still point where eternal love leaves all the fuss behind.

PART II

SPIRIT-ACCELERATED
SUCCESS

by Sharon A. Klingler

CHAPTER 8

YOUR SPIRIT, YOUR SELF

*"I call intuition cosmic fishing. You feel a nibble,
and then you have to hook the fish."*

— **BUCKMINSTER FULLER**

How many "fish" have you hooked by listening to your intuition? How many others have gotten away because you didn't trust what you heard? Whether you realize it or not, your intuition may be one of your most important advisors on the road to success.

If you were to interview the most successful people in the world, you'd likely find that their intuitive sensitivity is the best barometer for measuring their achievements. Individuals such as Oprah Winfrey, Bill Gates, and many others learned to investigate and study the research, and then listen to their inner voice to make good personal and business decisions. They probably also have the ability to build connections, which is another one of the cornerstones of creating success, wealth, and reputation.

Although it doesn't occur to most people, making connections is important in the spiritual world as well as the physical. You don't need to be aware of all your spirit contacts to succeed, but becoming so will most certainly accelerate your success, for the world of spirit sees far beyond what you can perceive, and it can tell you about opportunities that are just around the corner!

The world of spirit includes everything from your loved ones to the angel kingdom to your own spirit. In this section, you'll look at all of these, but for now let's examine the first and most important connection you can make—the one with your own intuition, the voice of your spirit. It's not only the key to your success, it's also the champion of your well-being and the catalyst to your happiness. In order to let your intuition do its best, you first have to learn what it is, how it works, and how it expresses your eternal spirit. Let's get started.

What Is Intuition?

Your intuition is the voice of your spirit, that part of you that exists beyond the physical reality. And because your spirit is eternal, it can share insight from a much broader perspective than what's available in the mere three-dimensional world. It's a gift that you may tend to disregard—even when you have a nagging feeling that you shouldn't.

About Intuition

1. *Intuition is subtle.* You must be willing and able to listen inwardly. This wisdom doesn't scream at you; it whispers. You need to maintain a calm mind and a peaceful temperament so that you don't drown out your inner voice with emotional angst and mental confusion.

2. *Intuition is spontaneous.* You need to cultivate both flexibility and spontaneity in your life so that you are able to respond to your intuitive voice and take action.

Quick! Close your eyes. What's the first spontaneous message that your intuition gives you about the next step toward your dreams? Don't analyze it or figure it out; just perceive it.

3. *Intuition doesn't happen to you; it happens for you.* Although intuitive events are spontaneous, you don't have to wait around for them. You can connect to your intuition *anytime* by just taking a breath and listening inside. It's part of you—indeed, it belongs to the most real part of you.

YOUR SPIRIT, YOUR SELF

4. *Intuition makes itself known by the compelling force that accompanies each intuitive feeling or thought.* Whether it's expressed through a "gut feeling" or a nagging thought that won't go away, you'll know your intuition through a sense of being compelled by it. Don't confuse this with emotional urgency when you're feeling clingy or fearful. It's common to experience neediness in a relationship or career directive, and then falsely define that need as being "guided by intuition" because of the passion or intensity. Urgency reflects a component of fear that's very rarely attendant with intuition.

5. *The intuitive mind expresses itself through the right brain or the imagination.* Many of these processes are right-brain experiences (utilizing visual and imaginative thought rather than deductive and analytical reasoning). Develop small exercises and longer meditation processes to cultivate your right brain while quieting the left-brain activity, which can actually sabotage intuitive perceptions with overanalysis and self-doubt. As Albert Einstein is reported to have said, "Your imagination is your preview of life's coming attractions." Practice using it frequently so that you can easily perceive what your intuition wishes to tell you.

> *Quick! Close your eyes. Your own coming attractions for the next week are on a screen in front of you. What do you see? Who is the star of next week's show?*

6. *Intuition works, even though the results may not be what you expect.* This is the case with *secondary intuition,* which occurs when you feel compelled to do something, but the results may be completely unrelated and unexpected. For instance, on your way to work you may feel the need to go back home because you believe you left the coffeemaker on. When you get there, you find that the appliance is turned off, but you'd forgotten your briefcase.

This type of secondary intuition happened to my friend Jane, who was in dire need of a new (and far less toxic) job. One day she felt compelled to go shopping at a bookstore several miles from her home. Always being sensitive to her intuition, she decided to make the trip. Taking a friend, she spent several hours looking through the stacks for an unknown book that she was sure she was destined to find. Although Jane felt guilty for disregarding her friend, she stayed and stayed and looked and looked. She felt as if she were mining for gold, and she was certain that she would know the precious book when she saw it.

Suddenly, however, she decided that enough was enough. She purchased the other books that had interested her, although she still hadn't found that special nugget she thought she was supposed to discover. Then while leaving the store, she literally ran into a former co-worker who had gone on to manage another business. Due to this synchronistic meeting, Jane found herself working at this woman's company within two weeks—all because she kept looking for a book she was never able (or even meant) to find!

7. *Intuition works even when there are no apparent results—ever.* One day you may feel compelled to shop for a book, although you may not find it or even run into your next boss. Still, you may have missed being hit by a drunk driver because you were delayed. Your intuition doesn't only help you get to the right place at the right time, but it also helps you avoid the wrong place at the wrong time. Even when your inner wisdom doesn't *seem* to get you where you're supposed to go, you must always trust its vision—for it sees quite a bit further than you do!

8. *Intuition is always available to you.* The more you connect with it, the more available it becomes. One of the best ways to become more aware of these perceptions during your working, active life is to carry a small notebook with you so that you can record insights and observations. This helps you build the habit of looking for the "little" thoughts throughout your day—the whispers that would have otherwise gone unnoticed because you were simply too busy. More than that, writing your insights down keeps you from forgetting them. How many times have you thought, *I need to remember that later,* and then you've lost it forever? As the great Sir Francis Bacon once said, "A man would do well to carry a pencil in his pocket, and write down the thoughts of the moment. Those that come unsought for are commonly the most valuable, and should be secured, because they seldom return."

9. *Your intuition helps lead you to your success by telling you what's not working.* If you were employed at a facility that was filled with toxic waste

or if you were married to someone who brutalized you, it's likely that you wouldn't need your intuition to tell you that you were in the wrong job or the wrong marriage. But there are times when the negative results of your choices and actions aren't so readily apparent. When this happens, your inner wisdom will let you know by giving you a nagging feeling that something's wrong.

There may be times when you disregard a feeling that you ought to leave a negative situation (often because the leaving seems too difficult). Even then your intuition won't shut up—no matter how much you want it to. At the very least, you'll feel uneasy or "off center." Over time, this sensation will grow to unhappiness, which will continue to expand. Ultimately, the persistent voice of your spirit will become impossible to ignore.

10. *Your intuition helps lead you to success by taking you to new areas of growth.* Your spirit is working all the time. You may find a book at a friend's house that leads you to a new career, or you may meet a person at a coffeehouse who teaches a class that interests you. These types of "coincidences" (which are never really coincidental) are all in your life's plan. Again, if you don't make the effort to pursue what you're drawn to do, you'll begin to have that uneasy feeling—and the longer you put off following your interests, the more that sensation will grow. But if you give yourself permission to enthusiastically investigate everything you find intriguing, you'll find that your growth and success—in your personal life, relationships, and career—will begin to carry their own momentum. And many more "coincidental" opportunities will start to fall into your life like dominoes in a line, falling one after another.

Using your imagination and with your eyes closed, picture this: Your intuition is handing you a piece of paper with something written on it. Open it up. What does it say? Make yourself see the message— even if it's just one word. Now your intuition is handing you a note about your success. What does this one say?

Stories of Inspiration

Spirit—whether it's your own or another's—is often the source of amazing inspiration. Great discoveries, artistic creations, and financial windfalls have been achieved when people were inspired. The higher Self unites with all of spirit in collaborating on your success. You can join this collaboration by opening up to spirit's inspiration just as the following people did.

Julia Ward Howe awoke one night with a poem filling her mind. It came practically without thought in the middle of the night. It began, "Mine eyes have seen the glory of the coming of the Lord," and it continued sometimes poignantly, sometimes joyfully to the last entreaty, "As he died to make men holy, let us die to make men free." Howe sold "Battle Hymn of the Republic," to the *Atlantic Monthly* for $5, and it soon became the anthem of abolition and freedom.

Although the eerie tale of *Dr. Jekyll and Mr. Hyde* came to Robert Louis Stevenson in a dream, there's another very interesting story that tells of an inspired drawing. This occurred when Stevenson was idly painting with a young student to pass the time during a rainy summer. He looked up to notice that he had just drawn "with the unconsciousness of the predestined" an elaborate map of an island, which he immediately named Treasure Island. He recalled, "The future characters of the book began to appear there visibly among imaginary woods . . . The next thing I knew, I had some paper before me and was writing out a list of chapters."

Stevenson wasn't asleep or in a trance during the time he was painting the map that turned out to be Treasure Island. His "unconsciousness" worked while his analytical mind was completely out of the experience. He was letting everything flow with no involvement of the personal mind—only that of the genius within his own spirit.

Success can come in many forms. The following story of inspiration (recounted in an episode of the Discovery Channel series *I Shouldn't Be Alive*) doesn't involve creativity and literature—it's about survival. A young American couple had taken a trip to the Amazon rain forest. They were hiking there and got hopelessly lost. Hour after hour went by—and then day after day. Their worst torment was being bitten by insects day and night. The couple covered themselves with mud in an attempt to protect their skin, but to no avail. They searched and searched, staying near a river for water and crossing it many times in their efforts to find a way back.

Finally, after a number of days, they became so weary, so infested with insects and raw with bites, that they began to think about suicide. After hours of discussion, they decided that it was their only way out. But the young man suddenly had what seemed to be a pretty crazy idea: If they were going to kill themselves, they had to clean up first! His girlfriend couldn't believe this. It wasn't in his nature to care about that kind of thing at home, much less in the jungle! Besides, what could it matter? The bugs and animals would consume their bodies in a matter of hours anyway, and no one would ever find them. Still, he was adamant. They *had* to "get clean" before they ended their lives, so they began their walk back to the river that had become such a large part of their lives during their days in the jungle.

When they got to the water's edge, right there—immediately before them—was one of the forest natives who lived farther downstream. He'd come up the river to go fishing, and the young couple's lives were saved because of the inspiration to bathe (secondary intuition at work!).

The Universe Within and Without

Connecting with your intuition begins with first believing that you are more than who you seem to be. To know yourself in a larger way is to understand the Universe more broadly—to know that you are pure and absolute potential in a Universe of possibilities. This higher comprehension of yourself and of your world requires effort and a desire for investigation. Yet life has become so demanding that it's often difficult to keep up with your own daily agendas, much less have time to study, to learn, and to expand your awareness of the world in which you live. Regardless of your time constraints, your life will grow if you make an ongoing commitment to the activity of discovery.

And while you're busy investigating the mysteries of the Universe— the stars, the seas, the worlds within and beyond this one—you must remember that the greatest of all mysteries is the one that lies within you. Your soul, your spirit, can lead you to unlimited discoveries if you just take the time to *discover* it. Pause a moment now to consider just what the higher Self is.

Many people think that the spirit (or the soul or higher Self) is just a part of the individual much like the heart or the mind. But the truth is that you aren't a physical being who has a spirit; you're a spiritual being who has a physical body and a physical life. Your spirit existed long before your body was born and will continue long after your mortal heart has ceased to beat. It is the highest expression of who you are. It has a conscious-ness with no limits in time or space; it has an emotional experience (the great essence of which is love) and a vision that sees with a scope well beyond your personal view. In this way, your spirit can share its heart and its vision with you, and it seeks to do so always. (One of the ways it does so is through your intuition.) Your higher Self is never apart from you, but you must learn to define yourself as this eternal being so that you can begin to make the connection.

How unfortunate it is that so many people go through life with a diminished connection to that great mystery of the spirit within. Sadder still are those who define themselves through *everything but* the eternal, glorious Self. They define themselves through what's around them (their car, their crow's-feet, the weight they need to lose) rather than what's deep within them.

If you define yourself in limiting ways, it immediately undermines your success because it prevents you from seeing all that you are and all that you're capable of doing. In order to succeed, you must get in the habit of changing all restrictive labels and self-concepts.

Changing Labels

You become the labels that you're assigned not only by believing that they're true, but also by believing that they define you *totally*—that they're *all* you are. A mom isn't only a mom; an architect isn't just an architect. Even the most famous, wealthy, and critically acclaimed actors, authors, or Olympic athletes will be *limited* by these grand and sweeping definitions—if these are the only ones they know.

Much worse than identifying yourself by a career or an activity is the near-suicidal practice of defining yourself through your emotional history. Have you ever thought yourself to be—even for a short time—a victim, a loser, a failure, worthless, unlovable, undeserving, or hopeless? If you've felt like any of these and have begun to carry them as your "truth" for any length of time, you've created your own designer label. And your pain-filled creation walks down the runway of your life in your energy and in your aura. Your negative brands stand out like beacons and attract others who feel the same way. You've built a world of false definitions that must be discarded. You aren't your emotional histories, and you aren't your career. You can't be summed up by your failures or even your successes.

You're an eternal spirit who knows—deep inside—boundless love; power; and the open, unlimited horizons of opportunity. The Universe stirs inside you. And if you truly seek the full width, depth, and breadth of the undiscovered country within, you'll achieve nothing less than your manifest destiny.

Your Manifest Destiny

Manifest destiny is the expansion that is born out of the innate conditions present for any individual or group. (In the development of the United States, it was thought that its manifest destiny was to extend to the Pacific Ocean; sadly that was achieved without care for the individuals who already resided within those lands.)

In terms of the growth of any individual, manifest destiny is a natural—indeed, unavoidable—evolution. For the human spirit, this isn't born out of any external events or influences but solely out of one's inherent nature or *beingness*.

Because you're who and what you are—a Divine, eternal being—all possibilities are open to you. And if you allow yourself to *be* and *live* the full measure of your truth, these opportunities aren't only available to you, they're *inevitable* for you. They're your manifest destiny.

In this section you'll learn about spirit connections and assistance, and there are many great and loving individuals in that world who seek to help you. Yet all of them combined can do little if you don't first and foremost know your own spirit. And far beyond that, you must *be* your spirit.

There are many people who don't fully understand this concept, thinking that personal discovery and success are solely functions of the mind. They've read all of the right books, pursued inner investigation, and even embraced new theories of thought—academically, that is. Yet they continue to say, "I've been working on this for years, and I still can't get the right job or find the right relationship. These Laws of Attraction just don't work for me."

The truth is that the Laws of Attraction do work. It's your manifest destiny to know the absolute best in every area of your life. (This isn't to say that once you've met your manifest destiny, you won't have any trials, but even those can turn to opportunities.) So what goes wrong? How can anyone's dreams fall so short that—even with exceptional effort—there's failure? The mental work is absolutely necessary to shift your beliefs, but that's not all you need to do. You must also shift your *being*.

At its deepest level, your manifest destiny lies in *becoming* absolutely who you are eternally. It isn't only thinking about it, understanding it, or even believing in it (although all of these are necessary). You must become your spirit and give voice to your intuition every moment of every day.

> *Your success, your manifest destiny, doesn't lie in meeting a goal; it lies in living your truth—down to your core. Close your eyes and feel the absolute power of your eternal truth moving through you. Go deep and know it completely. If you channel this power in any direction you wish, how far can you go? Let your intuition show you now.*

The "little self," or the personality, is often in the driver's seat, even for those who are well schooled in the Laws of Attraction. But to reach your highest potential, you must live from your soul. And in order to do that, you must first know the difference between your personality and your spirit.

How can you tell when you're academically comprehending your spirit (as well as the theories that help you realize it) and when you're actually *being* your soul and *living* those theories? The tell-tale signs can be easier to see than you might think. It's all in how you feel about yourself and about your life. Do you live in joy, or are you often depressed or lonely? Do you wake up in the morning with a sense of purpose and enthusiasm for your day, or are you lethargic? Do you make decisions out of a deep sense of what honors you (and the world) in the long-term, or do you respond to situations out of urgency and neediness?

The level of self-esteem you hold is a very strong indicator of how much you live the truth of your soul. Let's take a look at this particular yardstick of *Self*-awareness.

Self-Esteem and Your Relationship with Your Spirit— A Personal-Discovery Quiz

There are many clues in your life that can indicate how much you've *truly* realized your spirit in your experience (not just in your studies or in your thoughts). Following is a quiz that will help you assess your personal self-esteem and how you value your work. Although these two arenas of your life may seem unrelated, you'll find that they're significantly connected. All you need to do is give a rating from 1 to 10, with 1 being the least (or meaning *never* or *none*) and 10 being the most (or meaning *always* or *constantly*). It's important to be absolutely honest, so don't answer what you think you *should* do; answer what you *actually* do. (After all, you can't establish new ways of thought and action if you can't even acknowledge the old patterns!)

Your spirit is with you and, indeed, *is* you every moment of every day. That is inviolate. It's whether or not you *realize* this that makes a difference in your destiny.

Section 1: Your Life

1. Throughout your life in your significant relationships (both romantic and otherwise), how often and for how long have you upheld your own goals when they conflicted with those of others?

2. How often do you say no to doing things that you truly don't want to do (instead of doing them to make others happy or to prevent them from judging you)?

3. How many times a day do you think and say anything of a self-loving and appreciative nature?

4. How regularly and how many times a day do you act on the things that promote your own well-being (exercise, play, socialize, meditate, journal, read, and so on)?

5. How often do you feel joyful, enthusiastic, or happy?

Section 2: Your Work

1. How passionate are you about your career—not just about the money or the potential outcome of your efforts, but about the activities of your daily work?

2. How much do you feel "equal" to the other professionals in your field whom you admire?

3. How willing are you to take personal and financial risks to pursue your dream career?

4. How flexible and spontaneous are you about changing your work patterns and plans in favor of untried ideas?

5. How many times a day (or week) do you ask yourself, *Is this step of my plan also in God's plan?*

Scoring Your Results

The highest score that you can get in each section is 50. A low score is 1 to 25, and 26 to 50 is considered high. No matter where you land on the scale, it's helpful to read each score below so that you can recognize where you've been and where you're going. To raise your totals and attract greater success, it's helpful to create an intention out of any question that you answered with a 7 or less. For example, if you gave a 5 to the last question of Section 1, you might write: *I am becoming more and more enthusiastic about my life, and I am bringing joy to every experience.*

If you have a low score for Section 1 . . . This indicates that you may have had pain in your past (even in your past lives), and you're probably still recovering from it. Difficult events and hurtful people have brought you deeply into the personal perspective. You've measured yourself through others' eyes, and you've found yourself wanting. Although you may intellectually know yourself to be a Divine, eternal spirit, you don't yet feel the overwhelming love for (and from) that spirit in your heart. But fear not! You've been honest with yourself, which means that you're not hiding from the path that lies before you. It's time to take the steps through self-investigation, catharsis, and meditation to help release old, painful memories as well as the false beliefs that they caused. Your Divine spirit rests within you, and it's time to embrace it in your mind, in your heart, and in your experience.

. . . **with a high score in Section 2.** If you received a high score in Section 2 along with a low total in Section 1, it shows that you've had enough experience and have accumulated enough knowledge in your field of work to counterbalance—at least to a certain degree—a personal lack of self-esteem. Yet while your talents may ensure some measure of career success, it's unlikely that you'll really grab the brass ring until you know in your deepest heart that you deserve it.

. . . **with a low score in Section 2.** At this point, there's much work ahead of you. It's possible for an individual who has *either* personal confidence *or* vocational expertise to "fake it till he makes it," but when both areas of self-esteem are in short supply, obstacles to success may abound. This isn't a time to feel downtrodden, however. When you see the great truth of your real, eternal, and confident self, you'll find that unlimited horizons lie before you. First and foremost, take steps to tap the wellspring of your eternal power. Get to know it through meditation; come to believe it through affirmation; learn to act upon it by taking risks. Also begin to study and to practice the disciplines in the work to which you're drawn. In time, you'll find that self-discovery will turn to golden self-expression at every level.

If you have a high score in Section 1 . . . Congratulations! You've built a foundation for making every dream real. But no matter how strongly you're connected to your spirit and regardless of how comfortable you feel in your own skin, you're still a human being. You must be diligent in listening to your spirit, for your ego is also vying for your attention. Remember that you've done much work in discovering your truth and living it.

You may have put a negative history behind you, but history—as they say—repeats itself. Certain situations or types of people may trigger self-doubt and second-guessing. Conversely, if you enter into a new position of power, you may find that your confidence or expertise can spiral into arrogance. Self-doubt and arrogance seem to be opposites, since the first makes you feel bad, and the second makes you feel good—in the short term. Yet they're both fear-based responses of the ego, and they're both natural in the human dilemma.

A high score in Section 1 shows that you've made great inroads in discovering the Divine Source inside you, the origin of everything you need. But this isn't a destination you've reached; it's an experience to be lived. If you seek it every day, you'll know it every day. And through that regular discovery, you will also experience success.

    . . . with a low score in Section 2. Although you may not feel totally confident about your field of study, you have the personal self-esteem to pursue any endeavor successfully. All things come in their own time, and you may not yet believe that you have the work experience to put yourself out on the proverbial limb. But if you devote yourself to the right career steps, practice, and continue to align your personal agenda with your Divine plan, you'll make success a reality.

    . . . with a high score in Section 2. The time is here! You've put yourself well on the path of self-realization in both your personal evolution and your career. All you need to do is continue taking each next step as it comes (and as you're guided). Stay strong, stay flexible, and keep listening within!

> *Close your eyes. Your intuition has a list of your priorities—of people and projects—in front of you. Take a look at it, and see your name at the top. On the next line is what you're supposed to do for yourself. What do you see there?*

The Power and Vision of the Higher Self

Preparation: Defining and knowing yourself as a Divine being breaks down all barriers to your success. Meditation is the most dynamic tool to make your connection with your spirit and intuition real and more available every day. The following visualization is one that you can do anytime to tap into the powers of the higher Self. Remember, your personality is just a small component of your multidimensional Self, and it takes practice to focus inward and learn to still the personal mind. So stay out of your left brain—don't analyze or second-guess what you're experiencing. Trust everything you perceive spontaneously.

1. Take a deep breath and put yourself in a completely relaxed state of mind and body. Bring your awareness to your higher Self, deep at the center of your being. Feel this radiant, all-powerful, eternal source of all you need fill you with light, love, power, and grace.

2. You may feel larger, sit up straighter, or feel as if your arms and legs are longer. Whatever you experience, sense yourself completely and realize the force and power of the higher Self within. Notice all of the energies that are moving through you.

3. Feel the mind of the higher Self within your intellect; sense the sharing of confidence in the absolute presence of your eternal being; and perceive how this can help you step more strongly toward success in any endeavor. Take a few minutes to let your intuition communicate any new ideas and elevated thoughts about your endeavors as you get to know this broader mind.

4. As you know the eternal Self within you, experience the vision that your higher Self gives you about any particular situation—or about your life in general. Take a moment to view any temporal situation from your eternal perspective. Look at it with the eyes that see forever, and perceive it as your spirit does.

5. As you see the situation anew, consider any old methods that your personal self has used to deal with it, along with any of the past patterns and any limiting definitions that your personality used to hold. Allow the vision of your higher Self to blast apart these old paradigms, and see them floating away. Begin to release the personal perspective, history, and patterns. Know and understand how these stale, limiting structures undermined your success . . . then let them go.

6. Take a few minutes to perceive and understand all that lies before you in your new sense of self. Envision a path that lies in front of you, seeing it completely. It's the way of opportunity, power, and potential. Watch yourself as you walk down this path and start to utilize the force of the soul that you are and will be forever.

7. See yourself applying the powers of your eternal Self to the situations in your life that you thought you couldn't handle—those that you believed were too difficult to control or too challenging to affect. Watch as your higher Self handles these obstacles upon your path with confidence and strength. Do this now.

8. Continue to see your higher Self at work upon your path. Don't interpret or analyze—just take a moment to briefly look upon this journey, and let your intuition show you the many amazing powers you have and the successes that they bring forth into your life.

9. Don't try to predetermine where your path goes in the long run. It is eternal. If you don't understand something you see, just let it be there. The important thing is your ability to sense the new power and insight that you have in your choices and in your actions. With these, you begin to live and breathe each moment from the mind and heart of your soul, and you start to anticipate the opportunities for success that your spirit provides.

10. As you begin to bring your awareness back to your body, you also realize that shifting to this higher Self awareness is possible every moment. Affirm: *It is easy for me to absorb and channel higher and higher levels of power, love, and wisdom—from my spirit—to the world every day. I know the voice of my intuition, and I rise to meet it.*

Things to Consider

On a separate piece of paper or in your journal, write about your meditation experience and answer the following questions. (Throughout this part of the book, you'll use your journal frequently. For more information about different journaling techniques, see Chapter 14.)

1. List some of the past patterns and definitions that your higher Self helped you release. What new habits can replace the old ones?

2. How does freedom from the previous limits and pain afford you greater opportunities for success? List some of the potentials you'd like to realize, and consider a few steps you can take to begin the process.

3. How did your higher Self handle the situations you thought were too difficult? How did it feel to have the power of your eternal soul to deal with those challenges? How will you address them when they come up again?

4. Make your own affirmation to call upon your higher mind and energies when these challenges arise. Put it on a card and use it frequently throughout the day.

5. What were the directives shown to you by your intuition on the path that lies before you? What action can you take to pursue those purposes and realize their success?

Take Your Intuition to Bed

Begin to practice everything you've learned about your spirit and your intuition. Call to your spirit at bedtime and ask to be given all of the solutions you need. Keep a special dream journal (which can be separate from your daily journal) next to your bed so that you can record your dreams and note your insights upon waking. And while you're getting to know your own spirit, begin to open the door to the other spirits who wish to help you.

CHAPTER 9

SPIRIT ASSISTANCE—JUST PICTURE IT!

"The soul never thinks without a picture."

— **ARISTOTLE**

Your soul and those of your loved ones often use pictures, symbols, and other images to share messages. Although you may not feel familiar with this type of communication right now, it's easy to learn. With a little practice, you'll find that your spirit guides will be happy to bring you healing, share their counsel, and help with your success in many ways.

Connecting with spirit doesn't require any special gifts or family traits; all you need is to see the world with new eyes. Learn to still your outer senses so that your inner senses can perceive something that's already around you almost all the time. Like the Divine, those in spirit are with you—bidden or unbidden. And even mediums sometimes need to be reminded of that!

I remember when my mother came to take my son, Devin, and me to dinner, a week after my husband's funeral. When we got to the restaurant, my son, who was three at the time, ran to the table and climbed onto a chair that he seemed to have selected with great purpose. When I began to sit on the empty seat to his left, he grabbed my arm to stop me.

"Mommy, don't!" he exclaimed with great urgency. "You can't sit there. You're going to sit on Daddy."

I was happy to switch to the other side of Devin. And we all—including my husband, I'm sure—spent the evening in great love and peace.

You might be surprised to find out how often those in spirit come to the table, and you don't have to be a medium or a little child in order to connect with them. As with anything, the first step in knowing these glorious beings is to believe—in *them* and in your ability to sense them. Then, as Aristotle suggested, all you have to do is think with a picture.

Quick! Close your eyes. Someone from your spirit family or friends wants to help you make the connection. Let yourself sense it, feel it, and picture it. Find out who this is, trusting the first thing you perceive.

In this brief exercise, you just used three of the primary components necessary in working with your own spirit (your intuition) and with your guides and angels: *spontaneity, imaging* (or *pictures*), and *trust.* Not coincidentally, these aren't only the activities of spirit communication, but they also belong to your right brain—and that's the "right" brain for any intuitive experience!

As my sister and I have said, the left brain is responsible for deductive and analytical thought. It's the part of you that figures out the tip at a restaurant and that finds (you hope!) the file you seemed to have lost on your computer. Your left brain is also where you analyze your own success and failure—from the smallest events to the largest—measuring, quantifying, and evaluating.

Just as with the intuitive messages from your own spirit, your experience with other spirits will often be subtle, spontaneous, and visual; and it will always require your trust. Since the right brain is where you perceive images, it's also where you imagine. Consequently, when you first start exercising this part of your mind in connecting to spirit, it may feel just the way it did other times in your life when you've used your imagination. Because of this, you may think, *I'm only imagining this,* or worse, *I'm just making this up.*

Remember that the world of spirit is a beautiful realm of grace. There's nothing and no one outside your own thoughts that can separate you from it. That type of negative, doubtful thinking immediately undermines your ability to trust. It also instantly takes you *into* the left brain (where these analytical statements originate) and *out* of the right brain (where you experience spirit).

There are two *rules of thumb* in responding to this left/right dilemma about inner perceptions:

1. If you find yourself doubting, second-guessing, or in any other way measuring your experience, promptly realize that you've wandered into your left brain. Quickly let go of all such thoughts. Then simply open yourself up to the next spontaneous perception and trust it.

2. If it feels as though you're imagining something, it's only because you're *imaging* it. Pat yourself on the back and assure yourself that you're using the right inner senses (and the *right* brain). Then simply open yourself up to the next spontaneous perception and trust it.

About Spirit

As you begin to learn more of the spirit world, it's important to consider how to refer to its inhabitants. Spirits are individuals and can be referred to with terms such as *this spirit* or *those spirits* (just like *this man* or *those men*). And just like the word *man, spirit* can also be used as a collective—for example: *Man has a consciousness no other animal knows.* Throughout these chapters, you'll see the word *spirit* used in the singular, plural, and collective forms.

And how do you "see" spirit? Actually witnessing spirits with your physical eyes isn't what the terms *visualizing* and *imaging* reflect. The experience of visualizing refers to "seeing" in your mind's eye the images or ideas that your spirit guides telepathically "think at you." Unfortunately— thanks to the way spirit is depicted by Hollywood—most people expect to hear spirit with their actual ears and to see inhabitants of that realm as if they were three-dimensional people.

While it's true that your guides are very frequently standing right next to you, it's unlikely that you'll perceive them with your physical senses. Spirit people are—after all—not physical, they're spiritual. They share images in a mental way that reflects themselves and their messages. For instance, imagining your grandfather's pocket watch could indicate that he is present or that he's telling you to watch your time on a certain project.

The soul really does think with pictures, and so does most of humankind —it's no accident that magazines are comprised of mostly images. It's the same way in the experience of spirit communication. Such messages occur in many ways, but for most people, they come through inner visual impressions. For spirit, a single picture truly is worth a thousand words, and one image can have a number of meanings.

An example of this would be a perception from spirit (whether from your own intuition or from your spirit guides) of a simple image or idea of a three-leaf clover. This one message could represent a great number of things: a person from Ireland, a trip to that country, a lucky opportunity coming, a triplicity of some sort (such as a partnership of three), a spirit from Ireland, an event connected to March 17th, or many other events. It may even refer to something that you don't know about yet. It's up to you to note in your journal all images, feelings, and symbols that you perceive and then consider all possible meanings later.

Quick! Your spirit guide just handed you a flower. Close your eyes and "look" at it. What is it? Notice its textures and colors. What does it mean to you?

Learning to Read

All of the relationships in your life can help you move toward your success in many ways. The people who care for you in the physical world can do many things to show their support—from sharing their opinions to helping you make the right contacts. Your spirit loved ones can do all this and more, but first you have to learn how to communicate with them.

Spirit speaks to you telepathically. And you can perceive (or read) their signs in a variety of ways—all of which will be with the inner senses. Most people are *clairvoyant* ("clear seeing"), but others are *clairsentient* ("clear knowing"). You've already learned about the gut feelings that can accompany intuitive experiences—the inner knowing or compelling sensations, which are signs of clairsentience. *Clairaudience* ("clear hearing") occurs when words or ideas pop into your head. Despite the literal meaning of the term, you won't actually hear a voice; you'll usually just sense or know the words.

It's important to discover how you, personally, perceive things. Are you visual, mental, or feeling? Once you've determined your strongest tendency (clairvoyant, clairsentient, or clairaudient), you can expand your comfort zone by practicing with all of your "extra" (or inner) senses. Here's a little process to begin:

> *Imagine a red feather and close your eyes. Do you see a picture of it, think the words, or feel it? After a moment, also try to perceive it in a different way, then let it blow away. Which direction does it go? How do you feel?*
>
> *Now your spirit guides are sharing a song. Listen for it in your heart, and trust the first thing you get. Do you "hear" the music in your mind, recall the title of the song, or think of the lyrics? What does this song mean to you?*

Calling the Troops

Whom exactly should you call upon in the spirit world, and what can they do, anyway? Well, the answer is: anybody and anything. I have a friend who strongly believes in the intercession of those above. She cried out to spirit to help her find a job, but she couldn't release her financial worries. Later that day she asked again. The response she "heard" was: *Have we ever let you down before? What makes you think we're going to start now?* Days later, she got a call from a company where she'd interviewed more than three months earlier. She landed that job, and it was there that she met the person who was to be her future boss at yet another company. Without knowing it at the time, she had begun climbing the ladder of her success.

I asked my friend who it was in spirit who had told her not to worry. She told me that she didn't know precisely, but she knew it was a "higher intelligence." This is the way it goes—you don't always have to know exactly whom you're calling upon. Sometimes you can request help from your friends and loved ones; you can also invoke your higher guides, your angels, your own soul, and even the Divine.

Actor Denzel Washington revealed in an interview that while shooting the movie *Glory,* he needed to prepare for the scene in which he was to be whipped. He, too, reached out to the spirit world, saying, "All you men and women in spirit who've been whipped, come be with me. I'll let go and let whatever happens happen."

In this interview, Washington pointed to two of the most crucial steps in working with spirit. First, make the call! Your spirit guides certainly show up without your inviting them, but your request clarifies and crystalizes your intention—both for you and for them. *(Never forget: Ask and it shall be answered.)* Second, let what happens, happen! Let go of your need for control. Trust what you perceive and that you'll be led where you need to go.

The spirit people who helped Denzel Washington succeed in the movie *Glory* weren't known to him personally. And there may be many unknown spirits whom you can call to support your successes, too. You'll learn more about that later, but now it's time for a spirit party—so get ready to invite your family and friends.

> *Call to your loved ones in spirit and feel them gather around you; close your eyes and sense their presence. One steps forward with a gift for you. Notice who it is and open your present. What is it?*

Many people have sought spirit's help in their pursuit of success. Abraham Lincoln sat at séances, and industrialist Cornelius Vanderbilt had regular meetings with a famous medium to discuss his holdings and investments. But you don't have to do either of these things to get information from the spirit side of life.

I had a client named Bob who was an investment broker who'd been experiencing a smattering of success mixed in with a lot of very disappointing results. He first came to me for a reading about whether his accuracy in picking investments was going to pick up. But as our conversation went on, I started suggesting ways in which he could get the information he needed himself, including meditating and keeping a dream journal. He decided to try the technique of calling a spirit friend's name and asking a question just before he went to sleep.

A good friend at his company, Ed, had passed to spirit about two years earlier. Before that, they'd played golf together and spent a lot of time socializing in addition to their hours at work.

Bob had often felt Ed's presence since his death, and there were a few incidents where Bob felt as though he was getting some specific directions. Once he had a sudden urge to take the long way home instead of getting on the freeway as usual. When he was watching the news later that night, he found out that there had been a five-car pileup on his normal route. Although my client didn't know whether he would have been involved in that accident, he certainly would have been waiting in traffic for hours because of it.

Bob experienced several incidents like this, so he decided to ask Ed for help. As he went to bed each night, he thought of Ed's name and asked for any information he needed to make wise and successful investments. He did this for several weeks without getting any response—or at least anything he could understand.

Then one day Bob woke up with three letters floating around in his head. They looked just like the abbreviations that are used for corporate stocks, but he'd never heard of a company that used those letters. He asked his friends, but they had no idea either. So he wrote the letters on a sticky note and put it on the wall over his desk, and then he almost forgot about it—but not quite.

Several more weeks went by, and Bob was poring over several newspapers and financial reports, as he did every morning while he had his coffee. There, in a small article about a new energy company, were the three letters that he'd received. He quickly researched the business and decided to follow his guidance. He started investing in it, and he and his clients were soon making a bundle. As a result, he was assigned several large accounts.

Another interesting thing happened several months later. Bob had endured a long day of meetings, and he was exhausted—practically asleep on his feet. He was brushing his teeth while getting ready for bed, and when he leaned over to spit into the sink, he thought he saw those same three letters go down the drain! When he went to sleep, he asked Ed for more information about it, but he just kept dreaming about the letters going down the drain.

The next day, Bob knew what he had to do. He went to work and started selling off that company's stock. His friends thought he was crazy because the share price was still going up. But he was adamant, and when his clients and co-workers saw his fervor, they started following his lead.

A few weeks later, the press started to cover some questionable activities and business practices concerning that company. Within a very short time it went bust, and all the people who'd pinned their life savings on its success were devastated. Everyone in Bob's company wanted to know how he knew what was going to happen, and there was even some talk about insider information. Still, it was clear that my client had no connection to anyone at that company. (His "insider information" came from inside the spirit realm.) After that incident, people at work joked about Bob being the psychic stock trader, even though he'd never told anyone about his dream!

This experience speaks to many important issues where success and spirit are concerned. First, no matter who you are, you can learn how to get help from spirit. Second, you have to be willing to recognize and act on that wisdom. Third, spirit doesn't have to be weird or crazy. It's a wonderful source of assistance that you can make a part of your daily life—if you just give it a try.

That investment was just one of many experiences where Bob's success was helped by spirit. He's made a lot of money and gotten several promotions since that time, but one result was far more important than all the cash in the world.

Bob has developed a much more peaceful perspective since his first experience with Ed in spirit. Before that, he was struggling with grief over his friend's death. He'd also gone into a downward spiral about his own life, wondering what it was all for if it was possible to work so hard and then just drop dead of a heart attack as Ed had done. But this experience made Bob—a practical and even somewhat skeptical man to begin with—look for something deeper. He found incredible comfort in the profound realization that life goes on and our connections never die. This brought him serenity and certainty that he'd never known before . . . and Bob says that this life-changing inner peace is the greatest success he's ever known.

Family Reunion—Please RSVP!

You have many loved ones in spirit who have assumed your care as their own singular assignment. These are your "guardian angels" from your family and friends. And although they aren't technically angels, they are to you! They're angels because they serve and care for you. These loved ones in spirit make it their business to help you and to make you more aware of your options and patterns. They try to point out the areas where you need to create change as well as the opportunities that pop up in your life.

The first (and perhaps most important) thing that you can do to create an ongoing conscious rapport with your own spirit people is to believe. Still, that's only the beginning. Let's now climb the *steps* to the spirit world.

Steps in Spirit Communication

1. *Create the belief in spirit and in your ability to communicate with spirit.* Nothing ever happens without believing in it first. Know absolutely that you *are* spirit. The voice of your higher Self is always available to you, and so is your spirit mind. You're capable of perceiving all you need to perceive (including those in the spirit world) as long as your personal mind or ego doesn't block you with judgment and doubt.

2. *Make the call! Invite spirit's presence and participation every time you think of it.* Whether in life's large decisions or its little tasks, ask these assistants to be with you. Although your own personal spirit guides are often present without being asked, it's important to call upon them (as well as all of the spirit people who want to be with you). This helps you do a number of things:

- Focuses your intention

- Affirms your beliefs

- Builds the habit of spontaneous connection

- Opens the door to helpful spirit guides who may not yet be known to you

3. *Use your imaging skills.* Picture, picture, picture! Practice, practice, practice. Whether you tend to be clairvoyant (visual), clairaudient (verbal), or clairsentient (feeling), your right brain and your imagination are key. Use them often. Become familiar and comfortable with how they feel, and then validate your right-brain perceptions by following up on the information you get.

4. *Let go of doubt, judgment, and the need for control—in other words, trust!* The activity of relying upon your inner senses must be cultivated every day by quieting the mind and listening within. But trust must also be cultivated in the rest of your life as well. How can you count on the little, subtle communications from spirit if you don't trust the larger events in your life? The greatest step in building this quality is to relinquish worry and fear. Give your life to the Divine Spirit and trust absolutely in every step you take. All that you need is inside you. Believe it, feel it, and trust it.

5. *Act on your commitment to know spirit every day.* Do the things that help you realize your own truth as a spiritual being and also to nurture your relationship with other spirit guides. Study; meditate; keep a journal; and if you can, find others to share your journey of inner discovery. Most important, learn to keep an untroubled mind and a serene heart. Let go of reactionary emotions, and shift your focus from the little self to the large. Tranquility opens the door to receiving the telepathic whispers from your own soul and from all of the guides who seek to help you.

6. *Adopt a spiritual view of success.* It's not just about becoming rich or famous. Those are the personal world's definitions of doing well; and while they may be happy conclusions, there are many other ways to know success every day of your life. When you speak with people, do you strive to look for the spirit inside them? Do you go through the day seeking a depth of meaning behind the little events and the miracles in ordinary life? If you learn to live with a sense of wonder and a quest for a greater vision, you'll feel the presence of your own spirit more often and much more consciously. And every waking moment will be filled with living your highest truth, imagining your greatest success, and expressing the thoughts that speak to the world.

From Successful Imagination to Telepathy—the True Wireless

This is the story of a man whose imagination brought success to himself and to people all over the world. He also believed that telepathic thought was a force of attraction, and he used it often. He was the father of all wireless, the Italian physicist Guglielmo Marconi, born in 1874. In his early 20s, he first started to experiment with electromagnetic waves. Within a very short time, he was transmitting wireless signals across the English Channel and then across the Atlantic Ocean. In 1909, he and German physicist Karl Braun were awarded the Nobel Prize for physics. Later, Marconi also invented the devices for shortwave radio. Thus, the communication age was born.

Marconi was a man of many talents and even more interests. He believed in Spiritualism, the continuation of life after death, the ability to communicate with those in spirit, telepathy, and the ability to effect change in your life by the messages you send out.

In her *New York Tribune* interview, Mary Williams Reed (pen name: Kate Carew) asked Marconi if he believed that someday ordinary means of communication would give way to the extraordinary.

"I certainly do!" he said. "We'll be able to tune our minds. I am sure of it. We do it now in a measure, but some day when you go into a restaurant and the waiter asks you, 'Alone?' You will say, 'Oh, no; I expect somebody.' You will send out a wave or two, and soon the somebody will appear."

Without knowing it, Marconi was cracking the door open—not only on the subject of telepathy, but perhaps even more important, on the theory of mental waves and of how they can manifest successful results.

There was something else unknown to the inventor at the time of that interview. Although he'd already gained an amount of celebrity by winning the Nobel Prize, the Marconi wireless still hadn't been universally used and wasn't even that well known. Yet by the end of the following day, the name Marconi would resound in newspapers, offices, and households around the globe and for generations to come. This interview took place on Sunday afternoon, April 14, 1912. And somewhere, very far east of the Holland House in New York City, where they were chatting, the *Titanic* was speeding toward her destiny. Due to the arrogance, greed, and folly of a great many people, about 1,500 men, women, and children would drown that night in the icy Atlantic. Yet the saving of more than 700 lives would be largely credited to Marconi's wireless.

Before finishing the interview, Mary Williams Reed asked Marconi about the use of wireless for rescue at sea. Marconi replied, "In my imagination, it had happened a thousand times."

Imagination! He'd seen it, imagined it, known it. From Marconi to Einstein and beyond, imagination has been a highly valued (and, indeed, necessary) commodity in the world of discovery, invention, and success. These scientists and many others in every field of endeavor have relied on their imaginations to inspire their creativity and lead them in the direction of their dreams.

You must also practice using your imagination to create the successes of your personal life as well as in learning to communicate with spirit. Unfortunately, some scientists, many skeptics, and even your own analytical mind may try to tell you that the world of spirit is "just your imagination." The truth is that imagination is not just the key to success, it is the key to greatness.

All great art, thought, and science have forever stood upon the shoulders of imagination. It is, after all, the place where you can see the unseen and know the unknown. Close your eyes and let your imagination take you to the mountaintop. Take a look at the horizons and see, now, where you're meant to go and what you're meant to do.

Like Marconi, you can:

1. Imagine the possibilities.

2. Send out the telepathic thoughts that successfully manifest your intention.

3. Believe and receive the telepathic guidance from spirit.

Then the entire world will be at your door. Now you can practice receiving and using that place of imaging to greet your loved ones in spirit.

Spirit Comes to Life!

Preparation: Begin by first putting yourself in a relaxed position where you won't be interrupted by the telephone or by your family members (well, by your *physical* family members, anyway). Remember to give yourself permission to use all of your imaging—however *you* use it (in pictures, words, or feelings). Be spontaneous and *trust* your perceptions.

1. With a few deep breaths, feel yourself relax and move deeply into the mind and heart of your spirit. Feel the peace and begin to think about your loved ones who have passed.

2. Now remember a photograph of someone in the spirit world who loves you deeply. It's a picture that you've seen many, many times, and it's quite easy to recall.

3. This picture of your loved one begins to take shape. If you're seeing it with your mind's eye, it may feel as though you're imagining it because you're viewing it through the imaging side of the brain (clairvoyance). If you're simply recalling the memory of it, it may seem more like an academic or mental experience because you're holding the thoughts about it (clairsentience). No matter how you experience it, this is real for you. You can "see," feel, and sense the image of this photo and the person in it.

4. As you focus on this familiar picture, it starts to become animated. This loving individual's smile starts to grow wider, and from the twinkling eyes you can feel a message of great love.

5. As this person becomes more and more animated, he or she begins to move, then takes a step out of the photo and right up to you. This spirit wraps his or her arms around you, and you can feel the unfathomable love in this warm embrace. Take a moment now to sense that embrace completely.

6. As you feel the profound presence of this spirit, take a moment to ask the person any question about anything you want. You may perceive a mental answer in your own mind, or you might just get a feeling. You

may receive a fleeting image or visual symbol. Even if it's just a piece of a puzzle that you don't entirely understand, notice it. Trust whatever you experience—exactly how you experience it.

7. Take a few moments to have a little dialogue with this person in whatever ways come to you. And just for practice, ask to be shown a symbol—any symbol—about your actions for success, and make a mental note of it. Remember to write it in your journal later.

8. Now, this spirit tells you that another person whom you love is there, too. And suddenly, a second spirit steps forward. Sense and feel who it is as this individual embraces you also. Take a few minutes to converse with both of these loving beings now.

9. Thank these spirit people for coming to be with you, and make a commitment to them (and to yourself) that you'll call upon them and your other spirit loved ones and guides often. Create an affirmation declaring that you'll stay open to their approach—both in your meditations and throughout your workaday life. Tell yourself, *I am sensitive to my spirit guides and seek to know their presence every day.*

10. As you bring your awareness back to your body, remember all of the things that happened for you. Take some notes in your journal about the images and ideas you perceived. If you experienced anything that you didn't understand, that's okay. Just make a note of it, and come back to it later. The more you work with spirit, the more familiar and comfortable you'll be with the language.

Spirit on Purpose

Sometimes when people begin to connect with spirit and seek assistance, it's the higher guides who are sought and who are given more focus and more validity. But it's impossible to separate your personal evolution from your eternal evolution, your business success from your life success, your outer work from your inner. You can't make success real in your manifest life if you don't fully comprehend who you are inside—from your emotional histories to your highest spiritual truth. What you have within you are the raw materials that you use to build your life. Because of your history and experience, some of those materials may be tarnished, faulty, or cracked. With your effort, however, these can be changed and released. And just as you might employ professionals in the physical world to help you with these shifts, your spirit guides can help you tremendously, too.

Also inside you, bubbling and boiling at your core, is the power of your own eternal spirit that can manifest absolute success in ways you have yet to discover. But before your spirit can act with its full power, you must remove the blockages and boundaries established by the faulty belief systems from your past. Of all the spirit helpers in the world, your loved ones are particularly capable of helping you change your inner makeup because they know you and your life intimately. Some may have even contributed to those negative histories and wish to help turn things around.

Your personal guides (your spirit friends and family) are the key participants in the work that you have to do in this regard. It's the *internal* work that you do that provides the foundation for the *eternal* work you bring to the world. After all, if you wish to have influence upon the whole world, you must be able to effect change in your own life—and your spirit people can help you make change real.

> *Imagine that a spirit loved one is standing next to you right now. He or she is here to show you one thing that you need to change to help lift your energy, your confidence, and your sense of success. Close your eyes and see it in your mind's eye now.*

All aspects of your personal reality contribute to your ability to succeed. Your physical, mental, emotional, and spiritual makeup will, each in its own way, enhance or diminish your sense of confidence, your ability to take action, your belief in yourself, and your vision of the opportunities in your life.

Those who seek to assist you from the higher realms often have a tendency to work in the areas of your life with which they personally resonate—even at the most mundane level. If there are repairs or technical projects at hand, spirit fathers, grandfathers, and brothers will often participate; mothers and grandmothers enjoy helping with children.

Co-workers and bosses who have passed give a hand with work-related issues. And it's almost always the case that those who have unresolved emotional histories with you will wish to make amends. They often want to fill the roles that they may not have been able to fill when they were living.

I have a client named Mary whose mother had been a great source of pain through her criticism and harshness. Although it was difficult at first, Mary began to work with her mom in spirit. Mary discovered that her mother also had to deal with a history of great self-loathing when in this world. More important, Mary was able to meet the truly loving soul of her mother—something she'd never known while her mom was alive.

Of course, there are no set rules about what each spirit guide will contribute to your life and to your success. The lines of assistance aren't drawn by gender or occupation but by empathy and need. As a matter of fact, all of your spirit guides wish to help you heal. And if part of that effort includes reconciling your relationship with one of them (mending old wounds, speaking what had been left unsaid, and so on), that will be the first item on their agenda.

Healing the Past—the First Doorway to a Successful Future

If you're trying to create a future of success, the energy that you bring to your efforts must be clear, confident, and precisely intentional. If you're carrying difficult emotions from the past, they can cloud your present energy—even if you think you've successfully put them away.

The idea of recalling to mind the individuals who were hurtful, dismissive, or even just too busy to bother seems counterproductive to many people at first. They think, *Why should I do that if it will just bring up the pain?* The reason why, of course, is that the suffering (low self-esteem or devalued feelings) is still there no matter how much people try to ignore it. (On the other hand, many people seek therapy and talk about their trauma for years—even decades—yet they still have no relief because change doesn't occur only on the mental level. It happens on the physical, emotional, behavioral, and spiritual levels. Therapy must be proactive and include all of these approaches as well as their daily application.)

When I tell my clients that one of the things they need to do is to get in touch with the spirit of the person or people who (even remotely) may have contributed to their difficult emotions, many quite literally drop their jaws. Lots of them have said, "I don't want to talk to my [mother, father, uncle, or whomever] in spirit—what a horrible person."

You may feel that way about someone, too. But in every case, the desire to push somebody away indicates a history where the pain must still be healed. This must happen not only to mend the relationship but also to fix the ongoing sabotaging thought-forms that go with the hurt and that undermine your success. The need to push away loved ones in spirit also indicates a lack of understanding about how the spirit world works.

If you were to look into the many books about near-death experiences (NDEs), you'd find an overwhelming consistency in the reports by those who have been clinically dead and then have come back. First, of course, there's the ubiquitous tunnel of light, but even more important than that, there is the frequent occurrence of absolute joy, love, confidence, and peace along with the total release of fear and vulnerability. Why is this a common thread that runs through most NDEs? It's because in a near-death experience, the individual is having a full-throated, uncensored communion with his or her own eternal, invulnerable, imperishable soul. For the first time in this person's consciousness, there are no walls; no barriers; no measurements of the ego or priorities of the personal, land-locked, little self.

This is the reality of moving into spirit. Suddenly you see all of your eternal life, and you remember who you are. You get a chance to look back on your physical life with all of its urgent and temporal priorities, and you wonder why you made such silly and sometimes even selfish things so important. It would be just as if you were to look back today and recall a temper tantrum you had had in the fourth grade. Even if you could remember why it happened, you'd realize that whatever was so important to you then isn't even remotely so now. Just imagine the sublime clarity of suddenly stepping into a world where boundless freedom, power, and love define and fill you. The poet W. B. Yeats, who worked with spirit his whole life (and of whom I'll speak more later), called this state of clarity the *lucidity of the soul*.

This is the way it feels for those who pass into the spirit world. It is the higher Self they discover.

The higher Selves of those who have already moved out of this realm want to connect with you to heal the past, embrace the present, and create a future of happiness. Even if there were no deep wounds or words left unspoken, your loved ones in spirit want to help you do away with any hurt feelings and negative beliefs—no matter what their origin—so that you can lift yourself up to the highest realization of joy and success in life and in business.

Here's a process for healing with your loved ones in spirit. And all you have to do is bring a trusting mind and an open heart.

Healing with Your Loved Ones in Spirit

Preparation: Before you begin this exercise, determine which emotional and mental patterns most strongly work against your sense of joy, confidence, and inner strength. In your journal or on a separate piece of paper, write down a few of the self-diminishing thoughts that you experience most frequently. You can use some of the negative conclusions from earlier exercises in this book. These come from your old histories, and as part of your quantum psychology, they can often inhibit your future success.

1. Close your eyes and take several deep, calming breaths. Allow yourself to relax and call upon those in spirit who love you. Trust every subtle nuance as you feel their approach. Let yourself take a minute to notice everything that you internally sense about them.

2. Now recall the emotional feelings and thoughts that you've just determined are difficult or hurtful. Feel the spirit people who are there to help you, and notice who they are. Did any of them give rise to these feelings in any way when they were alive? If so, notice that you're now dealing with their *higher* Selves, their spirits who truly see the priorities of the soul. These spirits ask for your forgiveness now.

3. Also begin to notice your own higher Self. Imagine that you, too, have stepped into the spirit world, and you stand well apart from—or

even above—the little physical world. You begin to see your old history from the perspective of your eternal, invulnerable spirit.

4. As you remember the events and sense the individuals who gave birth to these negative histories, let these people show you how they were acting out of their own pain and vulnerability. Take a moment to see their former lack, understand their emptiness, and forgive.

5. Now watch yourself releasing those histories along with every thought and feeling that diminish your sense of the glorious spirit within you. With a deep exhalation, send those narratives, those thoughts, and any feelings of failure or lack away from you on the wings of the wind. Feel the great heart and mind of your own spirit. Affirm to yourself: *The heart and mind of my spirit are in my awareness always. I know only power, joy, and pure potential.*

6. Allow yourself to feel the great love from your spirit guides, and also sense the unstoppable and unimpeachable love from your higher Self. This source fills you so profoundly with unconditional grace and power that you know you can succeed in any endeavor and in every way. You feel yourself brimming over with energy, purpose, and new self-realization. This is your truth in the eternal heaven. It's your home every day. Feel it, know it, and remember it!

7. Allow yourself to slowly come back—bringing your awareness to your body and to the room, but still recalling and trusting every subtle perception and experience.

Conclusion: After you return to your conscious awareness, be sure to write down your reactions along with some affirmations that will help bring to mind your new perception of these spirits and of your higher Self. Make a commitment to release and redefine old thought patterns. And as you live your life more consciously, call upon these guides and your higher Self every day to reinforce your healing and your journey of success with spirit.

Life on (and with) the Other Side

Of course, spirit doesn't come *only* with life-changing advice or in times of dire need. As a matter of fact, just as every prayer shouldn't turn into pleading, you shouldn't make every communication with spirit a fact-finding mission or a call for help. Although these guides wish to assist, they're not your servants, and they want you to let go of urgency and desperate seeking. They wish a life of peace and joy for you.

Like your physical loved ones, these individuals want to be with you in the little moments as well as the large. Indeed, life is made up mostly of small events, so that's where you will find spirit the most—in your house, at your job, in your car, and even in your dreams.

There are a lot of misconceptions and questions about spirit. The following three stories will help you understand their world and how they connect with you a little bit better.

— My client Annie wondered why her sister often dreamed about their deceased mother, but Mom never seemed to come to Annie. I told her that not all people remember their dreams and that she should keep a dream journal by her bed to start building the habit. I gave her some meditations so that she could practice putting herself in a receptive state without falling asleep. I also said that, while spirit does visit when the family is sleeping, not all dreams reflect a communication with the other side. Some are the working out of your unexpressed emotions, which can include great grief over the loss of a loved one.

Annie began to keep a dream journal, and over time she started to remember her dreams, including those of her mother, as well as the ones that gave her insights about her hopes, her fears, and her life. In addition, she found that her meditations brought her great peace and gave her the opportunity to be with her mother in a more conscious and deliberate way.

— Shortly after his father's death, my son had dreams of being pushed down the stairs by his dad. His father in spirit certainly wasn't giving him these images! Instead, the dreams reflected the sense of abandonment that my son naturally felt from his father's sudden absence. Of course, his dad hadn't really abandoned him at all; he was as close to him in spirit as he was in life. My son's feelings were all part of the natural pain of grief. And as that healed, so did the dreams.

— My client Rick told me that he could often feel his brother's spirit with him soon after his brother died. But then his brother seemed to stop coming to visit. I explained to Rick that what actually had happened was that he was getting used to his brother's energy. The siblings' auras were starting to "blend." As I tell my mediumship students, when this happens, sensing the loved one's spirit is like looking for a white rabbit in a snow-storm. His brother was still visiting in spirit; Rick just needed to learn how to meditate so that he could begin to perceive spirit at the more subtle levels of experience.

Moving on or Being Held Back?

One of the most horrendous misconceptions about those in spirit is that they can be held back from their own growth or from "moving on to the light" if the family left behind grieves too much or even thinks about them too often. Consider this: If your brother and sister moved to California, would they stop learning, growing, or traveling if you were to call or visit? Do you think it's possible that the indomitable, all-powerful, eternal soul (which has no limits in time or space) could conceivably be held back by what you're thinking more easily than someone living in another state could? The thoughts of the people living in the three-dimensional world certainly aren't more powerful than the minds of those residing in eternity.

Nor are the thoughts of spirit stronger than yours. You're an eternal spirit yourself, so you needn't fear that you'll "lose control" if you work with the higher realm. All individuals—whether in a body or not—are held back by only one thing: the limiting beliefs they impose upon themselves.

If any people—even professional mediums—ever tell you that spirit is holding you back or vice versa, or if they in any way promote fear or impose limitations, know that they're *not* speaking for or about spirit. And they most definitely aren't speaking from the heart or vision of their own higher Selves. They're only sharing the limiting perspective of the ego, for the spirit knows only joy and power and grace. Your spirit people love you and want to be with you—in the moments and in the hours, in the grass and in the weeds, in the light and in the dark. Every day, they're there for you.

I remember one day when my son, Devin, was in the third grade, and he came home and told me about a special event at the church, where the taller kids had been seated in front of the little ones. Devin said that he stretched and shifted and stretched some more, but he couldn't see anything. Then he simply thought the words, *I wish I could see.*

Suddenly, he felt his dad lift him up. And although he could still feel the wooden bench beneath him, he felt taller, as if he were sitting on his father's lap. He saw everything that happened. And he recounted it all to me in the kind of detail only a third grader can perfect!

As with Devin, spirit is with you, even in the little events. When you're taking a walk, when you're driving your car, and when you're having coffee—spirit is with you! When you're writing a proposal, when you're looking for love, and when you're seeking success—spirit is with you!

Connect with them several times a day. Share a thought, ask a question, or just close your eyes and send them a hug. Then simply open your heart and your mind to receive. But how will you know that the guidance isn't from your ego? If it helps you to feel strength, if it gives you hope and love and peace, if it *lifts you up and helps you see,* it is—in every way—from the heart, the mind, and the reach of spirit!

✤ ✹ ☯

CHAPTER 10

YOUR HIGHER GUIDES AND ANGELS

"Outside the open window
The morning air is all awash with angels."

— **RICHARD WILBUR**

There are many different types of angels and higher guides who seek to help you with every success and in all of the areas of your life. First, you have your own guardian angels. Then there are the archangels, who provide particular service for the specific needs you hold. Yet besides the angelic realm, you also have those in spirit who resonate with a higher vibration than most of your family and friends because of their great impact upon humanity. These include great artists, composers, leaders, and prophets.

Just as they would in the physical world, your family members and friends in spirit often assist you with personal issues and some particular work situations. But also like the physical world, there are times when you need to employ the help of professionals—the higher guides and angels. Happily, the "professionals" in spirit are much more available than their earthly counterparts. And the only cost to you is the time and effort it takes to develop your relationship and communicate with them.

Although you obviously already know your loved ones in spirit, the higher guides who come to help you with your success and greater evolution may not have any previous relationship with you (at least not in this life). In these cases, it's the energy of your work that attracts your assistants. If you're a writer, you'll attract other writers from the higher kingdoms. If you're a healer, you'll receive guidance from fellow healers. If you're an artist, artists will seek you out. Just as your thoughts, energies, and activities act as a magnetic field of attraction in your physical life, they do the same in the spiritual.

> *Quick! Close your eyes. If your energies were to attract a higher spirit guide right now, who would that be? What purpose does he or she hold for you? Picture that person now.*

Your Higher Guides—Contacts for Your Success

As a medium, I often do public events where I teach attendees to connect with spirit, and I also bring messages from the spirit world to various audience members. I remember a recent case where I very strongly "heard" from spirit the last name Clark and the first name Hilda. I shared the names (in that order) with the crowd, and for a few moments there was no response at all. I walked to the section of seats where spirit guided me, and I said the names again. Slowly a woman in the third row of that section raised her hand.

"I know of a Hilda Clark," she said, "but I never knew her personally. She's not widely known, but she's my favorite writer."

Now I'd never heard the name before that day, but Hilda didn't seem to hold that against me. The messages flowed like water.

"Well, she knows you." I said. "And now she's showing me her pen, and she's handing it to you. She's telling me that you're a writer, too." The woman in the audience smiled and nodded enthusiastically. "You've drawn her to you because of your work and because of how much her writing resonates with yours. She loves working with you. She shows me the book that you're finishing now. She's proud of it and you. She wants to let you know that there will be another book to follow."

I continued to share more insights from Hilda. Then, excited and smiling, the woman confirmed what I'd said and thanked me for the message. "It's important that you learn to visualize and meditate," I told her, "so that you can connect with Hilda more consciously and really experience the contribution she's making to your publishing success and in your life."

With a happy new understanding of who her guide was, the woman promised that she would learn how to be more mindful of Hilda so that they could work together more directly in the future.

When dealing with the higher guides, you can call upon the greatest thinkers in history. You can choose to reach out to those who have inspired you personally, or you can wait to feel the embrace of those who come to you without being called. The spirit of Hilda had arrived unbidden in order to help that budding writer succeed.

Here's another story about assistance from unknown spirits from a young pilot in what may have been one of the most important flights in aviation history. After his journey was over, the pilot recalled having "visitors" during his solo flight—ghostly, transparent presences with vague outlines and no substance. He could "see" them all around and behind him without turning his head. (This is typical of clairvoyant seeing. Take a moment now to "look" behind you without turning your head and see which spirit helper might be with you.)

The pilot described how these phantoms came and went right through the fuselage. They "spoke" to him in friendly voices, advising him on his navigation, reassuring him, and giving him important messages that he thought would be unattainable in ordinary, daily life. This pilot was Charles Lindbergh, and his plane was the *Spirit of St. Louis.*

This was the experience "Lucky Lindy" had with spirit during that historic, first transatlantic flight. He embraced the help, but he was mistaken in one way. Such messages are very attainable in ordinary life—they only seem difficult to access because most people don't seek *to know* spirit. And even fewer learn the techniques of interacting with the higher plane and of meditating, which is the most helpful step in developing a receptive mental state.

Pursuing an ongoing interaction with spirit can alter your life forever. You've read about the successes to which spirit contributed in very specific events for Charles Lindbergh and Denzel Washington, but what could happen when you connect with such guidance every day? For the great poet W. B. Yeats, knowing spirit was an ever-present passion. And even though he carried that devotion throughout his life, there were certain periods where he focused exclusively on his work in his daily interactions with spirit. This wasn't a secret; newspapers of the time would congratulate him *and the spirit people* who helped him on "their linguistic accomplishments."

And even biographers of today describe those periods of daily spirit focus as Yeats's most prolific, inspired, and successful years.

Yeats sought inspiration "from above," and you can, too. The world's great minds from history seek to help those who seek them. Whom would you call upon if you could ask anybody to help you succeed? Would it be a poet like Yeats? Would it be an artist like Monet or an actor like Laurence Olivier? Consider it now, because here is a visualization to help you meet the higher guides and acquire . . .

Inspiration from the Ages

Preparation: Think of all the legendary individuals through the ages who have inspired you—the great artists, philosophers, poets, politicians, and leaders. Many people in ancient and recent times have lent their hands to your heart, to your mind, to your successes, and to your life. Think of one of them now, and prepare yourself to call to him. (You may choose a female, but for expediency we'll use the masculine pronoun.) As you hold this person in your mind, don't for a minute think that he's too famous or too important to respond. When he was in the physical plane, he sought to bring his vision to the world, and now he wishes to do the same for you. He seeks to lend his leadership and influence to your life, your purposes, and your dreams.

1. Close your eyes and breathe easily. Center yourself in peace for a few minutes, allowing yourself to relax deeply into the grace of your spirit. Call the person you chose to you now and feel his approach. Sense him completely; and begin to notice how you perceive his presence, power, and colors. Feel this person's energy move through and around you.

2. Ask him to indicate to you which situation or endeavor in your life he has come to help. It could be a current directive, project, or relationship; or it could be something about which you have yet to learn. Let this person take the lead and show you what it is.

3. Trust everything you perceive—even the little symbols you might not fully understand. Once you have an idea of why he's here, let him

show you the actions he would take and the voice he'd give to succeed in this project or endeavor.

4. After a moment, release all of that. Let him now share with you the energies of his specific talents. Even though you may not want to perform his precise skills (writing, composing, or the like), there's a creative force about him. Let him flood you with the talents he brought to his craft, his purposes, his successes, and his life. Take a few minutes to feel these.

5. As he shares his talents with you, feel how they want to move through you—through your hands, your heart, and your voice. Feel filled with these creative forces. Take a few minutes to really sense how you might express them yourself. After you experience those abilities as your own, simply let them all go.

6. Now this individual shares with you some of the elements of his personal life. Even if you don't know everything about his history, understand that you may somehow resonate with his experiences in life's lessons and trials. And as he shares his challenges with you, let yourself feel kinship with him. Know that even the great, the mighty, and the powerful have dealt with difficulties just as you do.

7. As you sense some of his difficulties, determine how they may somehow be reflected in your life. Feel empathy as you get closer and closer to this person and think about similar challenges you've known. And although you don't have to solve every problem, notice as he shows you how to deal with them.

8. Next, this great person of the ages wishes to share with you the values and ethics with which he tried to live. He may not have always been successful, but he wishes to share that integrity with you now. As he fills you with it, feel your life being lifted to a higher plane. Notice the quality of truth filling every corner and every goal—elevating you to more personal success and a greater sense of purpose and joy.

9. As you bring your awareness back to your body, thank this person for his help and guidance. And when you feel yourself slipping off your

path of truth, you can call upon him. You've opened the door to this relationship, and you can tap into the talents and the creative forces that this legendary individual wishes to share with you. Make a commitment now to reconnect with him. Also, decide to meet other great thinkers, leaders, authors, poets, and artists. They're available to you, and they wish to know their hand in the physical world again, reaching out to others through *your* inspiring work. Affirm to yourself: *The great legends of the world are available to me. They wish to help me succeed, and I am open to their touch.*

Making New Connections

One of the ways in which you can help build a greater relationship with the higher guides whom you seek to know is to find out more about them through books, movies, music, and memoirs. Familiarize yourself with their work, their lives, and their contributions to the world. My client Beth was a musician and composer who had felt a strong kinship with an early-20th-century vocalist. Beth told me that she'd sensed the spirit of this "nightingale," and it was then that my client began to perform the legend's work and get to know her favorite singer better.

Intuitively directed by this spirit, Beth ultimately (but not coincidentally) ended up portraying her icon in a play about her life. During the production's long and celebrated run, Beth told me that she knew she wasn't alone on the stage.

As you develop strong relationships with your individual higher guides, it's important to know that these are still members of a team. You must continue to nurture all of the bonds you have with your people in spirit. Each one, in his own way, has something to contribute to your success—emotionally, mentally, and spiritually. And just as you would in the physical world, you not only need to cultivate existing relationships, but you also need to stay open to fresh opportunities and new connections. There's always an opening for new players on the team.

Close your eyes and use your imaging to picture your team in spirit. See them all together and feel the camaraderie. Have a sense, just for a moment, of the general roles these spirit people play. Then

begin to notice that there are some spaces yet to be filled. Send out a
call to the higher guides whom you haven't met yet. Affirm to yourself
that you'll be open and receptive when the opportunity comes to meet
them.

Staying open to connecting with a new and unknown higher guide
proved to be quite an opportunity in my life, too. A number of years ago,
I was connecting with spirit for a client in New York City. (Most of my
consultations occur on the phone.) I described in detail one of the men
in spirit who said he'd come to thank my client for her healing help and
kindness. Because of the specifics in my description (how he looked, how
he died, and so on), my client recognized precisely who it was.

"Oh," she said, "that's Bennett Cerf. I was one of his health-care
workers before he passed." Bennett Cerf was the founder of the Random
House publishing company and a regular on the television show *What's
My Line?* That was all I knew of him, but now, in spirit, he impressed me
as a kind and devoted individual. For years he showed up (along with old
and new spirits alike) whenever this client called for a consultation.

In time, I began a few writing projects. On the days I wasn't seeing
clients, I was working on a book about intuition. Then I had another
appointment with this same client from New York City, and as always,
Bennett Cerf was among the spirit people who came to talk to her. Only
this time, after I hung up the phone, I asked Bennett to stick around for
a moment. I told him about the book on which I was working and asked
for his help in finding a publisher (who better to assist me?!). I thanked
him, let it all go, and went on to my next client.

A month later, I was in London to lecture at the Mind Body Spirit Fes-
tival. (Held each year at the end of May, it's one of the best international
conferences to be found. I've had the good fortune to speak there regularly since the 1980s.) Just a few minutes before one of my workshops, I
was setting things up in the lecture hall when a pretty young woman came
in and introduced herself as an editor from Random House, London.

"Something compelled me to come meet you," she said. "I'd like to
talk to you about writing a book for us." And within 18 months, my first
book, *Intuition and Beyond,* was published by Rider Books of Random
House in London. I have great gratitude and absolutely no doubt that Bennett Cerf, founder of the first Random House, had forged that connection
from the spirit side of life.

There's a brand-new, higher guide standing next to you right now. He or she wants to work with you on a new (or very recent) directive. Close your eyes and see who's there. If you don't know who it is, notice what he or she is wearing. What work is being handed to you?

Help from the Angels

The number of assistants (and types of assistance) from the angelic kingdom are legion, and so are the stories that tell of their intervention in the lives of people all over the world. I recently heard the story of a little eight-year-old boy named Anthony, which was recounted on *The Oprah Winfrey Show.* His abusive father had killed the boy's mother and had then begun stabbing Anthony.

"Angels told me to play dead," Anthony recalled. He did, and his father left him for dead. The boy also said that after his father was gone, "the angels lifted me up to the phone to call 911." Anthony is now a healthy, growing boy living with his aunt (and probably still with his angels).

This is just one of the many stories of life-saving intervention from the angels. Still, like the rest of the spirit world, the angels are also here to help us succeed with the little daily events as well. I have a young friend named Julie who's had difficulty taking tests her whole life. Even as a child, she began to call the angels to guide her during exams. After she completes all the questions she knows, she goes back to the rest. She's developed the habit of first taking a few calming breaths, and then she looks inside for the first *spontaneous* answer that she senses. With conviction, she writes the information down.

Here again are the ingredients in the recipe for success when working with the angels and with all in the higher planes. *Make the call to spirit. Get out of the worrisome, analytical left brain and relax. Look, listen, and feel for the subtle telepathic thought inside; then trust your perception enough to act on it.* (That last step is the test to end all tests, isn't it?) This little recipe will work for you just as it does for Julie, who's now excelling in college. She worked hard, and she made it—with a little help from her friends.

From saving lives and assisting with your studies to building your success and even helping you find the right partner, the angels are here for you. They participate on every level and in every way. The four primary archangels are also available to all for any reason or endeavor, but in the quest for success, each of them can be particularly helpful in his own right. Here's a look at the four archangels with their specialties.

ARCHANGEL	AREA OF EXPERTISE
Michael, the Warrior	Power, initiative, action, strength, single-mindedness, courage
Uriel, "Fire of God"	Transformation, growth, change, energy, transmutation, initiation
Gabriel, the Messenger	Communication, correspondence, teaching, writing, counseling, public speaking
Raphael, the Healer	Healing, love, relationships, release of negative emotions, travel

Meet Your Angels of Success

Preparation: Working with the angels can be a powerful experience. And as you can see from the preceding list of qualities, these archangels are uniquely able to help you with your success in any particular endeavor you choose. Just as with any spirit interaction, the most important aspect of your participation lies in your ability to trust everything that you perceive and to stretch your mental practice to fully image (or imagine) each perception as it comes to mind. Whether you experience this visually, or as words, feelings, or ideas, you must be confident that everything that occurs to you does so for a reason. (If you have a fear response, it indicates the emotional issues that still need to be healed.) Experience these angels now—get to know them and discover the help they bring. (The angels tend to be androgynous, but as with other visualizations, the masculine pronoun is used for expediency.)

1. Let go of all your worries and take a few deep breaths to center yourself. As you move into your relaxed, meditative state, call to one of the archangels: Michael, Uriel, Gabriel, or Raphael. Feel this radiant being

approach, and perceive his energy, power, and force. Notice the colors you sense with him.

2. Ask this angel how he comes to assist in developing your success. Which area of your life is he here to help you evolve and grow? Don't predetermine what that is. Let him indicate it to you now.

3. Now ask him which quality—innate to him specifically—he'd like to support you in having. Let him fill you with that particular power. Feel yourself fill up with it from top to bottom.

4. As you're permeated with this quality, begin to see yourself taking action in the area of your life he wishes to assist. As his energy pours through you, it then begins to flow out of your hands and extend to this situation. See how you'll *handle* it in a new way with his energy.

5. Let the quality he shares with you begin to cascade through your heart. Let it color every feeling you have about this area of your life. Experience the loving understanding of this Divine messenger filling your heart about this situation or endeavor.

6. The archangel now pours one of his own singular forces into and through your mind. Let it fill your thoughts. Begin to reframe the situation in this new perspective, applying these higher powers.

7. The archangel now steps aside. And as he does, you begin to sense the presence of another angel. Take a deep breath and experience his approach, fully perceiving all of his colors and forces.

8. Be filled with this new energy, and notice how it feels and the kinds of things that fill your mind as you do. Can you determine which archangel this is? If not, that's okay. Just let yourself receive this presence in your mind and heart.

9. Allow him to also indicate any new insights into this or any other area of your life. Ask him any questions, and notice every answer. Take a moment to have a brief dialogue with this second angel.

10. Begin to sense the presence of two more archangels. Feel them draw near. With all four around you, take a moment to recall their qualities —strength, transformation, communication, and love. Feel them all wrap around you.

11. Commit yourself to recognizing the strength and initiative within you, and affirm that you'll call Michael when you sense a need of these powers. Recognize, too, your ability to change and transform, like Uriel, anything that holds you back from your truth. Let Uriel show you the things you could alter to make your life succeed.

12. Make a commitment that, like Gabriel, you'll exert every conscious effort to speak only the words of Divine light, compassion, and tolerance. Decide that all communications that go forth from your heart to your own mind about yourself, others, and the world will reinforce the highest truth and the grace that is the eternal soul.

13. Affirm that it's your intention (as it is Raphael's) to bring healing to your own body, mind, and heart. The first step is the release of everything that's toxic and dark—all histories and patterns that cause you to stay in the ego and forget your spirit. Also commit to sharing this healing with all others by bringing it to the world.

14. Create a simple invocation that you can use to call upon these radiant beings when you need their assistance. Know that to find their powers you can also look within, for the forces that move through the archangels also flow through you, and it's their greatest wish that you discover these strengths.

15. Slowly bring your awareness back to your body. And as you walk through your day, know with assurance that the angel kingdom is at hand.

Conclusion: In your journal, write about your experience with these angels. Consider the new ways in which their energies can help you handle difficulties, embrace opportunities, pursue your dreams, and think about your life. Make a list of affirmations that help you build your conscious link with the angels throughout your day; then add a few more affirmations that help you focus your own "angelic" strengths that lead to success.

As you can see from this experience (if you were imaging and trusting, as I know you were), your angels really are here for you. Your personal success generates as much interest in the heavenly realm as it does for your other spirit guides. The sense of support and true assistance that these loving beings provide can bring you profound peace and powerful results—in every area of your life.

Still, outcomes don't manifest out of nothingness. They are, by their very definition, the consequences of previous actions and causes. To create ongoing relationships with these heavenly helpers, you need to be mindful of the many angels in your life. To that end, it also helps to recognize—every single day—the angel in the mirror.

Quick! There's an angel inside you who wants to aid the world. What service do you want to share? How will you do so?

Jenny's Success

Over the centuries, the greatest measure of success hasn't been defined by the wealth one has accumulated but by contributions one has made to the world. Do you measure your achievements in terms of what you get or in terms of what you give? I'm not referring to devoting your whole life to self-sacrifice or servitude. Instead, I'm speaking about finding a contribution that you can uniquely make, and it doesn't have to be on a global scale. You can make a contribution—a success—in many moments and in many ways.

Success can occur in healing, self-discovery, business, family living, relationships, and more. For actress and author Jenny McCarthy, her greatest success goes on every day. Her son, Evan, was diagnosed with autism, and it was Jenny's relentless (absolutely relentless) pursuit of every possible avenue of healing that, as she says, brought Evan "through the window." He can now laugh, play, and communicate his feelings like most other children, but it was a painful and difficult path, both for him and Jenny.

Part of that pain for Jenny had been the breakup of her marriage. Evan's father couldn't deal with his son's illness, so Jenny had felt very lonely both before and after the marriage ended. (Could there be a lonelier feeling than looking into the eyes of your child and finding no response or recognition there?)

When Jenny started to feel the need for loving companionship, she began to pray to Michael, the archangel, every night when going to bed, and she visualized meeting a new partner with an open heart.

Just as in her healing of Evan, Jenny applied one of her own greatest attributes—her persistence. She called upon the archangel Michael every day. And without any urgency, she prayed and visualized daily, too. In taking these actions, she began to feel a sense of trust and a greater peace. Happily, the angel heard her prayers, and the man with the loving heart came at last to the embrace of her little family. That man was Jim Carrey.

You may wonder, looking at the list of archangels, why Michael would assist Jenny in finding a relationship rather than Raphael, who's the patron of love. It's simple, really. Everybody, including the angels, is capable of doing more than a single thing (or even 2 or 20). Jenny had created a mindfulness of the angels, and she must have built a particular closeness to Michael, as she called to him for strength in dealing with Evan's autism. He was, in her time of need, the first angel she called. But even more than the angel Michael, Jenny had also built another relationship with spirit, and it was the highest. She'd forged a closeness—and a communication—with God.

Before he was diagnosed with autism, Evan had a history of seizures. In one case, he'd gone into cardiac arrest. Jenny called the paramedics, and they worked frantically giving him CPR. In spite of being in a state of absolute panic, Jenny suddenly felt a wave of strength come over her body. She heard God tell her to stay calm, that Evan would come back. Those words were right. The little boy did revive, and over time he thrived.

What would it be like if everybody listened for the voice of God—in good times and bad, for the minor decisions and for the major? The world would become a remarkable place. And if *you* learned to listen to God every day, your life would become a remarkable life.

Why don't more people seek to hear this voice? Is it because they can't? On the contrary, knowing the Divine intimately is a possibility for everyone. Not only is it a possibility, it may also be the single greatest success anyone could achieve—the success that leads to all of humanity's greatest achievements.

So with your angels in tow, let us now go in search of God, the highest of the higher guides and the wellspring of success.

✣ ✦ ☯

CHAPTER 11

THE SOURCE OF ALL SOLUTIONS

"Our humanity were a poor thing were it not for the divinity that stirs within us."

— Francis Bacon

Human and Divine—although they seem exclusive, they're insepa-rable for everyone. In previous chapters, you learned about the Divine Paradox, the somewhat ironic condition where being human causes needs but creating a link with the Divine source helps you satisfy those needs and create success. This incongruity is at the heart of the human dilemma, but—believe it or not—it also provides a springboard for the discovery of God. As you'll see in this chapter, understanding the Divine isn't only a spiritual quest. It's an uncovering of all that is human, an investigation of energy and of how to redirect the weak forces of the ego to the strong forces of Divine power. And God's forces move through (and illuminate and uplift) everything and everyone, including you.

Close your eyes. In a turbulent night, the lightning bolt of God illuminates the gale. Look quickly! Whom do you see that needs shelter from the storm? What higher force or quality can uplift and illuminate that life?

In Search of the Divine

Preparation: This process requires both left- and right-brain activity. Let yourself move between the two and hold each perception in a state of trust. Have paper and a pen ready.

1. Relax for a few minutes and consider what you think the Divine is. What qualities belong to God? Think of all the words that you would use to describe them. (Would they include *love, power,* or *peace?*) Write a list of *your* words on a separate piece of paper or in your journal.

2. Now take a few moments to think about what the Divine is *not.* Write down a list of words or ideas that you think would be contrary to God. (Would they include *hatred, jealousy,* or *greed?*) Write all the things that *you* feel belong on this list.

3. Read the second set of terms and really begin to think about these concepts. Concentrate on the strongest description of what does *not* belong to the Divine, and fill your mind with the idea of it.

4. Begin to let the idea move beyond your thoughts and into your entire body. Although it may be uncomfortable, *really feel* the strongest characteristics that oppose the Divine experience. Let them fill you, and notice how you may feel uneasy.

5. Observe everything that you're sensing, and think about your life for a moment. When was the last time you experienced any similar feelings—even in a small way? What was happening? Whom were you with? Why were you affected that way? Make a note about these experiences in your journal.

6. Now let all of that go. Release it all with a big exhalation, clearing your mind and body. Bring your attention back to your first list, back to the qualities that belong to the Divine. Read them all and really immerse yourself in them. Fill your mind at every level with the strongest qualities of God.

7. Now begin to let these higher attributes into your heart. Feel the qualities of the Divine envelop and fill you, move through every emotion, permeate your body, and color every part of you. Notice how you may feel the comfort and peace they carry.

8. Hold this in your experience for a few minutes, and notice everything you feel. Think about your life. When was the last time you felt this way? What was happening? How were you feeling about yourself? Write about it in your journal.

9. Bring your awareness to both your experiences of the Divine peace and of the opposing tension, and compare them. How often do you naturally feel the higher qualities, and how often do you feel the opposite? How easy was it for you to recall and sustain each? How familiar did each of them feel?

10. Consider all of these questions and answer them thoroughly in your journal. Write about your experience and about how you felt. Commit to taking time throughout each day to connect with the Divine. Feel that presence, and allow yourself to be embraced by that love and power. Affirm also that you will seek to define and experience your life through the heavenly forces.

In this process, there were probably some elements of each list that were familiar to you and some that felt foreign. For instance, in the descriptions of the Divine, you may have thought of the words *perfect, confident,* and *strong.* You may not often think you're perfect, and you may not even feel very confident or strong. Nonetheless, you can recognize that some of the words representing the Divine can also reflect the deepest part of you, at least to a certain degree. Why is that? It's because you're a child of God. Francis Bacon said that the Divine stirs within you. It's the part of you that's invulnerable, imperishable, and eternal.

Looking at your experience, you'll also notice that the words you chose for what opposes the Divine are a natural part of your makeup as well. You may have written down some words—say, perhaps, *evil*—that you think wouldn't describe you. In their extreme, some of those words would certainly never fit. But if you modified some of the harshest terms (for instance, changing *evil* to *mean-spirited*), you'd find that these, too, are a big part of the human experience.

Indeed, for many people, the list of "what *isn't* Divine" may feel more common than the list of what is. Yet both components are true elements in everyone's nature.

As you look at these two sets of words, you can see which qualities would be the most likely to help you succeed and to help you feel the greatest, most real sense of your power. Those are the forces that rest with the Divine. The higher traits reflect the eternal soul within, and the opposing ones reflect the perspective of the temporal self, the ego.

> There's no small irony in the fact that God is unmeasurable, and that the ego's primary activity is to measure. Close your eyes and envision what your ego might look like. See it however it appears. Now imagine that you have to try to fit God inside it. How possible would that be?

Why is it important to recognize the distinction between the Divine soul and the ego? If you want to be able to connect with God, to communicate with that sacred being and channel those forces in the world, you must learn to perceive and use the mind of your spirit. The voice of the ego speaks only in its own terms. It relates only to the temporal perspective.

It's the human conundrum to confront the duality between the personal, temporal self and the unlimited, eternal self. The first step in knowing God is to comprehend both selves, learn to understand both of their natures, and seek to make choices that reflect the highest expression available.

The Ego—Shooting for Success for All the Wrong Reasons

In the psychological makeup of every individual, the ego plays a primary role. Indeed, Sigmund Freud called the ego the executive of the personality—the part that supervises all other components of the psyche and that interacts with the outside world. The ego defines the self and all things in the world relative to what the self needs. Without this component, the individual would never learn very basic requirements of survival.

The ego is an essential part of the psyche, but it can quickly get out of control. It has a tendency to be a pretty bossy executive, always measuring the self and other people, places, and events in terms of how they reflect the self. And since there will always be somebody who has more than you, the ego's most frequent admonitions will be about what you lack.

Ultimately, this can turn into a droning voice quantifying everything that makes you great (because you don't feel good inside) or everything that's wrong with you (again, because you don't feel good inside). The achievements the ego seeks are primarily designed to overcome feelings of lack by placing more notches on your belt. These inevitably don't "succeed" in a more permanent sense of well-being because the notches on your belt are events outside yourself, and the lack you feel is still inside. If you choose the thoughts, feelings, and activities that fill your heart and release that sense of deficiency, your internal success will be absolute and the external successes will follow.

It's a common misconception that the ego is reflected in confidence, but real confidence isn't bluster. It's born out of a strong sense of self and an ability to make honoring choices. This type of loving the self isn't the same as vain self-absorption. As a matter of fact, vanity and arrogance usually compensate for a *lack* of self-love.

Another myth is that only arrogant people have big egos. In truth, those who lack confidence and feel valueless have just as large egos, for they're just as caught up in the action of self-measuring as the arrogant are. Oddly—or not—the actions of both the conceited and the woefully inadequate reflect the same two things:

1. They probably spend a great deal of time thinking about themselves.

2. They've determined that they're deficient in some way.

It's a sad and vicious circle. Those who feel weak are usually disconnected from their own spirits and from their Divine source, so they have a greater tendency to give more airtime to the ego. The ego's judgments and measurements keep the weak forces flowing through their lives, and these continue to decay their well-being and erode their connection to the Divine spirit.

Recognizing the Ego's Voice—the First Step to the Divine

Here are examples of some of the ego's measurements:

- *I need a bigger house (car, boat, or the like) to be happy.*
- *Other people might not like me, so I'd better impress them.*
- *I'm not smart enough to get ahead in the world.*
- *Why can't I do anything right?*
- *What an ugly dress she's wearing.*
- *I'm so much better than that person.*
- *If I show off my money and stuff, people will respect me.*
- *I'll never be in a happy relationship.*

All of these statements and any others like these (even the seemingly most innocuous ones, such as *I have bad hair*) work to decay the individual's sense of the true Self in favor of the ego.

Why would someone make the choice for the ego when it leads to sadness and weakness? Because it's a habit. It's the familiar belief system with which the person has grown up. There's a certain safety in staying with what one knows. It means that the effort to change can be avoided. And there is, after all, an ease in following the path of least resistance (although it *never* leads to success).

All of these patterns, however, are still only habits. The habits of the ego are fear, pridefulness, vulnerability, selfishness, self-diminishment, and the like. It's important to understand that the feelings of loss or rejection that caused these tendencies are valid and always were. But if you have chronic negative feelings, it shows that you've built a habit—maybe even an obsession—out of them. And more than this, it shows that you've begun (and continue) to define yourself through them and through the original events that caused them. Left unchecked, you'll create a self-fulfilling prophecy of minimalization that undermines any success you might pursue. So take a moment to look inward. If you feel unhappy, if you're incapable of making a shift in your perception, if you can't implement change or act on your own behalf, then you're living firmly in the realm of the ego.

Feeling God Feels Good

So what's the alternative to giving big airtime to the little self, the ego? It's finding the big Self—the higher Self, to be exact—and its connection to the Divine. You could also refer to this Self as your soul, your psyche, or your spirit. *What* you call it matters very little; *that* you call it matters very much.

Close your eyes. Your ego is writing a list of what's wrong with you on a blackboard. Next to it, your soul is writing a list of your glorious eternal qualities. Which entity is larger, brighter, and more powerful? Which list of words will lead to your success?

Now watch as the soul picks up the ego, pulls that being into itself, and fills it with the light and love that the ego thinks it needs. Feel your ego relaxing into that love, and notice that the negative words on the blackboard disappear.

You can connect with your spirit every day through:

- Meditation (choose a mental focus or use a CD, and if your mind wanders, bring it back)

- Frequent inner imaging and thought processes (like those in this book)

- Trusting your intuition and tuning in to it frequently throughout your day

- Affirmations that help you redefine yourself in your eternal power

- Physical activities that support your sense of well-being

All of these are habits, too. You'd be amazed by what would happen if you took the same time that you use on the ego's routines and spent it on these instead. You have the ability to decide which habits to cultivate. Just like the ego's patterns, the elevating habits of your spirit are built mentally, emotionally, and physically every single day. But unlike the ego, whose behaviors cut off your power, these choices of the soul lift your power. They build and build until they snowball into other habits—those of joy, enthusiasm, confidence, peace, and success. When you've developed these, there's nothing missing. You've found the strong force.

The higher Self is the strong force because it binds you, at your deepest core, to the Divine. There's no greater source of strength or love. All confidence, bliss, and energy are provided to everything and everyone by the force that unifies all that is. And the more you're aware of your higher Self and connect with it, the more you'll direct the strong forces of the Divine to your life and to the world.

Let's take a quantum look at the world of strong and weak force and at the theories that may unify them.

The Unified Theory

There are four fundamental forces in the universe: gravity, electromagnetism, strong force, and weak force. Obviously, the first two are quite commonly known. If you've ever stayed on the ground while walking or gotten a shock after shuffling across a carpet, you have a personal acquaintance with both gravity and electromagnetism.

The other two occur at subatomic levels. Not coincidentally, the strong force is the strongest of all by far (forming protons and neutrons by binding together quarks, the elemental basis of matter). The weak force causes certain atomic particles to transmute or change. The beta decay interactions in carbon-14 decay (which is used in carbon-14 dating) are examples of weak force.

It has long been a dream of physicists to find a *theory of everything* (or TOE) that would synthesize the theories of all force interactions. But gravity depends upon mass relative to the distance between objects, whereas the other three forces depend upon the exchange of particles. (There's a theory of quantum gravity that includes a carrier particle called a *graviton,* but the graviton hasn't yet been discovered in actuality and remains only a theory.)

Well, missing a TOE, one would naturally go for the GUT—or the *grand unified theory!* The GUT is a theory in particle physics that seeks to provide a single, unified predictability for both the strong- and weak-force interactions. Unfortunately, the energy levels needed for such theories to be tested exceed our present technology and would require a particle accelerator bigger than the solar system itself!

Still, the search continues. From particle physics to philosophy to the arena of self-discovery, there's a compelling quest for unification. Is there an inner personal science of unification? The answer is a resounding—and even uncanny—yes! Your energies and emotions aren't simply erratic reactions to the people and events in your daily life. There's a predictability of force in the human experience, and it's that quality that can help you know success in every aspect of life.

In order to work with these predictable forces, you must undertake a study of human behavior and motives and of the energies that reflect strong and weak forces in all people, including yourself.

Strong and Weak—Let's Take a Peek!

There's energy in all things—all matter, all activities, and all creatures—everything! Indeed, there's a great deal of power in emotions and in thought. In the human experience, it resonates in various ways and can express very different qualities.

Still, it's quite amazing to discover that many vibrations in human behavior that appear different are actually the same. When energy is expressed through the lower emotions or dishonoring behavior of the ego, it will then manifest in weak-force activities. But that same energy can be lifted up to become a strong force by making honoring choices and directing your thoughts and power to (and through) the higher Self or the Divine eternal soul. These strong-force energies and thoughts then lead to strong-force activities, which result in your manifest success.

If you make a study of your own energy patterns, you'll become intimately aware of what types of vibrations flow through you. You may know right away if they come from negative thoughts (weak force) or from Divine emotions (strong force). If you don't already know, an understanding of the energies and a consciousness of their patterns will help you start to manipulate these forces in ways you may never have thought possible.

Of course, this doesn't happen by itself. To recognize weak force, you must become keenly aware of the patterns that weaken your confidence, power, and success; being conscious is the first step. The second step requires you to redirect weak force into strong through your mind and your actions.

Within the unified nature of strong and weak force lies no less than the key to absolute and unprecedented transformation. Every single pattern, thought, and activity in your life resonates with a very specific energy. Once you anticipate what that is, you can redirect it to a strong-force experience and expression.

In quantum mechanics, the strong force binds, while the weak-force interactions allow decay. It's similar in the human experience. Strong forces bind you to your Divine source; weak ones decay your sense of power, your sense of truth, and your sense of Self. But how do you stop these decaying vibrations, these energies and habits that weaken your experience of life? It's simpler than most people realize (but not necessarily easy).

Changing Weak Force to Strong

Unified theory allows you to know energy in general as a predictable force. This is true in your personal experience as well. Your weak forces reflect the strong ones but are being expressed in lower ways. Once you learn how to redirect them, you can change your life—and the world! Understanding and using the following tenets will provide you with one of the most important keys in any transformation at any level.

- *DO NOT battle the natural forces and tendencies at hand. Use them!*

- *Each force has a weak and strong expression. Choose the strong.*

The strong forces that move through your life are the forces of God, Who works through you—they're the natural energies of your soul. The weak forces resonate with the exact same qualities and energies as the strong, but they are translated by the ego in very different ways. They're channeled into behaviors and thoughts that reflect only the personal perspective of urgency, need, and lack. You don't need to worry, though. These vibrations can be redirected back to their higher qualities, to more elevating actions, and to unparalleled success. The trick is to not fight them, but to *use* them. All you have to do is redirect the flow.

Take a moment to imagine that you have two distinctly different areas in your yard. One is on a steep incline, difficult to get to and harder to tend; there are many weeds beginning to spread in this area. Next to that is a space that's perfect for growing flowers, fruits, and vegetables. You're able to prepare the rich soil, and you plant all the seeds that will provide beauty and nourishment. You place your hose and sprinkler in this new garden. But then, without your noticing it, the hose slips away into the weeds. Over time, the fragrant and healthy plot of land begins to fail; the flowers and vegetables die. Yet the weeds grow thicker and mightier, even beginning to climb into the flowers—choking your opportunity for beauty and bounty even more.

The water that runs through the hose in this scenario is just like the energy that courses through you. You can use your power to grow the things that choke you and your expression in the world, or you can use it to create glory, success, and a great harvest. But in order to redirect the flow of energy—to reposition the hose, so to speak—you must first be *conscious* of how you're using your vibration already, and you must become sensitive to how different energies feel.

There may be times when you're lonely, angry, distracted, inert, or puzzled. As you can see, these all resonate with different qualities. If you wish to redirect them, you must know, in any given moment, what energy is moving through you. Then you can choose—first, which part of you (the lower ego or the higher Self) will act upon that energy, and second, which action best directs that force to its strongest expression.

The following chart and explanations outline the different common forces and how they can be altered. Remember, you're not trying to change what's present; you're simply redirecting the *same* energy into a much higher vibration—through conscious intention and choice.

Weak Force to Strong Force

Isolation and Loneliness (Being Only One)	→	Oneness (Being One)
Anger	→	Power
Sabotaging Behavior	→	Destroying Negative Habits
Inertia	→	Higher Inward Focus
Neediness	→	Receiving
Servitude	→	Self-honoring
Judgment and Self-diminishment	→	Assessment and Self-awareness
Distraction	→	Diversification
Fear	→	Trust
The Need to Feel Special	→	Being Special

How to Redirect Weak Forces

Isolation and Loneliness (Being Only One) → Oneness (Being One)

Loneliness stems from the ego's definition of the self as being *apart* from others and all that is. The Divine self knows you as *a part of* all that is. When you're feeling as if you're the only one, take a moment to remind yourself that you live in a unified collective. When you're one with all that is, there are no doors between you and the entire Universe—no barriers between you and your success. So when you're feeling isolated, allow your spirit guides to bring you their embrace from this united heart and mind. And then use a little process such as the following to expand yourself to connect with the bounty you are.

Close your eyes and see yourself and your energy expanding. Larger and larger it grows to include and embrace every tree, animal, thing, and person. Begin to know the comprehensive ONE that you are. Connect at the heart with your favorite people, past and present. Allow your energy to penetrate the depths of space, the universes beyond, and even the kingdoms not yet known. Take a deep breath, bring it all inside you, and feel ONE with all.

Anger ➤ Power

Being angry often means that you feel wounded by somebody. Since it's never healthy to repress your anger, the first thing to do is to give yourself a healthy way to vent those feelings—punch a pillow, write in your journal, or do some kickboxing. Then, after some of the steam has been released, apply your mind to reassessing the situation. Although much anger comes from feeling invalidated by other people, that can still only happen if you're looking to others for validation and your sense of well-being.

Your well-being comes from the wellspring of love that was born in you before the stars knew light. Although you may not be familiar with it, your eternal Self is perfect in every way.

Determine how the dismissive behavior from others also reflects their own weaknesses. How much are they living in their egos? And consider that your need for their approval means you're giving more weight to their opinions than you are to your own truth. Realize that your anger represents your intense will to achieve their validation. Change this to an intense will to achieve *your own* validation. Shift your anger to a higher power by focusing on the thoughts and activities that support yourself.

To discover your perfect, eternal Self, *take action*—read, study, get therapy, change the jobs or relationships that diminish you, meditate, affirm. Anger is projected at others because you have invalidated and disempowered yourself through them. Recognize this every time that you get mad. Then, in order to shift this weak force to strong, spend as much time—and use equal force—in doing the things that validate and fulfill *you.* Soon the opinions of others will matter very little.

> *When you're angry, close your eyes and get in touch with it. Imagine yourself as the volcano Vesuvius, and your rage is bubbling and churning inside you. Then, suddenly, all of that is released—blowing upward and exploding out of your crown chakra, scattering to the winds. Feel the emotional release as all of that emotion is expelled and dispersed into the ethers.*
>
> *Then take a deep, easy breath. With your next exhalation feel a sense of calm and peace being restored inside you.*

As you sit in this relaxed state, you can feel a new energy. It is the great, yet gentle, power of your eternal spirit—down deep in your core. And you know that this is who you are and that you can channel this confident power in ways that can fulfill you and contribute to humanity. Determine, now, the ways you'll express yourself to the world.

In peace and quiet strength, take another deep breath. Feel the eternal embrace from your soul that allows you to act on your own behalf and that fills you with the greatest love you can know.

Sabotaging Behavior ➤ Destroying Negative Habits

In this case, you're using the energy of habitual destruction. When this is present, you can either funnel it into habits that tear you down you, or you can use it to destroy the negative old patterns. These destructive forces are powerful. When you've minimized your sense of deserving through the ego's definitions of lack, the patterns that you create often destroy your success and thereby perpetuate your deprivation. First, redefine yourself. Let go of the lack that the ego wants you to measure and know yourself to have boundless power and love—that of the Divine. Affirm that God works through you. And since that's the case, every resource is at hand. You're capable of taking the highest action and making the greatest success. Then, when you see a sabotaging pattern begin to surface, immediately create a new habit that destroys and replaces the old sabotaging mechanism and reflects your highest source, the Divine.

Think of one sabotaging thought and one sabotaging activity that occur frequently in your day. Write down one strong new belief and an affirming action that you can use to destroy the old. Put what you've written in plain sight. Channel the higher force by speaking this new thought and taking this new action over and over again every day.

Inertia ➤ Higher Inward Focus

Long periods of inertia can indicate depression, which, if chronic, should be looked into with a therapist. But if you find that you go through brief, intermittent times of inertia, even these can be redirected. (It's important to realize that this energy isn't synonymous with relaxation. Relaxation and recuperation are necessary cycles of life and should be honored.)

To redirect moments of inertia, recognize them as reflections of your desire to take no action or to achieve no outer aim. Use these natural forces to go inward and experience an elevating yin (or receptive) phase by listening to music, guided visualizations, hypnosis recordings, affirmations, or even audio books. Take time to receive the peace-filled ideas, sounds, or pictures that elevate you. Allow yourself not to *do* but to *be* . . . and in so being, you become who you have been forever.

Close your eyes and take a deep, relaxing breath. As you do, feel all of your "to-do" lists and all of the items on your agenda fall away. With every passing breath, just let yourself be. Going deeper and deeper into your beingness, you feel greater calm and a happy ease. You have all the time in the world, for eternity is your home. You know the flawless, perfect peace in the eternal moment of now.

Neediness ➤ Receiving

As with all weak forces, neediness reflects belief in the ego's definition of the vulnerable, impermanent self and rests entirely upon a self-measurement of lack. Again, the first thing to do is shift your definition of self to recognize that the source of all you need is within you. Second, be willing to take steps to get what you need in the physical world. And third, call upon your higher Self and your guides by using processes such the following one to receive what you need internally. Soon you'll build the practice of receiving instead of the decaying habit of feeling needy.

Close your eyes and call your spirit team to you. See them all approach. Allow your higher Self and all your spirit guides to send their energies to you and wrap their love, guidance, and compassion around you. Become a sponge and soak it all up.

Now imagine all the stars of the Milky Way blazing forth their brilliance to you, filling you, and lighting you up. Feel the electricity within you. Now, begin to feel the waters of the mighty Niagara, like the power of God, thundering for you and washing around you. Receive. Receive. Receive!

Servitude ➤ Self-honoring

Servitude occurs when the will to serve is motivated by the desire to be liked or appreciated. Again, since the appreciation isn't internally sourced, feeling good relies upon the capricious response of others. But since it's the energy of service that resonates here, all you have to do in order to redirect these forces is to bring aid to yourself. This isn't being selfish; it's being self-honoring. You can't serve the children of the world in helping them find (and honor) the soul within themselves, if you can't do it for yourself. During times of servitude, you already want to help, and you want to feel good about yourself through what you do. So begin by feeling compassion for yourself. Determine what actions will serve and honor you and which steps to take on behalf of your own growth, success, and upliftment. *Do them,* and then feel good that you've brought yourself such loving service.

Close your eyes. Imagine that you're king or queen for a day. What would you ask for? Now imagine that you must serve all of your needs for just one day. What will you do for yourself?

Judgment and Self-diminishment ➤ Assessment and Self-awareness

All judgment comes from the ego; it's one of the first (and most common) indicators of weak force. Most people think of judgment just as criticism of others, but many people spend a great deal of time being critical of the self. Those who live in a frequent (or even moderate) state of self-diminishment are just as judgmental as those who think or speak ill of others, and this can have an even greater negative impact.

After all, when other people judge you, you don't always hear it, but you always get the message when you criticize yourself. If you have this habit (whether in diminishing yourself or others), you have a tendency to live life through the ego. You also spend a lot of time in the analytical mind, which naturally quantifies and supports the activity of measuring.

Happily, since the first task in changing weak force to strong requires redefinition of the self to the unlimited reality, you can jump right back into the left brain, which is where definition occurs. Consider all of the concepts, measurements, and ideas that portray your eternal, boundless soul. Think of the words you used at the beginning of this chapter to describe the Divine. Assess yourself in those terms, and begin to quantify your unlimited reality. (Can you count to infinity?) Then start to reassess every external event and every other soul in that truth as well. If you're able to catch and change every judgment of yourself and others in the moment of its birth, you'll succeed in transforming your life absolutely and forever.

> *Close your eyes. Imagine that your ego has a hammer and chisel, and it's banging away unthinkingly at the marble that is your outer and inner strength. With every stroke, the rock chips and cracks and breaks. Look and see the statue of yourself after your ego has done its work.*
>
> *Now imagine another block of marble that's the core of who you are. It's being shaped by your soul, mindfully looking for the edges that define its beauty, sculpting the curves that speak its grace. Tap, tap, tap. Just as David emerged from Michelangelo's tapping, you begin to be aware of the statue of Self that takes shape from within the rough-hewn marble that your soul has carved. What do you see?*

Distraction ➤ Diversification

Although a person can often get distracted because of an inability to pay attention, distractions can also play an important role in your life.

Unless you tend to be so scattered that you have great difficulty focusing, you can actually learn to use distractions to your benefit. Sometimes they'll simply help refresh your energy by giving you something new to occupy yourself, especially when you're fatigued or when your attention is waning. But even more important, distractions—like coincidences—can be attempts by your spirit and by your guides to lead you to new opportunities.

Diversification is an important element in everyone's growth and success. Without learning unfamiliar things or meeting new people, life would turn into a stale repetition of old experiences. Looking for fresh interests and ideas is how your spirit compels you to know yourself in different ways. Even a momentary distraction can give you a new perspective on an old problem, an alternative course of action when you're up against a wall, or simply a happier point of view on a mundane world. In these ways, what seems like interference can turn to diversifying moments filled with potential.

So learn to develop a sensitivity about when to be guided by distractions in order to enrich your life and when to let them go. (Even when you have an important agenda, a specific distraction can contribute to your task.) Just like intuition, a compelling force will identify the helpful events for you. Look and feel with your inner senses for the nuances of opportunity so that you can use a distraction to help lead you to greater success through diversification.

> *Take a moment to lift your head and look around you, allowing yourself to be distracted by one element you see. Even if you've viewed this object hundreds of times before, tilt your head, change your perspective, and look at it deeply in a new way. Ask, "What new idea or insight can I glean from this moment that will help me diversify and lead me to greater success?" Then listen and feel for the answer.*

Fear → Trust

This doesn't refer to the type of fear that occurs naturally in the body's fight-or-flight mechanism. In relation to weak force, fear means nervousness and apprehension brought on by excessive worry—worry about uncertainties, about "what ifs," and about things you can't change. At first blush, the energies of fear and trust don't seem to resonate with the same qualities at all. But in truth, they're both developed and supported by the exact same activity: repetitive and persistent reiteration of a singular belief system.

Fear is a mental attachment to the disruption and distress of the vulnerable. Trust is a mental attachment to the confidence and serenity of the unassailable. The energies of mental attachment are already present in the experience of being afraid. Simply attach to the higher belief in your unassailable, invulnerable, eternal power *every* time an anxious thought comes up. Affirm your indomitable strength through the imperishable soul that you are. No one and nothing can harm your eternal being, so become that Self and believe in it. Every time worry creeps into your thoughts, attach mentally (and immediately) to trust and to the idea of your confident, powerful, sublimely happy, and perfect Self.

> *Send your consciousness, right now, to the highest place in heaven your spirit has ever known or you could possibly imagine. Sense the physical world falling away from you completely. Take a deep breath, and feel your place in heaven. Notice the light and power—in you, through you, and around you. Take another deep and serene breath to move into this perfect state and know the unassailable Self you are!*

The Need to Feel Special ➤ Being Special

Do you remember the times when you were little, riding your bike or climbing the jungle gym and yelling to your mom or dad, "Look at me. Look at me!" You continued to call for their attention long after you were old enough to know that what you were doing wasn't all that different (or more special) than what the other kids were doing. Even as an adult, the need to feel special never seems to go away.

In this, as in *all* energies, there's an expression of weak (or ego) force and of strong (or Divine) force. Usually the ego makes the need to feel special relative to other people—when you shine from the little self, you want to outshine everyone else. The soul transfers the need to be special to a true comprehension of your specialness in God and in the unity of all that is. The experience is so powerful and so joyful that when you shine from the soul, you want to *share* it with everyone else.

You may be surprised to read this, but the desire to feel special is actually a gift from the ego to you, for it starts the enlightenment ball rolling. *This is the force that will ultimately and inevitably drive your personality to look for the soul.*

This will be true at some point in time for every individual in every arena of life. Since the soul is the only place to meet God, the truth of your Divine "specialness" will only be found there. Some people may seek specialness in money and wealth, some may pursue it through fame, and others may look for it in power and influence. When they're done looking in all these places and have found them wanting, they'll inevitably begin to seek it in the Divine heart within.

You don't need to go on a wild-goose chase for what you already have. Through study, meditation, and peaceful introspection, you can find the brilliant glory inside you. And then you'll discover that being special demands only that you be you.

> *Close your eyes. Are you looking for success to make you feel special? Or are you looking to express your Divine specialness successfully? Visualize God's power flowing through you without any barriers or impedance. See how it will manifest in your life, and visualize that success in every detail now.*

Strong Force Is God Force

As you can see from all of these shifts from weak force to strong, you'll only be able to make these changes if you live consciously in every moment. Indeed, you're required to stay in the now in order to use the energies at hand. Urgency against what's happening or attempts (even mentally) to get to or think of another moment will prevent you from: (1) changing the mind-set that puts weak force in action, and (2) elevating the energies to a strong-force expression.

In any shift from weak force to strong, *the first action necessary is to change your definition of the little temporal self to the eternal, luminous, sacred*

Self. You may at first feel so weak, bitter, devalued, or sad that it might be difficult to perceive yourself in this way. Indeed, saying affirmations about your power, beauty, and grace may even feel like lying at first. Still, doing all that you can continually throughout the day to change the old, weak-force descriptions of yourself is imperative. With each new elevated thought, you'll raise your energy. You'll experience the Divine working through you, and you'll be able to take higher and higher action and enjoy greater and greater success. You can (and you will!) put an end to the downward spiral of weak force and ego.

With each new step and thought, you'll perpetuate the upward spiral of strong force and God. The expression in your mind and in your actions of love, compassion, and strength define the understanding of the sacred within you. With this, you can give all of the tasks at hand to the eternal source.

God offers you the Divine perspective every day. The more you look for it, the more you'll find it. But in order to make your path easier, you must give no quarter to the ego—make no judgments of yourself or others. Every soul exists in a state of perfection. The flaws you witness in the world are not only temporary, they are the ego's; and they're always softened in the presence of love. Make no imposition of your will upon others. No matter how buried it seems, God's will is in all, and it will emerge out of the darkness for each individual someday.

You can lift the light on the planet by illuminating your life. All you have to do in any given moment is ask yourself, *Does this thought, action, feeling, or belief perpetuate my ego's weak-force expression?* If it does, then don't internalize it—*eternalize* it. Immediately find the strong force and reshape the moment in terms of your eternity. You'll see a new way if you look with fresh eyes. The foundation of your highest success is to allow absolute power (Divine force) to move through you in all that you do.

Success Through God's Force

1. *Live consciously. Know* yourself, your histories, your habits, and your motives. In the business world, corporate troubleshooters can't lead their companies to success if they don't know what the problem is. Be clear about what you feel and think and what you need to shift.

2. *Change your definitions.* Every time you give yourself evidence that you are what the ego believes you to be, remind yourself to let that weak image go. Recall the truth you were before the stars were born. Define yourself as the soul and force that allows pure potential to manifest every dream in its highest way.

3. *Redirect weak force to strong.* Take action and elevate all of your actions to their highest forms. Fill every thought and deed with a new sense of purpose in your Self realization, your service to humanity, and your ability to succeed.

4. *Meditate.* You'll find the path to God (and to your Divine truth) through your soul. It isn't in your paycheck or your body, and it isn't in or of the world. Meditation will create the steps to your spirit and to your bliss. There are those who say they "can't" meditate, but they simply haven't practiced enough to build their success with it. God's force is the strongest there is. And although you might be able to sense it while watching a sunset or walking in the woods, you can know it absolutely and channel it in any endeavor and toward any success—if you learn to meditate.

As Emanuel Swedenborg said, "It can in no case be said that heaven is outside anyone; it is within him." The following visualization will help you find the doorway to God inside you.

Across the Threshold to Heaven

Preparation: The place of trust in your mind and heart is your springboard to knowing Divine peace and presence, both in meditation and in daily life. Every time you trust, you build even greater trust and a greater connection to the source of all solutions. So use your vision, your imaging, and your trust right now to meet the Divine.

1. Close your eyes and take several deep, cleansing breaths. Feel yourself let go of all tension with each passing inhalation and exhalation.

THE SOURCE OF ALL SOLUTIONS

2. As your body relaxes more and more completely, begin to feel a sense of stillness coming to your mind and heart. As you move more profoundly into your spirit, the troubles and challenges of the physical world seem to drift away, for they all belong to the personality that you are in the world of time. And soon you start to notice, in the depths of your soul, a sense of timelessness. In some way, you begin to remember how it feels to belong to no time and to every time.

3. Feel yourself spread through the past and before it, beyond the future, and across the universes. Allow yourself to be filled with the great breadth and width and volume of this immortal truth. How does it feel to have no beginning and no end in time or space?

4. Take another deep breath and call to yourself the God of your understanding. Whether that may be a force, an individual, a collective mind, or a presence, call that Divinity now. Allow yourself to see and feel the approach of consummate radiance, love, and power.

5. Even though, just a moment ago, you were unlimited in your own breadth and scope, you're now overwhelmed by the boundless, unmeasurable force and mind of the Divine.

6. Allow yourself to feel this brilliant presence moving through you, penetrating every cell, every thought, and every part of you. Experience the unbounded joy and embrace from the God Who knows you and Who loves you beyond reproach. Take a few minutes to feel it all.

7. This is the force that works through you, the power and mind that seek to be known and to be expressed in all that you do, think, and feel. Ask how you can better implement God's design through your plan. Are there any new directions you'd like to pursue, any shared successes you want to make real, or any new horizons to be discovered?

8. Take a moment, as you drift in the peace and awe of this glory, to recollect one of the challenges that may have been troubling you in your personal or business life. From your current vantage point, observe how distant it seems and how apart from it you feel.

9. Remember whether there were any weak-force responses that you (and your ego) were making in this situation. See yourself letting those go, and begin to channel the powerful God force that fills you right now. Notice how the presence of God helps you see things in a new light and how you feel and act toward these circumstances in a confident, powerful, yet peace-filled way.

10. As you take another deep breath, commit to bringing this blessed, sacred energy to every situation where you might have had a weak-force response. Affirm your ability to know and connect with God and to direct strong force anywhere and anytime. And make a promise to touch in with your own timeless, limitless scope often throughout the day. Remembering who you are is the first and most important Divine revelation of all.

Conclusion: Slowly bring yourself back to your body, remembering all that happened for you and knowing that God stands beside you and stirs within you always. Write about your experience in your journal.

If God Works Through You, You'd Better Get Working!

Your success with the Divine starts and stops when your conscious connection to the Divine starts and stops. Every time the ego takes charge in your life, you give little recourse for the higher energies to work through you, for you're already too busy with the little self's agenda. The greatest step you can take to relieve the ego of its "executive" duties is to stop criticism of yourself and others—even in the slightest ways.

The most constant and most detrimental decaying force in the human experience is judgment. The ego's incessant inclination to measure can result in a stream of judgments that can fill (and ruin) the day—not to mention the vibration you send out. These criticisms can run the gamut from the innocuous to the severely damaging.

As you've learned, the first way to deal with such thoughts is to change them to assessment—the assessment of life based on the eternal point of view. Another action you can take is to tap the powers of nonjudgment often throughout the day. Taking time to consider and comprehend nonjudgment may seem unnecessary if you aren't a particularly critical person already. (After all, why bother to build a new habit if the negative behavior doesn't seem to be present?) Still, it's important to really understand how subtle yet pervasive judgment can be.

All judgment limits—it limits the self, others, and opportunities. Where limitations thrive, success can't be achieved, for the very nature of success compels you to stretch and move beyond boundaries. Bringing an end to every judgment not only helps you get rid of a weak force; but it's also a significant step in your success and evolution, as well as the successful evolution of the entire planet.

The release of judgment gives birth to the strong force of compassion, which may possibly be the most powerful of all strong forces. For it is compassion, the deepest form of love, that binds you to your soul and to the souls of others. Compassion for yourself channels Divine love to you. Compassion for your brother directs that same love to all humanity. So take time, several times every day, to know yourself and your world through the power of compassion. Hold it in your heart for the saints and for the sinners, for the weak and for the strong—and also hold it for the face in the mirror. Know that the face looking back at you is just a little hint of your eternal image. (And discovering that eternity is the greatest success you can achieve, for it is the father of all successes.)

I recently read a commentary by Harold Bloom about the Gospel of Thomas. He said that the Jesus in that Gospel was looking for the face he had before the world was made; I know of an old Zen koan that reflects this sentiment, too. Yet this great quest isn't only Christian or Hebrew or Buddhist. It is for every faith, for every culture, and for every human to find the sacred spirit they always were. And it is for you, too.

Do you remember *your* face before the world was made? Try. And try to recall what you felt when you looked upon the coming of the universes—the good you could do, the opportunities you had. These are not gone . . . *you* are not gone. To find your greatest success all you have to do is look. And if you discover the face you had before the world was made, and if you seek it in the faces of all humanity, you'll know compassion, you'll find God, and you will change the world.

PART III

FLIP THAT LIFE!

by Sandra Anne Taylor

CHAPTER 12

DECONSTRUCTION: GETTING RID OF THE OLD TO MAKE WAY FOR THE NEW

"The strongest single factor in prosperity consciousness is self-esteem: Believing you can do it, believing you deserve it, believing you will get it."

— JERRY GILLIES

There's a hot trend in real estate known as "flipping." In fact, a very popular television show documents this process, demonstrating how someone purchases a run-down, low-value property and then fixes it up, adds high-value items, and sells it for a profit—sometimes even a considerable profit. The suggestion is that you can make some pretty remarkable changes in a relatively short period of time, ending up with something far more attractive and salable than what you originally started out with.

I love watching the show because I'm so fascinated by the process. It's often amazing to me how much potential these dilapidated places have. No matter what state of ruin they may be in, they're always capable of being transformed in both beauty and functionality—and it usually doesn't take long!

I think this is a wonderful metaphor for turning your own life around. No matter how much work you think needs to be done, you can achieve a significant reversal—and it doesn't have to take forever! Even if you've totally given up the hope of ever being able to make something lovely and valuable out of the raw materials you have, you can still find a gem hiding deep within. Of course, you may have to be willing to put forth some effort in order to uncover it.

If you watch one of the many programs about flipping, you'll see that the first big step in turning a property around always involves demolition. In fact, some of the "flippers" are rather ruthless about what they tear out, embracing the attitude that if it's not working at the moment, it's got to go. Many of them take great delight in destroying walls, floors, and anything that may be bringing down the value of the property.

In terms of flipping your own life, you may have to be pretty aggressive about what you need to demolish, too. In the quantum psychology that makes up your mental and emotional structure, you could find that some of the cognitive walls that have been closing you in will have to go completely. Your thoughts and beliefs may have been significant influences in limiting and devaluing your life, so don't be discouraged if you have to gut everything in your belief system. At least you can rely on the fact that you'll start with a good foundation.

You may think (as many do) that the underlying material of your life comes from your parents or other significant authority figures in your primary family. This isn't so. Your foundation goes back long before that, back to your spirit, to your eternal soul—and to the source of all consciousness creation. Sure, it's true that your parents established the mental groundwork, but anything that's learned can be unlearned—anything! That's what this book is all about, creating a new psychology, learning a new consciousness and energy, reclaiming your truth, and aligning that with the reality and exquisite power of the Universe.

The most fundamental Universal truth is that you were spirit first—pure energy! In fact, you still are spirit—no less than when you're in your pure energy state. It's just that now you've added a physical dimension to it. And your earthly life brings a lot with it, including your parents and their entire lineage, your environment and all of its influences, your brain and its patterns of thought and chemistry, and your body and its physical and emotional responses, just to name a few. So you picked up a lot when you were hitchhiking from the other side of the energetic realm!

Not to worry—you can get rid of all the unwanted baggage you've been dragging along with you on this trip. It just has to start with your realization that that's all it is! You've simply accumulated some heavy and cumbersome luggage in the form of your persistent thoughts and behaviors, and you absolutely don't have to keep dragging it around.

You can start right now to flip your life. Take charge of your thoughts, and rip out everything that doesn't honor you or create real value. When you've gotten rid of the low, drab ceilings of limitation, knocked down the fences of self-doubt, and dug up the creeping vines of worry—underneath it all you'll find the beautiful, unencumbered, and eternally solid foundation that is your soul.

Transcend Your Childhood Drama!

What was your childhood drama? Almost everyone has experienced some sort of emotional upheaval. Out of this comes the imprint of your present psychology. Were your parents divorced? Statistics show that children from broken homes have a very difficult time trusting in their adult love relationships. Were either of your parents critical? If so, it's likely that you could become a self-critical or perfectionistic adult—even if their judgment was directed toward others and not at you. If your mom or dad was worrisome, you could grow up and become a fearful or even catastrophic thinker. If they were absent or neglectful, that could lead to adult isolation, depression, and even hopelessness.

There's one important thing that you need to do in order to change your quantum psychology—that is to identify and release your childhood drama, whatever it may be. This isn't an attempt to cast blame or encourage a sense of victimization. It's merely the first step necessary in your deconstruction phase. After all, if you refuse to identify what needs to be changed, it will be impossible to flip the energy and the consciousness of your life.

I once had a client named Bess whose mother repeatedly told her, in a very strict fashion, "Watch your figure! No man will want you if you don't watch your figure!"

Dreading the thought of spending her whole life alone, Bess became fixated on her weight from a very young age. By the time she was in high school, she was deeply indoctrinated in the habits, beliefs, and biochemistry of both anorexia and bulimia. These issues became the main focus of her life. By the time she hit college, she was hovering around 90 pounds and had to quit school because she was so weak. Of course, her mother's prediction that no man would want her came true. She was so thin and so stressed out that she couldn't create any energy of attraction. But she obediently did what her mother demanded—she "watched" her figure until it almost cost her life.

When Bess wrote about her childhood drama, she aptly titled it "Food, Fear, and Rejection." Her mother was basically an absentee parent, so obsessed with her own looks and status that she was always out shopping, exercising, and social climbing. The only thing that she seemed to be available to provide for her daughter was constant criticism and contempt. In fact, Bess's experience was so difficult, uncomfortable, and life altering that it was far more of a trauma than a drama.

Maybe your situation doesn't seem so extreme, but it could have been a powerful influence, nonetheless. Perhaps it was just a little criticism here and there or a passing comment of fear. Perhaps your drama was only related to one issue, like not being good enough at school or not being social enough to escape other children's barbs of judgment. Don't dismiss the challenge of looking at your past just because you weren't seriously abused. Childhood fear, negation, or dismissal—even in seemingly small doses—can be poison to a truly successful adulthood.

Deleting the Drama

Some people might be reading this, feeling hopeless about getting past all of the trouble and misinformation from their youth. They look at their past and see it layered with toxicity. But I've worked with hundreds of individuals who have been the victims of many levels of mistreatment, from indifference and skewed priorities all the way to horrific abuse— some of it so heinous that I wouldn't feel comfortable addressing it in these pages, even with my clients' permission. But I can tell you with unqualified certainty that whether you have drama, comedy, or serious trauma in your childhood, you *can* get past it.

You have the right and the power to change your reality. You can begin the process of cleansing and clearing with just the intention to rewrite your truth. The following process will help you deconstruct your old, unhealthy drama. You're already aware that you need to change your thinking, but doing the entire exercise will help you reframe the very structure and energy of your life. Let yourself take some time with this, for it's nothing less than the reconstruction of your quantum psychology, the rebuilding of your present happiness, and the positive programming of your future.

Step 1: Identify and Release Your Drama

In order to rebuild something with long-lasting and positive results, it's often necessary to take it apart first and find out what's underneath. When flipping a house, it may seem that only cosmetic changes are necessary, but when you tear down the drywall, you may find more serious problems that require much more significant changes.

This applies to people, too. Many think that all they have to do is change something on the surface, like their appearance, in order to achieve success, but life force goes much deeper than what they see. Quantum psychology—the hologram of consciousness and core of personal energy—has much deeper roots, and more often than not, those roots can be found in the dynamics of one's earliest years.

It may be easy to look back and acknowledge the general source of your present attitudes and beliefs, but transcending your childhood drama requires a more systematic approach. I usually recommend that my clients spend some time investigating their drama in their journal, using one of two formats. The most effective way is through writing a narrative, a story about the experiences of your past. Using the real-life characters that you were surrounded with, write a play or short story about what happened to you. Make sure you jot down the feelings that the various events evoked, and if you can identify some of the conclusions you made at the time, that would also be very helpful. If you have lots of upsetting events—and therefore lots of negatively defining influences to your consciousness—you can break down the format into chapters that represent those situations.

You may find that writing one or two stories will stimulate your memory of other similar experiences. If that happens, allow yourself to keep adding to your narrative. Whenever the memory or mood may hit, let yourself dive into the experience and write about it. As you do so, allow yourself to vent any unexpressed feelings of lingering anger, hurt, or fear. It's likely to bring some tears, but don't let that stop you. This is the negative part of your history that you're choosing to release. So let the tears come, and continue to narrate your young life.

You may not have the time or the inclination to write a long and involved reproduction of your personal play. If that's the case, use the format of a timeline. Draw a line down the center of a page, and starting with the first event that you'd like to deconstruct, place your age at the time of the event on the line. To the left, write a few sentences describing what happened. To the right (at the same place, the same age), write a few of the conclusions or reactions you had as a result of that experience. Many people have created timelines, but few have used them to locate originating conclusions, which is an integral part of the process.

Continue to move down the line, briefly addressing each event in this way until you've covered all of the experiences and conclusions that you want to expunge. Again, if this process evokes more memories that you'd like to include, simply continue to add them as you go along.

Some students of the Law of Attraction might say that these exercises will shift your focus to negativity, but this is an important first step in transcending and releasing the source material of your present-day energy. As we discussed earlier in talking about the long-reaching power of your feelings, *you carry your previous experiences with you in two significant ways: first, by harboring unexpressed emotions; second, by continuing to make conclusions based on those past events.*

Writing your narrative or timeline will help you vent any residual feelings as well as analyze their influence. Plus, you'll be taking yourself out of the picture and looking at your old drama in a more objective way. Of course, if you become obsessive about writing and rewriting your early hurtful experiences, you'll be seeing yourself as a victim and moving into paradoxical intent. Be careful not to define yourself in that way. Some people think their suffering makes them special, and if that's how you've seen it, it's time to leave that self-perception behind. So let yourself be analytical and honestly acknowledge and release each important event. Write it down once and then move on to Step 2.

Step 2: Accept This Truth—It Was *Never* about You!

This piece of the process is hard for most people to grasp. Even though your childhood story revolved all around you, the way the principal players acted was actually never *about* you. In fact, it was really *their* drama! They were the writers, producers, directors, and supporting characters in a full-scale production that you were unwittingly forced to play the lead in.

The word *drama* calls to mind a play that's scripted—and for the most part that's true in this case, too. All of the adults had learned their lines, but the children were thrown into a kind of improvisational situation—in their minds, there was chaos and confusion, and they had to come up with their own responses themselves. But kids are quick studies, and it doesn't take long before their parents' dialogue becomes a significant role that the child is willing to replay.

This is what happened to Bess. The input from her mother had nothing to do with her looks or even her potential looks in the future. The misguided insistence that Bess should watch her figure (or else!) was all about her mother's fears and insecurities. It had nothing to do with the little girl's value, abilities, or worthiness to have a relationship; it was all about her mom. And poor Bess was placed smack in the middle of the adult's misguided perception. But where did this script originate? Somewhere along the line Bess's mom was taught that she wasn't good enough, that she had to fear rejection and strive for perfection. This was her mother's childhood drama, which she had never learned how to transcend herself.

> *Realizing that your childhood drama wasn't about you is a very important step in your process of rebuilding a healthy quantum psychology. It's a necessary part of rediscovering your genuine worthiness and really embracing your true value—which are key elements in creating a success consciousness.*

You need to look at the events of your drama from a different point of view. Your objectivity will turn your understanding around and allow you to reverse the resulting beliefs. So if you reflect on the conclusions you made back then and find that you assumed things such as: *There must be something wrong with me if they can't love me,* or *If only I could somehow be different, be better,* or *It's all my fault—I must not be worthy,* you need to redefine those beliefs. In the next step, you can create a present view and an accepting understanding of your worth and value, because—believe it or not—whatever happened back then was never about you!

There are just two cautionary comments I want to make about this issue. First, this truth doesn't minimize the difficulty of the experience—and it doesn't reduce the power and influence the difficult situation may have had on your life so far. However, when you can finally understand that there was nothing you could have—or even should have—done differently to force the players to change, you can free yourself from guilt and self-inflicted responsibility for the past. This will also release you from continuing to doubt yourself and your power in the present.

Second, when some people finally realize that their childhood treatment wasn't about them, they assume that it should no longer be necessary to deal with it. They think they should just be able to forget about it. But this is just another form of denial. Remember, as long as you're carrying toxic conclusions from an earlier event, those thoughts could be affecting your present vibrations.

This is what reconstruction is all about. Your beliefs, thoughts, and conclusions form the framework that holds everything else together. If they're rotten, your life can't help but fall apart. But when you mentally take control, you'll find that you've taken back enough of your own power to start to build a fresh psychology and a whole new reality.

Step 3: Identify the Related Toxic Conclusions of the Present

It must be patently clear by now that the absolute minimum you can do to issue a harmonious consciousness and magnetic energy is to make sure you're *not* engaging in fearful, limiting, or self-judgmental thinking. Whether you merely choose to jump into adjacent possibilities of optional perception or decide to establish a whole new belief system of optimistic assumptions, you simply *must* become the master of your own thought process. Some people say that all you have to deal with is emotions, but the two go hand in hand in a cascading connection of cause and effect. And in order to intervene in the negative pieces of this process, you simply have to find out what you're thinking.

The current thoughts that are connected to your childhood drama follow similar types of conclusions, although they may manifest in different ways. For example, if your parents made you believe that you were faulty in some way, you may now take that notion to work with you, expecting to be judged and worrying about making mistakes. If you were exposed to a lot of fear as a child, you may be presently entertaining false, negative conclusions about your safety, your future, or your health.

If you've done the exercise in the chapter on emotions, you may be well aware of your present toxic patterns of thinking. But it's helpful to see which thoughts came out of your childhood drama—and even more beneficial to know that you can transcend that line of thinking that was so misguidedly scripted for you. So take some time now to look at your narrative or your timeline and see which conclusions from the past might be connected to your present false beliefs. You can recognize your erroneous conclusions by the way they disempower or dishonor you or make you uncomfortable, fearful, or judgmental about yourself or your life. If you need help in this identification part of the process, use your journal to complete the sentences below. They can be very revealing.

- *When I was a child, I used to worry about . . .*

- *Now that I'm an adult, I tend to worry about . . .*

- *I used to see myself this way . . .*

- *Now I tend to see myself this way . . .*

- *In some ways, my parents taught me to feel this about myself . . .*

- *Some of the things I still believe about myself are . . .*

- *When I feel bad, I'm usually worried about these things . . .*

- *If I could reverse any conclusion from the past, it would be . . .*

List all of the false and counterproductive beliefs that you can think of, even if they don't seem to have any connection with your childhood drama. From now on, you must never acknowledge a degrading, judgmental, or limiting statement as true. When you fully embrace the nature of your eternal and energetic consciousness, you'll know without a doubt that there's no limitation, no reason for judgment, and no validity in dishonoring. These are just your *false negatives,* and it's time to let them go.

The phrase *false negative* is often used in medical testing, indicating that a negative test result was not correct. I like this term because it makes me realize that everything that's dismissive, debasing, or negative in some way should be seen as untrue; and with that realization, I'm free to move on to a higher truth. When it comes to your value, there are no false positives. In terms of your worthiness, personal power, and unlimited potential, there's only the forgotten truth. So when you consider your conclusions, remember that you always have two options: the false negative or the true positive. Throw all your false negatives away, open yourself to the positive truth, and move on to Step 4.

Step 4: Rewire Your Mental Direction

Your old cognitive patterns may be very tempting indeed. After all, they have your history and emotional conviction behind them. But the important thing to remember is that your false assumptions stem from misinformation received long ago, and it's time to identify it as such once and for all. It's time to acknowledge the truth about the old lies.

It may seem simplistic, but once you consciously label the worries, fears, and self-criticisms of the past as *mere misinformation,* then you're free to not own them anymore. To make this surprisingly clear, try this exercise. Take each of the negative beliefs that you listed earlier and write down a statement declaring that it's misinformation. For example, if you have the sentence *I'm a failure,* write: *The old belief that I'm a failure is just misinformation.* If you listed: *I can never be happy,* then write: *The belief that I can never be happy is misinformed. I can let that false belief go and choose to be happy now. In fact, it's my thoughts and nothing else that determine my happiness, so I am choosing a new belief now.*

When I worked in a private psychological practice, I saw all sorts of people with serious problems—from paralyzing phobias to bitter relationship rejections. I consistently found that the individuals who were willing to work on changing their thoughts were the ones who moved on. Those who didn't were destined to stay in the same unhappy emotions, repeating their tired, old, unhealthy patterns over and over again.

The same held true when I added the quantum influences into the mix. Those who controlled the thoughts at the center of their consciousness not only got happier, they also got increasingly better results. Although they may have had some setbacks, eventually both their inner and outer life would change in wonderful ways.

The hologram of your accepted truths cannot be resisted. Your life will unfold in strict accordance with your beliefs, so with every negative notion you encounter, write it down and label it as misinformed. No matter what may have happened in the past, you must be in charge of your own truth from now on.

Belief Relief

As you look at your list of relabeled beliefs, you'll probably get some mixed feelings. A part of you will feel relief, yet you may sense some opposition. Underneath the relief is a nagging sense of disbelief that much of what has guided your emotional life has been false. Don't worry. The resistance is natural, but you can—and will—break through it.

One woman told me that when she did this relabeling exercise, it felt as though her entire life had been a lie. She'd always worried about what people thought, and she wondered what she was supposed to think and do next. She actually told me that in spite of the fact that the labels of misinformation made her feel better, she didn't think she could choose to embrace new beliefs because she wouldn't know how to define herself without her fears. She felt disoriented when she told herself, *The belief that I must live according to others' expectations is false!* She'd spent so much of her life trying to impress everyone else that she didn't know what she should focus on now.

Another man told me that it made him feel disloyal to his parents to throw out their deeply held negative beliefs in this way. While he recognized that they were neither true nor healthy, he felt that he had to hold on to them merely because they'd come from his parents. *And besides,* he wondered, *maybe Mom and Dad were right. How could they have been wrong about so many things?*

In time, both these people—along with countless others who felt the need to hold on—were able to see how truly destructive the misinformation of their past had been. Once they allowed themselves to become their own loving guide, they were able to let go of their misdirected motivations. After all, the need to cling to the familiar was just another function of false belief, one that said they weren't in control of their own destiny and for some skewed reason they had to choose to continue to live in pain.

Are you ready to stop suffering? If so, let yourself build some new neural pathways of healthy, optimistic beliefs. After you've labeled your conclusions as either false or misinformed, add a releasing intention along with a new conclusion to counter the old. For example, you might say, *My old belief that I'm a failure is false; I choose to let it go. I open myself to a new, loving view of myself, and I see myself as valuable and successful.* Rewrite each assumption in this way, then repeat them often.

You can be rewired to think new things and react in new ways. Your neuroplasticity—the ability of your brain to change—is encouraged by regular movement and meditation. So when you're stuck in a thought that you want to change, get up and move. Meditate every day; and always, always be mindful of your cognitive options.

Every time you repeat a new optimistic conclusion, you redirect your mental activity to a different neural pathway. With enough repetition, these new beliefs will take over as your spontaneous, automatic responses, so you won't have to work at it so much. Imagine how wonderful it will be when the peaceful, positive assumption becomes your natural response to everything!

Don't Do It Later—Do It Now!

I know it can be difficult to shift your deeply indoctrinated thought patterns, but it really is your decision. *A choice is a moment when you hold two options—and you also hold the power to consciously pick the best one.* Changing your thoughts doesn't have to be all that much different from making the decision to turn right or turn left. Don't make it bigger than it has to be just because the belief has been around for a while. Your assumption that it's impossible to come up with healthy, stable perceptions is another false thought that simply has to be reversed.

Remember, the more emotionally charged a situation is, the more control you give away. So if a new situation sweeps you up into your old reactions, take mental command as soon as possible. Don't fault yourself, though, if your initial response is negative. It's totally normal to get emotionally involved when you're placed in the middle of an ongoing drama. The fact is that life can be one crisis after another, but you'll find that the sooner you consistently master your conclusions, the less chaos you'll be attracting to you.

Some people actually get addicted to the turmoil. The emotional intensity seems to feed their energetic power. It's a fraudulent sense of power, though, and it leads to a very dangerous self-definition of victimization. I have a friend who has been in that place for years. She has a running feud with a co-worker and constantly crows about it with righteous indignation. She goes on and on about her aches and pains and illnesses, much to the consternation of anyone who spends time with her. She seems to love the drama, but she's losing friends—and considerable power—by choosing to define herself in this way.

Whatever your situation is—even if you're still lingering in your old childhood script—don't stay addicted to it! Take control, no matter how easy it may be to get swept back in. Whether it's past or present (or even in the imagined future), you can and *must* step out of the drama, make clearer conclusions, and then write yourself a new self-dialogue.

Be ever vigilant about considering your adjacent possibilities. When you feel stuck, close your eyes, relax, and take a deep breath. Tell yourself: *I don't have to make this a big deal. Whatever happens, I will be okay.* Even if it *is* a big deal, you can always rein in your thoughts and widen your perception. Never take anything personally. See the situation from a more distant and objective viewpoint and always add the spiritual element. Affirm: *I open myself to my spirit's capacity to relax. I let this go and develop a new understanding of things. At any moment—no matter what is going on—I can switch to a thought that is more peaceful and empowering for me.* Be persistent, and remember that your power to change everything in your life is centered in this choice.

I recently found myself in a very challenging situation involving past betrayal and future demands with someone I was very close to. I was angry and hurt, and I didn't realize that I'd been brooding about it much of the time. There are crucial events in life, but we can always bring ourselves in to the safe harbor of spirit—and that's precisely what I forgot to do. I lingered in my mental and emotional upheaval for weeks, and I talked about it all the time. (Just like my friend with the aches and pains—be careful what you judge because it will always come back to bite you!)

Finally my husband said, "I can't believe you're going on and on like this. I know it's huge, but you can't keep doing this to yourself. Don't you always tell people they have to redefine it?"

Of course, in my highly emotional state, my first reaction was to become defensive and tell him he didn't understand what I was going through. It always amazes me how we tend to hold fast to the very thing that depletes us. Then when I realized he was right, I laughed and said it must have been hormones. (That's my story, and I'm sticking to it.)

But he was right, indeed! I'd gotten caught up in the enormity of the situation, imagining worst-case scenarios and assuming that I had no way out. I'd forgotten to redefine it and choose some new conclusions. Realizing this was like a light going on in a place that had been dark and scary, revealing that when I took back my powers of cognitive choice, there was nothing to really be afraid of. While a lot was going on, I didn't have to panic, lose power, or live in anxiety. I was free again. I switched my thinking, and the quality of my life shifted overnight.

Now I can look at that problem and not be drawn back into the angst, although in an ongoing provocative situation, it can be difficult to stay centered. So when I'm tempted to fall into the fray again, I remind myself to step back and focus on the present, take command of my thoughts, and acknowledge everything for what it is—a passing interest that helps my spirit evolve.

Remember the old saying I mentioned earlier: *Be careful not to suffer over your suffering.* This speaks directly to the Paradox of Experience. No matter what's going on—even if it's very difficult—be cautious not to add another layer of anguish through mental turmoil and emotional unrest. Deep inside, your spirit knows that it's only your response that matters. In the eternity of all time, the exact moment that you're in is the door to real peace. Step out of the storm and into the calm center. Simply watch as the issue swirls all around you. Express your emotions, then bless everyone involved and let it go.

Remember Bess? She had a very debilitating upbringing, a childhood drama that she carried around for years. When she came to see me at the age of 33, she'd already been to some clinics to treat her eating disorders. She'd gained some weight and reduced the episodes of purging significantly. But she still had lingering thoughts of self-negation and fear. She narrated her drama, although it was a long and painful process. But when she saw that she could label her fears as someone else's false beliefs, she knew that she had based her whole life on a lie.

She attacked her unhealthy perceptions with a ferocity I've rarely seen. She simply refused to be shackled by her mother's drama, so she wrote an entirely new script—one where she valued herself just as she was, where nothing was determined by her weight so it was finally safe to eat and actually enjoy food. She was tireless in her determination not to sit and stew in the old fears and judgments—and eventually her effort paid off. She gained more weight and became a healthy size 10—which was finally okay with her. She was happier than she ever thought possible, and her joy and newfound freedom broadcast an incredibly magnetic energy. In accordance with paradoxical intent, she *stopped* "watching her figure" and actually got what she wanted. She's in a job that she loves and is married to a man who—like Bess—loves her just as she is.

Your old mental and emotional patterns don't have to hold sway over you anymore. Erase the CD (Childhood Drama) and let the past go. Redefine your life and your *Self* according to your new unconditional and spiritual consciousness. And with each present challenge, take control of the direction you let your mind go.

Don't give up, even if your old issues keep resurfacing. Never stop reversing the negative conclusions that no longer are your truth. As you continue to revise your mental direction, you'll be rewiring your neural pathways, creating new and consistently healthy responses. You'll find that your happiness (and your magnetic energy) will keep getting stronger and stronger. With your old limitations cleared out of the way, you'll really be able to flip that life!

CHAPTER 13

UPGRADE FOR ADDED VALUE!

"Thoughts create a new heaven, a new firmament,
a new source of energy, from which new arts flow."

— **PARACELSUS**

You don't have to be finished clearing out the old, unwanted stuff of your life before you start installing the elements that will increase your energetic value. In fact, if you've been following along with the suggestions so far, you've already significantly upgraded the mental and emotional structure of your life. Now you can continue to raise its vibratory value by attending to the finer details of energy and consciousness enhancement. Your new psychology spreads out in waves of information and emotional vibration, connecting your inner truth with the Universal forces of abundance.

So let's review the key points of quantum psychology:

1. Your mental and emotional makeup creates the energy of your life force along with the details of your holographic projection to the world.

2. You have the power to change your psychology and shift the resonance of your life force as well as the nature of your holographic consciousness.

3. The present switch in thought and emotion to a more
    peaceful and empowered state immediately activates more
    positive patterns of attraction and manifestation, resulting
    in increasingly beneficial life results.

This process of changing your quantum psychology isn't really a materialistic pursuit, although it can end up seeming that way, because your
shift in energy gets external results. But when it comes to self-empowerment, it's the internal results that really matter. Once the self-mastery
is achieved and a steady sense of purpose and contentment becomes
your present state, then your consciousness rings clear with unconflicted
expectations; and your life force belts out powerful vibrations of peace
and love. This isn't just a pretense of happiness, but a genuine inner joy
that radiates from within. When this type of pure, self-generated energy
connects with the infinite and nonlocal flow of abundance, the Universe
can't help but respond. As always, the key to experiencing magic in the
world can be found by going within.

Interior Design: Mastering Your Inner Life Intentions

When people flip a house, they can't just focus on the exterior; it's
what's inside that counts. The same is true for you, too. Instead of ignoring what's going on within and just worrying about your external goals,
you need to consciously add value to your interior design.

Through your quantum psychology, you build your life every single
day. So when you put a positive mental and emotional intention at the
center of your awareness, you activate the energetic world accordingly.
Of course, things happen, and you can get distracted and easily diverted
off course. When you notice that occurring, you need to realign your
focus and remind yourself of your primary intentions. Take control of your
quantum psychology by filtering any issue that may come up through
your authentic power and self-honoring. Use the cognitive restructuring
steps in the previous chapters to realign your thinking whenever necessary.
Never forget that mastering your thought is the core of all you create.

The following four types of intentions will help you stay on track. Build
a higher consciousness of these intentions in your daily life, and when

something comes up, deal with it in light of these four guiding principles. You'll soon find that the answers you need will become clear.

1. Personal life intention: Just as you have your own unique childhood drama, you probably also have a personal issue or pattern that you feel you need to work on most. So it's helpful to design your own life intention according to the primary inner goals you want to achieve. These aren't the material aspirations that involve monetary wealth or even career success; these are states of being that you wish to achieve on a consistent basis. For instance, if you live in perpetual fear of the future, an important assertion for you would be: *I intend to live in the present and trust in the future.* Then, whenever you find yourself going back to your old pattern of fretting over the future, just gently bring yourself back to the present by reminding yourself of your guiding pesonal goal.

When I was in my 20s, I created a life intention that was structured more like a motto. I guess I was impressed with the three-word motto of the French Revolution: *liberty, equality, fraternity.* I wanted to choose some equally lofty principles to guide both the minor and major decisions of my life. The three-word motto that became my life intention was: *integrity, autonomy, equanimity.* I chose integrity because I'd been deceived in a very hurtful way, and I knew that if I wanted honest treatment, I needed to be stringent in my truthfulness with myself and others. Perhaps the desire for autonomy, my second guiding principle, came from being a twin, but I truly desired to be able to take care of myself and live an independent life. Finally, equanimity was the most important life intention of all. To me, this meant the ability to find peace no matter what might be going on and to stay centered, purposeful, and calm—even in the eye of a turbulent storm.

Equanimity is the guiding life intention that I've prioritized the most. I've worked on it every day of my life, and even now when issues come up, I try to ask myself what I need to do, think, or say to bring equanimity back to my life. By understanding and consciously determining my thoughts, and by connecting with spirit presence and Divine love, I try to make this central pursuit of peace an ever-present practice.

You can choose a one-word life intention or an entire mission statement, but whatever your decision, make this a high priority.

Focus on the energetic and emotional quality you want to achieve and intend to make that a reality. Here are some examples:

- *If you know you have the tendency to live in urgency and obsess about your goals, choose: I intend to live with peaceful surrender and trust in the future.*
- *If you're always working and stressed out, say: I intend to relax, let go, and be playful in my everyday life.*
- *If you need to honor yourself more, decide: I intend to recognize my value and live with self-love.*

This is so helpful, I recommend it as a matter of course to anyone who wants to achieve real, heartfelt prosperity. Your external goals are always accelerated when you focus on what it is you desire to achieve internally—whether it's a quality, strength, or even prevailing emotion. If you want to consistently create the emotion and vibration of happiness, then make sure authentic happiness is in your life intention.

This provides a central focus for your intentional energy, personal development, and higher-vibrational lifetime goals. When you're in the middle of chaos and confusion, you can turn to your own life intention for direction and guidance. Make it important, make it personal, and make it a priority! You'll be amazed by how stabilizing and helpful your personal life intention can be.

2. Value-creating intention: The goal to bring greater value to your life and to the world could be one of the most powerful life intentions that you can engage in. Value is the energy you bring to yourself and others through an honoring and caring heart. You do this through your respectful self-talk and honoring decisions. You create this with others by letting go of judgment, seeing everyone as equal, and demonstrating genuine concern for their well-being. It's important to ask yourself—at the beginning of the day or anytime an important situation comes up: *What would create the greatest value now?*

When you're involved in a difficult encounter with others, you might ask: *What creates greater value in this situation—confrontation or compassion?* In some cases it's clear, but never forget the issue of self-honoring. If you consistently dismiss taking care of yourself out of some false sense of obligation, you'll be projecting an energy that invites the world to use you and dismiss you, also. Oftentimes the question of value comes down to creating balance. Sometimes confrontation is exactly what you need to honor yourself, and the real value comes from doing it appropriately— with clarity and compassion for all involved. Remember, it never dishonors others to be truly honoring to yourself.

Here are some questions concerning value creation throughout your life. Try to refer to these often to give yourself a greater awareness of your choices and consequences.

- *How do I want to spend my time today? What activities would nurture me most?*

- *What are the consequences of this decision, and will they really create genuine value for myself and others?*

- *Does the energy of this thought, comment, or action bring more or less worth to myself and the world?*

- *What can I do to make this very moment more valuable for me?*

- *What would create the greatest value in my life now?*

Spending a few minutes investigating the answers to these and similar questions about your many choices will bring greater and greater focus to your intention—and in time will shift both your consciousness and your energetic frequency to a more positive direction.

You have the power to create value every single day in every thought, word, decision, and deed. There are many choices that will instantaneously accelerate your value production. When you take such paths, you automatically speed up the vibration of harmonic flow because the Universe greatly resonates with choices such as courage, honor, generosity, action, communication, caring, patience, grace, and acceptance. Such value-creating intentions will always move you forward on your path.

The following primary intentions of gratitude and love also create value; but they're so important that they each generate a formidable current of positive cause and effect on their own, so they need to be considered separately.

3. Appreciation intention: This is the choice to consistently and consciously acknowledge and be grateful for all the wonderful things present within yourself and your life. Most people merely have a sense of gratitude when something special happens, but that doesn't create a strong enough frequency to really build any momentum. Real appreciation notices all the little things of joy and value and then reaches down into the depth of the soul with thanks for the most important blessing of all—life itself.

This kind of intention—to recognize even the smallest, most fleeting gift that the Universe bestows—produces a voluminous and expanding consciousness, one that fills the world with your light, love, and receptivity. Yet the opposite happens when you ignore the little gifts and take things for granted, whether it's the beauty of a sunny day or a loved one's sweet smile! Such dismissal creates a shrinking, shriveling energy, and your openness to receiving is blocked because the Universe knows that the value of your blessings will only be ignored.

The energies of appreciation and happiness are inseparably connected, creating a powerful force in the energetic world. Your level of attraction will always match your level of appreciation. The Universe thanks you for every thankful thought.

As I write this, I can see the sun setting through my west window and the crystals hanging there are casting rainbows across the walls. The sunshine through the lace curtains and gently moving leaves create a beautifully dappled, lacy pattern, and as I stop to look at the details, I truly appreciate this moment. It's a precious gem of time to me—the soft breeze, the warm weather, the lovely lace curtains, my beautiful home, and the rays of sunlight—the actual light waves of which I cannot see. But the outcome is before me in a stunningly beautiful splash of color dancing on the page in my hand. And to think that this experience should be gifted to me at the very moment that I'm writing about appreciation!

There are no coincidences, just energetic returns and gentle reminders from the Great Loving Consciousness. Some people reading this might consider such a sentiment saccharine, but I mean it sincerely. It's moments like this that I feel the most "successful," when I'm connected to—and grateful for—the everyday blessings that fill my world.

I've heard of an Eastern philosophy that says: *Learn to contemplate just one thing of beauty each day.* It's a wonderful suggestion, but let's not stop there. I always encourage my clients to keep an appreciation and acknowledgment journal, where they jot down the things in their life that they're grateful for as well as record what they appreciate or acknowledge within and about themselves.

This daily practice shifts your focus from tedium to blissful energy expansion that the Universe loves to see. There's no doubt about it—your daily intention to enlarge your sense of appreciation will be duly noted in the energetic realm.

4. Loving intention: This is the highest purpose of the human experience. Love adds reverence to appreciation in profound recognition of life-affirming value and worth. In its purest state, love is accepting, tolerant, and forgiving. This is true whether it's directed toward yourself or someone else.

Self-love is at the nucleus of all kinds of love. Unfortunately, in its absence, there's a desperate longing to fill the soul's need. Every intention that comes out of a dark void like that becomes soured with striving and skewed with discontent. Self-loathing creates such a chaotic confusion of vibration that the affectionate support so desperately needed gets sent spinning outward in waves of unwitting rejection.

The key to your quantum psychology and emotional stability has to be a core of self-love. Almost every type of fear, depression, and anxiety comes from the inability to cherish and trust yourself enough. As I discussed in the last chapter, this usually stems from childhood drama. People learned to love themselves when they were young, if they had models for self-love and were encouraged to see and appreciate their own unique value.

Yet people who have never been shown their own worth suffer from low self-esteem that permeates their lives. Their psyche is riddled with worry, doubt, and hostility. They could be quiet and submissive or arrogant and power-mongering, but unhappiness is their predominant emotion. And so often they find themselves striving for external things, seeking material gain to prove their worth and compensate for the loneliness that always exists within.

Perhaps you haven't been shown how to really love yourself, or maybe no one has ever encouraged you to see your inestimable worth—but it's never too late to learn. In fact, if you really want to flip your energy and consciousness, you absolutely must make this your first priority. You're entitled to hold yourself in high esteem, to prioritize and care for yourself. Just because you were never taught that, it doesn't make you less deserving—that's an eternal truth that never changes.

Whatever conclusions of low self-esteem may be gnawing at you as a holdout from your childhood drama, you must aggressively resolve to reverse the power of this misinformation in your life. You can no longer torment yourself with criticism and self-doubt. Every single time such thoughts creep into your mental patterns, you must aggressively cast them out. *You need to have as much compassion for yourself as you have for others. Forgive and encourage yourself; acknowledge your own value every day.* Your choice of self-love creates a cascading energy of loving consequences that move out in the Universe in beneficial blessings.

From the place of genuine self-love, you're free to engage in the unencumbered affection for others. This isn't necessarily romantic; it's the willingness to accept and respect people the way you'd like to be accepted and cared for yourself. But you can't come from an open heart if you're continually perceiving others as a threat to your power or a source of competition. When you're envious or fearful, you're always living in a stressful state of striving. Let go of the stress, see everyone—including yourself—as valuable, and know that your power comes from within.

Let go of judgment, too. Your tendency to criticize others will only come back to you, leaving the bitter fear that you may be judged yourself. In addition, the act of devaluing creates a serious loss of your own dignity, compassion, and grace—a radical disruption to the magnetic energy you're longing to create.

The solution is to see yourself and others as equal spirits on similar paths of personal discovery. At the heart of each individual's drama is the light of the eternal soul, and that's what must be appreciated and even revered, no matter what else may be going on. This type of reverence is tolerant of diversity and empathetic to others' suffering, and your intention to bring this kind of love to the world moves out in global proportions, returning unending waves of Universal appreciation.

Whenever a problem comes up, send love to it. Just sit, smile, send love, and let go. Harbor no hateful intentions; just keep saying the word *love* whenever thoughts of the issue arise. Then sit back and see what happens next. You may be very pleasantly surprised!

The final form of this connection is Divine love. Just as this heavenly spark dwells in each and every person, it also thrives in the physical and spiritual world around us. Your life is an expression of Divine love, and that extends to all of nature, the planet, and the Universe beyond. This spiritual love perceives life as a blessing and always sees the inherent worth of all of the people, places, and things that are brought into your life.

Meditation on the mutual loving source of all people brings a unity and harmonic resonance into your heart-center that broadcasts outward for wonderful connections. Let yourself contemplate the all-loving source that everyone shares. Breathe in the love that transcends all time, and when you're in that blissful state, feel the power and profound peace that surpasses any other kind of needing. Sit in the sublime silence of your eternal soul's blessed source, and know without a moment's hesitation that you are now—and will forever be—loved.

When you live with the intentions to love, appreciate, and create value, your entire life becomes an affirmation. Your energy is buoyant with joyous expectation, pulsating with increasingly higher vibrations of all-consuming peace.

These intentions—along with your own personal life intention—can become a significant part of your daily experience. Filter both the mundane and the important situations you experience through these four considerations, and you'll become amazingly empowered in dictating the positive direction your life takes.

Every day you face a thousand choices that may (or may not) lead you forward. Always keep your inner intentions in mind. The following sections also offer a variety of suggestions for adding value to every part of your life. Whatever the time of day, always remember your adjacent possibilities—sparkling with options and pure potential.

New Awakenings

Every time of day offers its own special opportunity for consciousness creation and energy expansion. Morning is the re-creation of everything new. In the first hours of each and every day, you have a new chance to live with joy and intend love. When you wake up, don't just jump out of bed and race to get ready. Instead, let yourself stretch out and do some deep breathing. Give yourself time for at least a five-minute meditation where you focus on the following:

- Appreciation for the day ahead, rejuvenating sleep, your bed, your home, and anything else you'd like to acknowledge

- Your intentions for the day—not only what you want to get done, but also how you want to experience it

- Your daily action toward your goal—spend a moment visualizing yourself taking joyous action and being pleased with what you've accomplished

- Your personal shift. Ask yourself, *What do I want to be conscious of today? What's the energy I want to create? What's the emotion I want to live in today?*

Plan the emotional experiences of your day. As you think about the hours ahead, visualize yourself engaging in the activities and feeling the emotions that you desire. See yourself approaching everything with confidence, joy, enthusiasm, love—and any positive emotion you prefer. Instead of settling for a reactionary emotional existence, start to live an intentional life of feeling. Pick your emotion and make it your mantra for the day.

Affirm your emotional intentions, for example: *I am very happy today. On my drive to work, I feel relaxed and peaceful. I enjoy the work I do. I really love spending time with the kids.* Remember, the emotional quality of your daily routine dictates the energetic effects of your life force—and that's the real presence and producer in the Universe.

As you're showering, dressing, or commuting to work, try to be more conscious of your thoughts and the direction they're taking. Release negativity and move into an adjacent possibility of optimistic assumptions. *Whenever* you see yourself in the mirror, acknowledge your value and give yourself a loving and encouraging comment. Smile, wink, and blow yourself a kiss! It sounds silly, but it's great for your energy!

Conscious Eating

Whether it's a quick breakfast, a big dinner, or a late-night snack, bring your consciousness to it! I don't think there's anything that modern Americans do more unconsciously than eat. Take a moment to bless and appreciate the food in front of you. Give yourself time to really taste each bite, and stop periodically—put down your fork, relax, breathe, and enjoy the experience.

Don't shove down your food; that only creates a sense of urgency and a lifestyle of paradoxical intent. After you're finished, take some time to sit quietly—even do a two-minute meditation on the activity you're going to start next and what kind of consciousness and emotional experience you want to bring to it.

At mealtime—and throughout the day—drink plenty of water. Anchor an intention to this activity. Whether it's peace, productivity, healing, or bliss, affirm it with each swallow. Water cleanses your physical energy, and the intention you attach to it purifies your emotions.

Day-tripper

As you go through your day, make sure that you move leisurely and keep your focus calm. Hurrying only projects a cloud of urgent, fragmented energy that pushes beneficial solutions away. So let yourself breathe, relax, and take your time. Statistics show that you actually get more done and make fewer mistakes when you work in this fashion. More important, your energy is much more settled, tranquil, and gently magnetic that way.

At the beginning of each new activity, create an intention around it. Even if it's just vacuuming the rug, affirm: *I am dancing with this vacuum, and I am having fun!* If you have a challenging task, such as an important sales presentation at work, remind yourself that you don't have to make it mean too much. Way more important than the specific outcome is the emotional intention and energy you bring to it. You'll make many more sales over time if you shift your vibration out of worry and your consciousness into peace.

Stop periodically and do a one- or two-minute meditation, during which you drop your consciousness into your heart and connect with your spirit in appreciation. Remember to take little breaks throughout the day. Carry a booklet of affirmations and let yourself stop to rest, regroup, and read just a few to get yourself back on course. Bring the intention of love to each experience and each person around you. Say the word *love,* and direct it where you want it to go. This is your most fluid energy, and it creates harmonious connections and truly brilliant results!

Homeward Bound

Whenever you're heading home—whether it's after long hours of work or a day at the beach—use the journey to shift your focus. Give thanks for the action you've taken and the pleasure you've had, but then let go of what has happened. Be sure not to take any worry about work into your home environment. Let yourself shift gears and start to slow down.

If you have a partner or a family, think about how you want to spend your time together. Create the intention to open up and connect with your loved ones in a truly caring way. If you're planning to spend some time on an avocation, sport, or hobby, let yourself look forward to the experience. Plan when and how you're going to create some time for yourself and your personal goals. Try to establish balance in your life; consider the importance of self-care, leisure, and relationships. Remember that real prosperity is success on all levels.

Night Light!

In this rapidly paced and highly demanding modern world, it's rare to have an evening that doesn't contain at least a few tasks requiring our attention. It's important, though, to set aside at least some time to unwind, relax, and center yourself. It's very difficult to live with intention if you're running from activity to activity just trying to get things done. And if you don't give yourself some time, you'll find yourself feeling resentment, an emotion that you really don't want vibrating in your energy field—or in your home and family!

If you work at a nine-to-five job, the evening may be your only opportunity to work on your other goals. Try to structure enough time so that you can feel you're taking action, but not so much that you lose sight of everything else. There may be cases, of course, where a temporary period of high activity is unavoidable—like tax time for an accountant or a teacher grading finals. Don't spend long stretches of your life under such stress, however. It broadcasts a very clear message to the Universe, saying not to bother sending the things that you can enjoy at your leisure because you have no intention to make free time a priority.

Evenings offer a great opportunity to spend time enlightening your consciousness and energy direction. Make it a priority to meditate, write in your journal, acknowledge and appreciate your life, do thought restructuring, or exercise. Even just one such activity can do a world of good for your energy and consciousness creation.

As you're winding down toward bedtime, let yourself shift gears again. Entertain peaceful expectations for a quiet and rejuvenating sleep. Don't watch television right up to the moment you close your eyes, and try not to have the news or violent programs be your very last show. They agitate your vibration and increase the likelihood of unpleasant dreams, an energetic influence that can last throughout the night.

> At the end of the evening, take a few minutes to think back on the day with conscious appreciation. If you recall some nagging problem, send love to it and let it go. Do this often—at any time of day—until you see that it's starting to become resolved. Keep love in mind as your ultimate solution. That word and intention has the power to permeate even the toughest situation. Whatever the problem, love is the solution.

If you look back on your day and find that your thoughts or energetic choices weren't what you would have liked them to be, create an intention to be more conscious and in control tomorrow. Then truly forgive yourself and let it go. There's absolutely no value in self-condemnation, so release all your fears and self-doubts. Bless yourself and your day, and get ready to move into the creative and magnetic state of sleep.

Dream Team

The earth's vibrations are methodical and slow, and they tend to align with human vibrations most at night. You have a team of helpers whose energy can assist you more easily when you're relaxed. Therefore, night is the best time to connect with the energetic realm, get access to the information you may need, and receive real assistance in turning your dreams into a reality. Do the following just before sleeping to help get inspiration, answers, and results:

— Before you fall asleep, write an intention for the night in your journal, something like: *I sleep peacefully through the night and wake up refreshed and enthusiastic, looking forward to the day.*

— Just before bed, read your goal intentions. Then as you're falling asleep, visualize your desired end results. Picture all the wonderful details, and put yourself in the picture. Feel the joy and excitement it brings. Release the image to the Universe with surrender, trust, and blissful expectation.

— Take a few minutes to meditate. Open yourself to connecting with spirit, the Divine, or your higher Self. Forge a relationship with the loving helpers all around you. They long to connect and communicate their love.

— If you need information or an inspired idea, ask for the answer to come in your sleep. Affirm: *I am receiving the wisdom I need in a way that I can recognize and understand.* Keep a notebook by the bed so that if a flash of insight comes, you can write it down. Also use it to write down your dreams in the morning; the answers you seek may arrive through them. You may even be surprised to find that a thought will come during the next day, so be open to receiving and notice the response.

Life Song

Each of us lives in the hologram of our own making, our resonance and results swirling around us in an endless symphony of cause, and effect. From moment to unconscious moment we feel, react, long for, appreciate, and regret—waiting for our silent expectations to be met. We're the composer and conductor, too. We write the music that we live, destined to hear it over and over again. If we don't like what we hear, we need to change our tune.

Whether it's the blues you've been playing, a driving march, or a lonely ballad, you can rewrite your music and change your life force. This is the time to reclaim yourself, to sing your song of self-love and renewal—and to script a quantum psychology that shapes itself more surely and sweetly with each passing hour.

Your beliefs, your thoughts, even your emotions are ultimately up to you. Although you may need to remind yourself often that you are indeed in charge, every blessed return to that one realization brings freedom anew. *Choice is the most important form of prosperity,* and every moment you can choose *for* rather than *against* yourself. You can pick love rather than hate, trust rather than fear, peace rather than concern. Each of these moments of choice expands your wealth, and in that flash of self-empowerment, real prosperity—now and forever—is yours.

CHAPTER 14

QUESTIONS, ANSWERS, AND CONTINUED ACTION

"If one advances confidently in the direction of his dreams and endeavors to live the life he has imagined, he will meet with success unexpected in common hours."

— HENRY DAVID THOREAU

Over the many years that I've been teaching these principles, I've been asked countless questions about energetic change. The volume has greatly increased since the recent resurgence of interest in the Law of Attraction. I get e-mails from all over the world asking me why things happen the way they do, and there are some common threads in the themes of those questions.

A lot of people have genuine concerns, so I've taken the most compelling and common questions and tried to answer them to the best of my ability. Some of these are combinations of related issues. For example, I get a lot of queries from parents about why bad things are happening to their children; and I've answered that in conjunction with the question of why bad things happen to good and positive people in general. Whatever your question may be, I hope you find a helpful answer here.

Q: Why isn't it working? They say that if you ask and believe, then you'll receive, but it's not happening. Why?

A: This is one of the most common questions I receive. As you've read, it's a much more complex process than people realize. Since attraction responds to life force rather than individual intention, the reasons for delays will vary with each person. Having said that, I find the answers usually come down to one of three issues: paradoxical intent, low life force, and limited action.

The first possibility is paradoxical intent: You may feel very urgent about making your desire happen—and the longer it takes, the worse the sensation of immediate need can get. It's so easy to fall into desperation, but that will only poison your energy and make you miserable in the meantime. If you're not receiving what you want, check your urgency first. If you don't rein it in, you'll only keep sabotaging your results.

Second is life force: You simply *must* support your goals with your whole consciousness and life energy. While success may seem to be about the future, it's really about the present. Your vital vibration every day is what determines the results. If the way you live, think, and treat yourself contradicts your basic intention, it could take forever to get what you want!

Third is action: You can't just hope, you have to *do*—and keep on doing whatever it takes to make your goal a reality. If you've finished all the action that's necessary, yet the results still feel far off, find out what changes you can make in your plan and see what new results those tweaks could bring. Be flexible, persistent, patient, and optimistic. These are intentions and energies that move you forward.

Q: How can you tell exactly what you need to change in order to make your energy better?

A: The Universe often speaks your language in very exact terms. I've worked with individuals, couples, and even corporations by investigating the words they used both in daily life and in more formal situations. So listen to yourself for a while. Jot down any verbal patterns that could mirror your inner thoughts and emotions. For example, I had a client who often complained that everybody hated her. In looking at her beliefs, we found that she hated herself. Another client said his boss was always ignoring him, and we discovered that he'd been ignoring himself—never taking action on his own behalf and even being totally unaware of his own needs. So pay attention to your words and ask yourself how they could be reflecting the inner realities of your life.

You can also do a check on your emotions: Identify your feelings and see if they represent any thoughts of hopelessness or limitation. Let yourself work out the details and then reverse the thoughts aggressively, repeating the new options until you're saturated with the new, positive view. If you notice a particular negative thought resurfacing over and over, this represents an important issue for you. Make sure that you counter it with firm intention. *Remember that each and every thought is a new choice, even if it's a thought you've had many times before.*

Q: I recently heard someone say, "It's not enough to want something. To activate the Law of Attraction, you have to think, *I can't be happy without it!*" Do you agree?

A: I absolutely do *not* agree! If you tell yourself that you can't be happy without something, it won't ensure that you'll get it—it will only guarantee that you won't be happy! I imagine that whoever said this was trying to tell people to not give up. But you need to be able to stay motivated without being unhappy, or you'll completely reverse your energy.

Having the attitude that you need anything to be content will only make you focus on your lack, which can't be good for attraction. If anything, that kind of misery and desperation is more likely to make you give up, especially when you hit some obstacles. The bottom line is that unhappy people get unhappy results. So pursue your goal with joyful expectation and never give away your ability to enjoy life now!

Q: A lot of the Law of Attraction books talk about going to the "feeling good" emotions. Is it possible to feel good all of the time? What's wrong with me if I can't make that happen?

A: There's nothing wrong with you if you can't feel great at every moment. Human beings feel all sorts of things all of the time. Your emotions are natural reactions to the people and conditions around you. Never fault yourself for an honest response—whether it's good or bad. Honor your feelings and find out about the conclusions that are causing them.

I understand, however, what this "feeling good" intention is supposed to indicate. The idea is that the Universe will return your emotional energy to you, so if you want to get good things, switch to feeling great right now. There's a lot of validity in that suggestion, but you must be aware of some important considerations.

First, your ability to switch your feelings has to come from changing the negative or toxic conclusions behind them. Your real strength doesn't come from emotional denial but from cognitive control and healthy mental views. Your emotional power starts here.

Second, you have to make sure that the good feeling honors you. Some people find comfort when they engage in their addictions. In fact, the only time some individuals experience pleasure is when they're drinking, eating, spending money, or doing drugs. This isn't the "feeling good" intention that's being suggested here, and you have to always be aware of the honoring choice.

Finally, never be afraid of your difficult emotions or thoughts. There's a backlash to all of this that has created a wave of fear, self-blame, and dread over having experienced any negative feeling at all. Many people have some pessimism and think they've ruined all their chances at success. Yet no single thought or emotion—even if it's repeated—has the power to ruin everything!

You must stop being afraid of fear and negativity. Quit blaming yourself, for that only digs you in deeper. Even if you feel utterly convinced that some gloominess of yours has created a problem, you have to forgive yourself and let it go. Don't be so severe—just see it all as a process. Life is for learning, and the best thing you can learn is self-love, self-valuing, and self-compassion. In the end, understanding that will far outweigh all the negativity you've ever had.

Q: How does the Law of Attraction explain why bad things happen even to innocent, undeserving people like children?

A: The most heartbreaking e-mails I get are from parents who have a sick child and are trying to figure out how they could have attracted this. They're filled with guilt and self-blame, convinced that it was impossible for their innocent young child to think things like cancer and autism into existence, so there must have been something horrible that they as parents thought or did to manifest this. But thoughts are not the source of all sickness. Environment, nutrition, genetics, and even karma are all in the mix.

Since the dawn of time people have been asking why bad things happen to good people; why infants and children have to suffer; and why whole groups, families, cultures, and communities are forced to endure hardship and torment. While I'm certain that the Laws of Attraction and Manifestation are consistent, I know that we still have a lot to learn. I don't believe that every single adversity is brought about by negative thinking. Nor do all benefits befall only positive thinkers. So many factors go into making up someone's destiny that it just cannot be simplified to only one cause.

The patterns of attraction indicate what's likely to happen; they reveal the general direction and momentum of life. But they aren't the only influence over our experiences. Life is a complex process. Good and bad things happen to everybody. Death, illness, and difficulty can touch even the most positive and peaceful people.

In fact, this conundrum is what first sent me on my spiritual quest when I was young. After much study, I realized that the most compelling and logical explanation for such apparent inequities could be found in the concept of reincarnation—not as a punitive reason for suffering but as a source of learning and reversing energy. This became apparent when I used hypnotic regressions in my practice to try to discern clients' original problems. There were many cases where the person automatically went back to a previous life, without ever being directed to do so.

This is such a compelling piece of the puzzle that I've spent years researching it. In fact, my next book is devoted to the topic of past lives and how our eternal conscious becomes encoded with information that influences what we're experiencing now. It's a fascinating element of cause and effect, and this type of exploration can be a great source of understanding and healing.

But whether you think the source of your difficulties may be present pessimism or an unknown history, you need to know that life isn't a punishment. As hard as an experience may be, there's some underlying purpose to it—although we may not be able to see it at the time. In the mystery of existence, sometimes bad things just happen. It's not your fault, and anyone who tells you that it is needs to be dismissed. That person is only promoting fear and judgment—more energies that make the problem worse, so please don't go down that dark road!

It's hard enough to go through difficult times, to watch a cherished child or another loved one suffer. Please don't torment yourself with thoughts of guilt and self-recrimination. Have courage. Open yourself to seeing the lesson or the opportunity that may be the unknown purpose. Seek assistance from loving angel spirits. And don't—even for a passing moment—blame yourself! It's what you do with this experience that counts. Bring love, prayer, and learning to it, and in time you'll find your way.

Q: What about free will? How do the Laws work when more than one person is involved?

A: I've been asked this concerning several different types of situations, the most common of which is romantic attraction. People have wondered if setting their intention on a relationship with a specific person can force that individual to change his or her mind or become attracted in the first place.

In this situation, the answer is clear: You *cannot* force your desires upon another, especially if that person's will doesn't align with yours. Attraction is based on resonance; that's the only thing that creates long-lasting results. So fine-tune your energy and open yourself to connecting without manipulation. Whatever you're wishing for, the Universe may have something even better in store!

A similar question addresses the phenomenon of people who are connected in some way but have very different desires. Whether you're partners in business or in life, having divergent goals could be a problem. In cases like this, you need to talk to each other and see what options can help you meet in the middle. If you want to live in the mountains and your spouse wants to be in Hawaii, you should both put your intentions out, but work together on somehow making each dream a reality at least some of the time. Be careful not to hope for the other person's failure just so that you can get your way. Wishing for another's downfall—no matter who it is—only draws loss back to you.

Q: What about people who seem to want to block your goals, your success, or even your happiness? Why do you attract that, and what can you do about it?

A: Unfortunately, it's not uncommon to meet with resistance from others. If you've attracted that, don't fault yourself, because it's what you do once the resistance is handed to you that really matters. Perhaps you drew negativity to you because of your own fears, or maybe it's due to the fearful energy that permeates the hearts and minds of so many others. But the sad fact is that unhappy individuals don't like to see others be happy, and those who are unsuccessful long for others to fail, too. There may even be lots of people who feel that they get their power by keeping you down.

Whatever may be motivating them, you have to take a stand. If you really want to make some changes to your energy and your life, you have to intervene on their negativity in some way. First, assert yourself and tell the naysayers that you don't want to hear their predictions of doom. If you can, reduce your exposure to those involved. If it's someone close to you, like a spouse or parent, you may have to have a continuing dialogue requesting support—or at least demanding that the person cease his or her criticism.

In the meantime, place an energetic aura of protection around yourself. Visualize a light sphere of gentle energy all around you, sending any negativity back to the source. From time to time, affirm that their vibration has no influence over you, and that you're always free to move confidently in the direction of your goals. Continue to take action, and become your own greatest advocate and supporter.

Many people have faced such difficulties and still succeeded. Famously, Thomas Edison tried dozens of times to perfect the lightbulb before succeeding. Abraham Lincoln was often laughed at, so he began making jokes about himself. Some of the greatest successes in history endured terrible negativity and moved on to prove that the resisters were wrong.

Q: I really feel as though I'm changing my energy, and I often notice that I don't seem to want to be around some of my old friends as much. What's going on?

A: This is a very common response to arriving at a new consciousness and energetic vibration. The friends who used to resonate with the "old you" may not be a source of comfort anymore because they match your past unhealthy line of thinking. In fact, you may find that you're getting into little squabbles with both family and friends. When vibes don't match, they can actually make people feel jittery and irritable.

As you continue to change, you may also find that old friends resist even more and try to bring you back to your previous patterns of negativity. They like things the way they used to be because everything was familiar and probably empowering to them. You may even be tempted to return to "business as usual" where they're concerned. Fears of loss, the sense of potential grief, and even just a need to please can all be driving influences in that direction.

But don't give in! As your new resonance gets stronger and stronger, you'll attract new friends who match the healthy frequency. And in time, your old pals may come around a bit. Even if they don't, you need to honor yourself and keep moving forward. Your light will be bright enough to draw much more love, support, and camaraderie than you've ever experienced before.

Q: What should I do when I just don't know *what* to do?
A: People experience this sensation at a number of points: when they're overwhelmed by the changes they're working on, when they become so overattached to their goal that they get a bit hysterical, when a major emotional event occurs, or even when they just get off track and lost in the process.

If you reach this state of energetic disorientation for any reason, you have to shut down and reboot. First, do a little meditation where you turn everything over to spirit. Give it all—the goals, the changes, your thoughts, everything—to the Universe. Release it with the intention that your loving, unseen assistants will unscramble things and make it all clear. Send love yourself; bless the situation with no concern for outcomes. Then send the same love and blessings to your own heart, and feel it expanding in peace and release.

Then when you've let it all go, let yourself take a break. Do something where changing your energy or working on your goals is *not* on your mind. Have fun, meet some friends, listen to music, go to a movie, or take a weekend vacation. Take some time away from everything.

When you do come back to it, write down any initial responses to your time off. Create some new intentions about staying balanced, focused, and relaxed. Read them each day while taking a few deep breaths. Remember, never make *anything* mean too much—even when the "anything" has to do with energy and consciousness shifting. As soon as you become attached to it, whatever "it" may be, you push it farther and farther away! So relax, let go, and always follow the path of peaceful pursuit. A happy, tranquil heart will make everything new again.

Continued Action

That journey toward real success requires two types of action:

1. The kind that we've been talking about in this book—the action of consciousness and energy change

2. Specific goal action—the actual steps you need to take to achieve the outcome you desire

Both of these are necessary parts of your continuous process and personal evolution.

Some people have asked me these questions: If consciousness really does create reality, shouldn't we be able to manifest actual results without external action? Aren't our minds powerful enough to do things like lose weight without diet or exercise, levitate in spite of gravity, and attract a million dollars with no outward action?

My answer is qualified. Yes, we should be able to do all that, and our minds and spirits are probably powerful enough—as long as our beliefs, histories, and psyches don't get in the way. The problem is that in our present state, most of us aren't enlightened enough. Just as most kids couldn't perform successful brain surgery, most of us haven't learned enough of the power of consciousness and spirit to defy the physical laws of this world. (At least I know I haven't—or I would have found a way to think myself thin by now!)

This is another paradox of life—what I call the *Paradox of Power*. We have amazing, unlimited abilities, but we've also chosen to live within the physical Universe and the parameters that it creates. For many of us, our expectations of power are limited to our earthly experience of it, and until we're demonstrably more enlightened about our deeper, more profound, innate powers, we'll have to deal with the physical laws and chemical and energetic patterns of our physical Universe. For all but the most enlightened of our species, we have to be willing to take real action if we want to achieve external results.

To facilitate that, make a list of all the steps you need to take. Examine it often and update it as you go along. Set aside time in your day to work on your goals. Visualize the end results of your achievement, but don't forget to imagine yourself in a daily process that's enjoyable and exciting for you. Don't give up, but always be flexible about your plans. This patient but persistent attitude will keep you going.

Remember the hologram! In addition to your goal actions, it's also necessary to take the inner steps required for real personal achievement—the success of the heart and mind. Don't forget that through your own quantum psychology, this type of work is equally influential in the process of getting significant results. So keep in mind the following activities that on the surface seem to have nothing to do with your specific intentions for success, but in reality are all important:

Action of the mind	Optimistic and valuing thoughts, positive and pure intentions
Action of the body	Exercise, deep breathing, rest, healthy nutrition
Action of the spirit	Meditation, prayer, intuition, connection
Action of the heart	Love for self and others, compassion, caring, service

Energy Action

In order to help keep your energy and consciousness goals on track, here are some reminders of things you can do at any time. You can copy these onto cards and also create some of your own. Carry one with you to be the focus of your action intention for that day.

1. Start to develop an awareness of the energy that flows between you and others. Release separation and let the vibrations move. As you allow yourself to feel this resonant connection, greater harmony and synchronicity will bring unexpected blessings to your life.

2. Now and always make the choice to *let go of judgment.* Release comparisons. Recognize the worth and special value that's always inherent in you and everybody else.

3. As you go through your day, remember to make the conscious choice to release attachment! Whether you're obsessing about an old love

or a future goal, take a deep breath and affirm: *I bless that and let it go. As I release, I attract more to me. I choose to live in the energy of a trusting, peaceful presence.*

4. Many times today, stop and appreciate! Think about what you have to be grateful for—whatever you may be doing. Give thanks, breathe deeply, and feel a deep sense of gratitude in your heart.

5. Practice getting in touch with your emotions. Vent the feelings that you become aware of—whether they're about present issues or past events. Make it a priority to write in your journal. Get your emotions out so you don't carry their energy with you.

6. Bring an attitude of quiet peace to the tasks of your daily life. All of life is a meditation, so relax and breathe deeply. Smile and choose to see the peace and beauty all around you.

7. Whatever your goal or desire may be, it's time to let go of the hurry and urgency. Relax and practice the art of surrender. Remember that peace and trust will always get better results than fear and worry. So let go, be patient, and have faith.

8. Take some action toward your goal today. Do so with joy!

9. As you go through your day, remember to keep your focus on the present. Notice when you may be ruminating about the past or worrying about the future, then consciously—and purposely—*let it go!* No matter what you're doing, every moment is a gift. Value your present *now* to create a valuable future.

10. Throughout your day, remember to practice the art of playfulness. Smile and have fun! Be more spontaneous, seeing your life as an adventure. As you bring more joy to your routines, you'll attract much more to enjoy.

11. Spend some time today reconnecting with the power and presence of your own spirit. Meditate on your sacred and eternal identity. Breathe deeply and feel the presence of spirit all around you.

12. Remember to ask for help and guidance, and try to be aware of when and how you get your answers.

13. Remember to make your own goals and happiness a priority. Try to create a balance in your life, and spend at least some time every day taking care of yourself.

14. Intervene in your negative thinking—without condemning yourself for it. Just let it go and step into a positive adjacent possibility. Know that you're choosing a higher and brighter truth.

15. Live in the emotion you want to attract. Look for the things that bring you joy. If you seek success for the happiness it brings, choose that happy outlook right now!

16. Remember your option to *be affirmative*. Read, write, and recite your affirmations every single day. Declare support and positive intentions for yourself, your life, your process, your worthiness, and your value. Say an affirmation now and many times today. Make this your new addiction!

Affirmative Action

For decades, affirmations have been an important force in my life. Although they're often dismissed as being too simplistic, when you repeat them often and with emotional conviction, they can be a powerful tool in redirecting your neural pathways. Following are 50 statements that can help you shift your focus and come to some new conclusions. If you have a hard time embracing any of them for any reason, start the statement with phrases such as these: *I am beginning to, I am learning to,* or *It's safe for me to . . .*

Read these often and add some of your own. Conscious affirmation is always, *always* better than unconscious negation!

1.   *I am comfortable with silence. I use my quiet time to reconnect with my own spirit.*

2. *I affirm myself with a gentle and loving voice each day.*

3. *I am learning to think more highly of myself. I know that I deserve my own high regard.*

4. *At every opportunity I let go of negative thinking. I choose positive, trusting, and nurturing thoughts instead.*

5. *I value my life and myself more and more each day.*

6. *Through my own energy, I have the power to make my life better in every way.*

7. *I know that I have all of the talent and resources I need to magnetize everything I desire.*

8. *I attract respectful people because I send out self-respecting energy.*

9. *I know that I am worthy of a wonderful life.*

10. *I always take responsibility for my own happiness. I find many wonderful things to be happy about each day.*

11. *Every time I look in the mirror, I affirm and acknowledge my value and my deserving.*

12. *I am a worthy and valuable person, deserving of wealth, abundance, and real happiness.*

13. *I create a spirit of self-reliance and self-fulfillment in my daily life. I always take care of myself.*

14. *I truly believe in my ability to accomplish my desires.*

15. *I am releasing urgency and living with trust. I value what I have.*

16. *I embrace my ever-present connection to the Divine.*

17. *I adore my life and my self-loving energy.*

18. *I believe in myself. I value my integrity and my worth.*

19. *I know that I am strong, honest, confident, peaceful, and resourceful.*

20. *Abundant wealth and happiness flow through the Universe, and I am worthy of receiving all that I desire.*

21. *I am one with the Universe. I open myself to the flow of love and blessings all around me.*

22. *I release conflict, and I choose peace.*

23. *Every day, I am becoming more and more aware of my own eternal spirit. I live in the peace my spirit brings.*

24. *I see the Divine in all people. Higher Consciousness connects us all.*

25. *Divine Love fills me up. My life is a meditation and a peaceful prayer.*

26. *With every tranquil thought I think, the energy of peace expands.*

27. *I know that my own energy expands in my life and in the Universe. I choose unconflicted energy now.*

28. *I send my love to all I see. Many times a day, I think, feel, and say the word <u>love</u> with a heartfelt intention.*

29. *I walk and move at a leisurely and comfortable pace. I do everything in an easygoing manner. I am relaxed, and I carry that calming energy to others.*

30. *I embrace a peaceful attitude. I let go of worry, hurry, and the need for control.*

31. *I release competition and choose to see people in a different light. Everyone is a blessing to me.*

32. *I look for the opportunity to help others, to show compassion, and to be of service in many ways.*

33. *I see the value in everyone around me. Together we share the energy of the world.*

34. *I look for the joy in my life and take action to create it in all that I do.*

35. *Every day, I am increasing my focus of appreciation and self-acknowledgment.*

36. *I am learning to appreciate myself and my life more and more each day.*

37. *I enjoy the present and trust in the future. I see my life as an adventure that I create myself.*

38. *My life is full and fulfilling. I look for value in every experience*

39. *I release the need to worry about the future or relive the past. I focus on the present from now on.*

40. *I always take the time to see value in the current moment and activity.*

41. *I am becoming more and more conscious of all that I have to be thankful for.*

42. *I am letting go of lack and only choosing to see value and grace from now on.*

43. *I am proud of myself and my achievements. I acknowledge the effort I make in my life.*

44. *I acknowledge and enjoy my present possessions. I feel a sense of fulfillment right now.*

45. *I know that I have what I need and I am resourceful.*

46. *More and more, I am bringing an attitude of playfulness to my life. I smile, have more fun, and take more risks!*

47. *I am a wonderful, valuable person, deserving of all good things.*

48. *My spirit is strong and present. Divine love is with me now.*

49. *I am choosing to live an affirmative and optimistic life in all that I do.*

50. *I find joy and happiness in the present. I am truly blessed, and I draw endless blessings to me!*

Intention Action

Your intentions are the directional force of both your energy and your consciousness. Therefore, it's extremely helpful to write down your specific goals. I can't count the number of people who have told me that they found an old list of intentions and every one of them had been achieved.

I recently ran into an investment broker who took a seminar of mine five years ago. At that time, he wrote the following intention: *I work for a small investment company in California where six people handle $3 million to $10 million accounts. I am married to a wonderful, gorgeous woman, and we have two healthy kids. I live in a great house with a beautiful yard that a landscaper takes care of.*

None of these conditions were the case at the time. This man had been employed by a big company with lots of "worker bee" brokers who handled relatively small accounts. He lived in a condo and was dating, but he hadn't settled down yet.

When I met him recently, however, he told me that all of the items on his intention list had taken place—right down to the number of people in his company and the size of the accounts they handled! He told me that he had a fantastic wife, a two-year-old boy, and a newborn baby girl.

He said the only detail that didn't happen was the location—he still didn't live in California. But it no longer really mattered to him, because he got what he really wanted and was so very happy. I'm sure he could make that location change happen in time, though. When you focus your intention, the Universe becomes aware of exactly what you want.

So write your specific intentions down. Even if you never look at them again, you've given very clear directions to the current of manifestation.

And don't forget your life intention, which I wrote about in the last chapter. Choose a principle, single quality, or emotion that will help guide the decisions of your life. Write that down, too.

Finally, the following focused intentions—like the earlier energy actions—will assist you in creating and projecting a truly powerful life force. Let these sentiments guide you. Focus on a different one each day, and you'll slowly see some major inner changes that will manifest wonderful experiences in the outside world.

Focused Intentions

1. I am learning to walk the path of peaceful pursuit. I always take joyous action toward my goals, all the while releasing any attachment to the outcome. I create a happy life now and draw more and more happiness to me.

2. I always have the option to do—and think—something different. I constantly remember that I am the one who chooses what I think. Today, I will consider my many adjacent possibilities and begin to choose more self-honoring, loving, and nurturing thoughts.

3. Today I am choosing to value myself, my life, and the people around me. I release separation and notice good things everywhere. I see the worth in all that I do, and I always choose to create a valuable perception of myself and others.

4. I am no longer willing to view myself as a victim. I reclaim my power and choose to take action on my own behalf. I am powerful, capable, and resourceful. I am all that I need.

5. I live with hope. I embrace my goals with excitement and enthusiasm. I always choose to believe in myself. I know that I deserve to have the kind of life I desire, and I expect that the abundant Universe is bringing it to me.

6. Ever moment of my life is a *defining moment* for me. It's the accumulation of all the small choices and everyday thoughts that creates the

energetic current of my life. From now on, I am taking control of all of my "little" moments and defining myself in a new, conscious, and self-actualized way.

7. Today I am choosing to spend more time in silence. I am comfortable with my own company, my thoughts, and my feelings. As I breathe deeply and relax with the stillness around me, I will create a quiet, peaceful resonance within and an attractive vibration in my life.

8. Today I am truly letting go of the attitude of lack. I choose to notice the big and little blessings of my life. I acknowledge and appreciate *all* that I have each and every day.

9. Today I am choosing to live with patience, compassion, and flexibility—both for myself and for others. I know that my energy expands in my life and in my family. I consciously choose to amplify the vibration of love in the world. I send love to all—in my thoughts, my words, my smile, my energy, and my intentions.

10. I am focusing on the energy of honoring in my life. Today, I will look at my choices, behaviors, and thoughts, asking, *Does this honor me?* No matter what, I will muster up the courage to choose the self-honoring action and thought.

11. Tonight when I go to sleep, I will affirm my life and myself. I will visualize my desired outcome and peacefully release it to the abundant Universe, trusting that *this or something better* is coming to me in just the right time and just the right way.

12. Today I am creating a heart-centered consciousness in my approach to life. I let go of analysis, take a deep breath, and let my consciousness float from my head to my heart. Instead of worry, I choose release; instead of fear, I choose trust. I rest in the energy of peace and appreciation, and I let everything else go.

13. Today I am choosing to live with reverence. I look around me and see the Divine in everything and everyone. All of life is a blessing; all of

creation is valuable. I choose to see and appreciate the spark of Divine Love that lives within and unifies us all.

14. Today I look for opportunities to serve. I move through my day with joyous intentions to bring assistance and happiness to others. Whether it's a smile for a passing stranger or some greater opportunity, I know that in the oneness of all life, the energy I give to others is what I also give to myself.

15. Today I am becoming more and more conscious of the energy I am creating. I am more positive in my thoughts, emotions, and choices. I am letting go of *all* negative thinking, and instead I am choosing a higher, brighter vibration and greater optimism in my attitude.

Written Actions and Reactions

Keeping a journal is, in my opinion, absolutely essential if you want to really understand what's going on in your life and your mind. I started my first real journal when I was 19, and I haven't stopped since. Of course, I may miss some days, weeks, or even longer if I'm super busy, but I always go back to it to record and address what's going on.

Use your journal to vent your feelings when they run high and to analyze your thoughts when you catch yourself worrying or brooding too much. The following approach is designed to increase your energy awareness. Add your own questions and comments, and leave plenty of room for self-expression.

This journal starts with a section dedicated to your own personal prayers. You don't have to rewrite them every day. Just add to this part when needed and refer to it often to focus your heartfelt intentions.

Following the prayer list is the daily journal. Try to take at least a little time each morning to write a daily intention or affirmation to focus on that day. You can choose some from this chapter or make up your own according to what you're dealing with at the time. Also pause a moment to decide upon your emotional intention. If you think about it ahead of time, you're more likely to make it happen.

The next section is designed to help you investigate your energy and consciousness production. Some awareness questions will assist you in focusing on what kind of life force you're creating and remind you that you have options when your energy gets off track.

In the evening, remember to contemplate your *appreciation and self-acknowledgment*. Write two or three things or experiences you were grateful for each day, and at least two things you appreciate or acknowledge about yourself. This will help enhance your magnetic energies immensely.

Finally, make sure you think about the image and the thought that you consciously choose to end your day with. This energy will be repeated in your subconscious frequencies—and will be broadcast into the Universe as you sleep. This is one of your most creative times, so use it to build real value.

If you can't write in your journal every day, try to do so at least a few times each week—especially when you're attempting to change your energy. This tool is one of the important ways that you relate to yourself, and it sets up a positive resonance of self-priority and self-awareness that will create an energetic momentum, influencing all of your results to come. Vent, affirm, visualize, and pray. Remembering that your conscious energy determines your destiny, it's time for you to take control.

Here are templates and prompts for you to use in your journal:

Prayer List

1. Every day I send my prayers and loving intentions to these people:

2. Every day I send my prayers and loving intentions to these issues and situations:

3. Prayer for global healing: *Together we join our energy and send our own caring and healing intentions to all the world. May happiness, peace, and Divine healing bless all those who need it now. May Divine Love bring peace to every conflict and healing to every confusion or pain . . . with love in every intention, amen.*

Daily Journal

Morning Reflection

1. Today's affirmation or intention:
2. What emotion am I choosing for today? (For example: patience, relaxation, peace, trust, forgiveness, love, happiness, and so on)

Consciousness and Energy Awareness
(Choose a few of these questions to answer each day.)

1. What have I been most conscious of lately?
2. What can I choose to focus on in order to create a more peaceful and positive consciousness?
3. What has my recent emotional energy been like?
4. What can I do differently to change my feelings and my energy?
5. What have my thoughts been like lately?
6. What new conclusions can I make to create a more positive vibration?

Appreciation and Self-acknowledgment

1. List at least two things you appreciated during your day.
2. List at least two things you appreciated or acknowledge about yourself today.

Evening Reflections

1. Evening image or visualization:
2. Bedtime prayer, affirmation, or intention:

Icons of Adjacent Possibilities

In order to remember my many adjacent possibilities, I like to keep things around me—such as pictures, words, pieces of art, and jewelry—that draw my attention to some optional ideas. The images you've seen in this book are three of the icons that I have in my environment for this purpose. Their symbolism is helpful to me, so I'd like to share their meaning with you now.

The Seven-Pointed Star

All stars are a wonderful metaphor for me because they represent distant suns. Our sun (our closest star) with its life-giving light and heat, has long represented the Divine to me. In fact, I collect representations of the sun and have them all over my home to remind me of our ever-present heavenly source. My nephew tried to count them once, but he gave up when the number was so high that he couldn't keep track. Some people might think that my sun collection is extreme, but everywhere I look, I'm reminded of the Divine light that shines love within and all around me.

The seven-pointed star is a special sun. It represents the seven chakras—or energy centers—of the body, and reminds me to meditate on the power flowing through me. It corresponds with the seven colors of the rainbow, and prompts me to look for the beauty and diversity within my life. It matches the seven days of the week, helping me to never hurry or worry—there's always tomorrow.

The seven points represent the seven heavenly bodies that have influence on the Earth: the moon, the sun, Mercury, Venus, Mars, Saturn, and Jupiter. This reminds me that all of space is my playground, and the energy of all the Universe beats within my heart. The seven points stand for the seven notes of the musical scale, prompting me to listen to the music all around me—the chirping of the birds in the early morning, the wind through the trees on a beautiful spring day, and the laughter of my own children.

The number seven has always been a magical, mystical one, and I look at this to remind me of the magic all around. Life is a mystery—we never know where it's going to go next. The hope of the future is an adventure of our own making, and the star of our own purpose can gently guide us there.

Yin and Yang

The yin-and-yang symbol is an ancient icon that represents the duality of all of nature. Earlier in this book, I talked about the wave/particle duality and the Divine/human duality, two important concepts that I like to keep in mind. The first reminds me that energy is everywhere; the second tells me that God is everywhere, too, and that the spirit and human exist within me in equal measure.

Yin and yang represents the coexistence of the manifest and the unmanifest, what is and what will be vibrating in both the physical and energetic realm. It's a great metaphor for the power of intention. Our thoughts and our life force direct reality now and always.

This symbol also represents the balance that we can create in our lives through our consciousness and intention. Typically speaking, the yin represents the feminine and the yang represents the masculine, but it's important to know that we all have both of those energies within us. We're both active and passive, creative and receptive, logical and intuitive—but it's up to us to choose which energy we want to express at any given time. I like the way this icon reminds me that I can call upon different powers in different circumstances—even if I'm not naturally inclined toward that energy.

So if you tend to be passive, call upon your yang vibration, and focus on being active whenever the need arises. If you tend to be logical and find it difficult to get in touch with your intuition, call upon your yin to open to your intuitive guidance.

Here are the things that yin and yang typically represent. Keep in mind that you can call any of these energies up from your inner self and use them whenever you desire

Yin	Yang
Receptive	Creative
Passive	Active
Dark	Light
Yielding	Firm
Moon (reflective)	Sun (self-illuminated)
Following	Leading
Intuitive	Logical
Right brain	Left brain
Night	Day
Endings	Beginnings
Female	Male
Mother	Father
Soft	Hard
Completion	Initiation
Bringing in	Sending out
Absorptive	Resistant
Expansive	Contracted
Being	Doing

Practice picking an energy from the above list, and focus on it for a few moments several times a day. Just say the word, take a deep breath, and feel what power comes along. In time, you'll be a master of your energy production, and whenever you see a yin-and-yang symbol, you'll always remember that you have the power to choose.

The Calatrava Cross

The history of the Calatrava cross is said to go back more than 4,000 years. Its exact origins and previous meanings are unknown, but it was believed to have secret powers of protection and great good fortune. It came into the hands of the Popes and was passed from one Pontiff to the next. Finally, in 1158, Pope Gregory VIII used it as his standard in a desperate attempt to save a Christian church against an oncoming attack. Short on soldiers, he commissioned shepherds from the fields to fight as knights. They were known as the knights of Calatrava, named after an old Moorish bastion that was being defended.

The Calatrava cross was designed with four anchors, resembling fleurs-de-lis, that unite at the center. This standard was given to the shepherds with the encouragement that it would bring them protection and victory in battle against the superior forces of the Moors. Outnumbered more than ten to one, the knights were still victorious. Since that time, the symbol has represented power, victory, and good fortune. But it also has a deeper meaning, and that's really what I'm reminded of when I see this symbol.

The cross is said to stand for the four triads, with each triad symbolized by each fleur-de-lis. The fleur-de-lis is a three-pointed flower, two outside points facing downward with the center point facing out. This reminds us that we have many options. Some options lead us backward, but some lead us straight ahead. We are all always free to choose which direction we want to take. Here is the story of the four triads.

The Triad of Time

As you've learned, time is an important element in the process of attraction and manifestation. How you perceive it determines your approach to life—and often your results. Therefore, it's important to identify your place in time.

— *Past people* are often reminiscing about some wonderful bygone period that the present just can't live up to, or even more often focusing on a traumatic event that has frozen them in their former misery. Living with old longing, regret, anger, or blame totally disempowers your present moment—the only time that really has any value or strength in your life. Furthermore, if you live in the past, you close the door to your options to experience new events. Your backward focus keeps you from moving in a forward direction.

— *Future people* share a fate similar to past people in that they spend very little time in the present. Instead, they fantasize about or dread what's to come. People believe that it's okay to live in the future as long as they view it positively, but be careful not to fall into the assumption that tomorrow is destined to be better than today.

As you learned regarding the law of paradoxical intent, that belief is toxic to the energy of the present. It sabotages your future intention by creating an energy of unhappiness now. Contentment isn't something that happens; it's something you decide to be now—not tomorrow—because in the reality of time and space, tomorrow never comes.

On the other side of the spectrum, negative futurists are so consumed with fear and worry about the future that they can't bring themselves to really live fully today. They brood and ruminate about the catastrophes to come, always trying to keep control. This thinking only makes the present utterly miserable, an energetic vibration that will ensure more suffering—whether the disaster comes or not.

— *Present people* are free from both of these traps. They realize that they aren't their past, and no matter what has happened they don't have to let it affect how they experience or appreciate this very moment. Smart present people also realize that predicting the future is a waste of time, and they shouldn't worry about events that may or may not become a reality. Losing the potential for joy in the moment is like ignoring a sunny day because of anxiety about the rain.

When you've mastered time, you've mastered the moments. You allow the past and future to be part of your life but not the focus of it. Let go of your history and plan for the months to come, but spend most of your days being in the moment—loving, living, and appreciating now. In the span of your life, it's always now, so live it and enjoy it.

The Triad of Life

The second fleur-de-lis represents the triad of life, the three functions of human experience. As you learned in the chapter on the hologram of success, there are many ways to experience life. As a human being, you vibrate in three important ways—body, mind, and soul. While it's important to prioritize each of these things, the type of energy and focus you shower on each will influence the results of your life.

— *Body people* focus on the physical, and many of their decisions concern some sort of physical obsession. Some examples are alcoholics, anorexics, junkies, binge eaters, "sun worshippers," and even bodybuilders. These folks are obsessed with the experiences of the body. They may be unaware that their fixations consume most of their attention and energy, but the reality is that most of the time, these addictions become their primary concern. In the end, body people can't sustain happiness. Whatever quick fix they get from their momentary indulgence eventually levels off. While it's okay to prioritize your physical health, obsessing about material experience only takes you out of the other powers in your life.

— *Mind people* tend to be overly analytical; every decision must make sense. They worry and work things out, often ignoring their intuition and inner guidance. While living an objective life seems practical, there are very few things in this world that are entirely without gray areas. Relationships, love, joy, sadness—all are hard to put a quantitative spin on. They need to be experienced and understood.

Mind people are rarely happy because they're too analytical to just relax and enjoy. They focus on perfection, worry about success, are concerned with safety, and always try to protect themselves. Spontaneity is rarely experienced when you're living in your mind. Everything becomes a part of a puzzle that has to be solved. There's no room for beautiful sunsets, relaxing meals, or leisurely activities—and even when these are allowed, they're often completely missed because of the analysis that's going on inside.

So much of this book has been about how to best use the powers of your mind. You have strength there, but you have to direct it. The conclusions you make can free you from worry and bring you happiness instead. In fact, the best choice your brain can make would be simply getting out of your head!

— *Soulful people* live in experience, not in analysis. When you drop your consciousness from your head to your heart, you release the mental analysis and get in touch with your soul. In order to master your life, you must be soulful. If you're in this category, you have a great respect for the mind and body, but your soul knows it will never die. It sees its eternity and trusts. It lets go of striving because it knows that all of life is merely a journey back home.

Soul-centered people rarely see anything as a problem. Everything seems to take the form of an opportunity—to grow, to learn, and to remember their truth. This is because they see everything from a wider perspective, an eternal view that knows there's nothing really to worry about when they're in the safety and eternal love of the Divine.

This magnificent energy of the spirit can lift you up and bring you peace and joy. In fact, all of the feelings you long for are yours when you realize that how you feel is only a decision away—the decision to live in your heart and soul.

The Triad of Awareness

Mastery of time and life are necessary if you want to be a happy, joyful person, but they represent only part of the puzzle. The third piece is awareness, the triad of desire and consciousness creation.

— The *hopefuls* seem to believe that they have little control over what happens in their lives. They can be extremely hard workers, but believe that chance plays an integral part.

Hope is fine if you feel it with excitement and enthusiastic knowledge, but if you use the word *hope* to signal to the world that you're unsure, you relinquish your power to move forward with certainty. You need to elevate your state of awareness and come from the emotional energy of being definite. Even if you live for the moment and act from your heart and soul, as the two previous triads suggest, you can never truly be happy if all you do is linger in uncertain hope.

— Next are the *believers,* who are on a higher level of consciousness. To believe in something is far stronger than to just hope for it; it's a defining statement, not a wishful one. These folks tend to live happy lives because they've chosen to stand for something. They trust in themselves and their capabilities, and that moves them forward.

While these people are much more aware of their surroundings and their ability to change what happens, belief can still leave the door open to some doubt and regret. And when the outcome doesn't meet their expectations, even this group can get very upset. This is because they honestly believe that they know the preferred conclusion for every situation. Their belief is so strong that they often try to impose their will with rigid inflexibility. This is where they lose their power.

Believers are a thousand times better off than hopefuls, but it's better still to come from a consciousness of knowing—that you are safe and that there's no wrong outcome. This reflects the Paradox of Experience, the fact that although the reality of any event may be indisputable, the quality of the experience lies solely in your own interpretation.

— *Knowers* have the ability to look at any result and find the beauty and opportunity in it. Nothing is good or bad. Either something honors them or it doesn't; and if it doesn't, they can let it go.

To know is to be fully conscious and to be aware of all the power you truly have. To come from a place of knowing is to exclude any other possibility—to recognize that you can be happy in spite of what may be going on, you can be strong no matter what befalls you.

This means mastering awareness—taking control of your consciousness and bringing wisdom and equanimity into your life. *Know* that you're the peaceful and purposeful creator of your own destiny.

The Triad of Creation

For something to be created, it must first be conceived in thought, put into expression in word, and set in motion through action. All of these things must happen, but it's important to process your consciousness creation all the way to the end.

— Some people stay in the contemplation stage for much of their lives. These are the *dreamers,* who may have a lot of mental activity, but often get stuck right there. They contemplate a better life and a better existence, but are very slow in doing anything about it. This group is often stopped by inertia, the simple inability to just get going. They also can let fear and distraction keep them from their dreams. They're afraid to take risks, and although they can easily visualize their goals, they often can't figure out how to get there. Although dreaming is the first part of desire, they have to move on to find success.

— The next part of the triad gets stuck in words. The *talkers* have the concept and are able to express it, but they don't seem to be able to follow it through. Dreamers and talkers are in the same boat in the sense that their energies stop short of really achieving their goals.

These are the "woulda, shoulda, coulda" people—many have good intentions but not the willingness to do the work. In truth, the biggest failure isn't to try and fail, but to fail to try at all. Talkers may plan and brag about their projects, but all too often they make the stories more important than the adventure of the action at hand.

— The third part of this final triad is about *action people.* Thought, word, and action are the three elements of creation. To act without thinking or planning can be dangerous, but to plan without acting leads nowhere. All three energies work together: Get the idea and plan it out; then act and keep on taking action. Some people wait for happiness to come along, while some chase it in the external world. If you're an action person, you decide to create happiness for yourself, and you're willing to do what is necessary to bring authentic joy to your life in a myriad of ways.

This is the secret of the four triads: When you can be in the moment, use your heart as your compass, know that there are no accidents, and act with joy and purpose, then you've found your power. When you live in this way, you've mastered time, life, creation, and consciousness—all from exercising your power to be present, soulful, knowing, and active.

Keep in mind that you always have these four choices. Whatever difficulty may be going on, choosing one of these powers is guaranteed to get you unstuck. Ask yourself, *What do I need to bring to this situation? Is it presence, a sense of my eternal spirit, a consciousness of my own power and choices, or an action that I need to take?* Think of these options and pick one. In doing so, you'll soon become the master of your life, for there's no problem that one of these powers can't help you solve.

Herein lies your prosperity: It's finding your power in the process that counts. The measure of real success is living in the peace, pleasure, and purpose of pursuing your own eternal truth. Live now in the happy ending you want to create. For in the long reach of your life, you will find that the option of love and joy lives in every moment—and every success begins with that choice.

EPILOGUE

Deep within you is the voice of your eternal Self saying,
"Remember me? I am the Source of all you need."

— **SANDRA ANNE TAYLOR**

A lot has been written about the Laws of Attraction and Manifestation. When you get into the science, you'll invariably find that the common denominator is always thought. Yes, it really matters what's in your mind, so when you're talking about success, this is always the place to start.

It's easy to say, "Change your thinking," and sometimes it's actually quite easy to do. But there are times—especially when you're in the thick of a difficult situation—when reversing your fearful conclusions would be like trying to turn the tide of the mighty Mississippi River. Yet these are the periods that need your intervention the most! Don't worry about the river of issues swirling all around you; just turn the tide of *one* moment— just one. An instant of letting go, of not needing to have all the answers, of trust and self-love—just one moment changes everything.

Honor your feelings, but beware of the times that you want to hold on to your righteous indignation and victimization because those vibrations will never take you where you really want to go. And there are times when you feel so hurt and betrayed that you just don't know what to do next. I know—I've been there! It's a paralysis of mind and heart that stops your energy cold. Let yourself ride it out. Take some time to cry and brood, and then gather your resources. Vent all of the hurt and angry feelings, but *don't* give in to the conclusions around them. Instead, stand up! Stand up for yourself and for your life. Be your own best friend, be your greatest advocate, and give yourself gentle love.

The inner secrets of success can be found in your thoughts, and not just the ones about what you want, which are actually a very minor part of the process. (And they're a relatively easy part once you've mastered the other thoughts of daily life.) The real secret of success can be found in the sense of your own value, your worthiness, your amazing power, and your eternal beauty!

Never forget your eternal source—and your timeless identity. This is, in fact, the most powerful part of your holographic consciousness. When you activate this connection and infuse your whole life with spirit, your inner light will shine through every intention, goal, and desire.

Your consciousness moves through the Universe, creating your destiny —connecting with the consciousness of all others to co-create the destiny of humankind. Just as your thoughts have power in your life, they also have the power to influence the direction of all people.

We're in constant connection with each other, an inseparable and undivided whole. And our joint energy has the power to move mountains, start and end wars, travel through time, and determine the very future of our planet. In this we must take mutual responsibility. Every thought of ours—along with every choice—moves into a field of consciousness that expands and influences everyone else.

So your choice to love yourself, your refusal to fear and hate, your encouragement of self and others—all of these move energy into the field of loving consciousness. And when that expands, all of humankind will move in a new direction toward a stronger intention of peace, compassion, and understanding. To make that happen, though, you must first create that powerful intention for yourself.

You no longer have to live in fear and self-doubt. However strong they may be, your old beliefs can be turned around with each and every conscious choice of thought. Reverse the concepts that no longer honor you, and you'll start to create a new psychology—a quantum psychology that connects your highest life force with all of the Universe.

So remember this as your truth: Your soul is a brilliantly shining light in the firmament of eternity, and your journey here is one of adventure, growth, and expanding love. Your spirit knows—and it's time for you to remember—how truly, flawlessly, and impeccably valuable you already are. When you embrace this truth, every kind of success can be yours.

ACKNOWLEDGMENTS

First we want to thank Candace Pert for her loving and supportive words in the Foreword and, along with her husband Mike Ruff, for wisdom, laughter, and newfound friendship.

For the caring, supportive love of our family—Sarah Marie Klingler; Benjamin Earl Taylor, Jr.; Vica Taylor; Jenyaa Taylor; Devin Staurbringer; Yvonne Taylor; Kevin and Kathryn Klingler; and Rosie and Carol Staurbringer.

Unending gratitude for the incredible people at Hay House, including Louise Hay, Reid Tracy, Jill Kramer, Jessica Kelley, Jacqui Clark, Richelle Zizian, Christy Salinas, Charles and Summer McStravick, Diane Ray, and *all* of the lovely people at this wonderful publishing company.

For the tireless effort, industry, and creativity of our business manager, Noreen Paradise; and for the long hours, late nights, and always good humor of our typist, Rhonda Lamvermeyer.

To our inspiring colleagues: Wayne Dyer, Donna Eden, David Feinstein, Peggy McColl, John Holland, Colette Baron-Reid, Carmen Herra, John C. White, Barbara Freedman, Drs. Jeremiah and Deanna Freedman, Tom Newman, B. Anne Gehman, Wayne Knoll, Ben Gleisser, and Dennis Kucinich.

To the family of our heart—Barbara Van Rensselaer, Marilyn Verbus, Ed Conghanor, Julianne Stein, Melissa Matousek, Tom and Ellie Cratsley, Karen Petkac, Michele Dregas, Valerie Darville and Julia White, Esther

Jalylatie, Delores, Donna and Kathy Maroon, Thomas Bagiackis, and Pat Davidson—so much love to you all.

To our Lily Dale family: Sue Glasier, Joanne Taft, Barbara Sanson, Alpha Husted, Norve Loomis, Martie Hughes, Shelly Takei, Connie Griffith, Stephanie Turachak, Elaine Thomas, Jaccolin and Joanne Franchina, Tim Brainard, Carolyn Sampson, Jessie Furst, and to all our friends at the Dale.

Very special thanks to Fred Cuellar of Diamond Cutters International for the fascinating conversation and for my first Calatrava cross—thank you for the information and the reminder of adjacent possibilities!

To Jeff Garton and Cathy Yin, thank you for the beautiful poem.

To the wonderful coaches, consultants, and counselors I've worked with, including Michael Freedman, Tom Cratsley, Kathy Atkinson, Jason Barton, Mariana Cooper, and Robin Gardner.

A very special thank-you to my friends at the Tivoli Lodge, Diane and Bob Lazier, Ed Moulton, and Mark Asoian. Thanks for giving me a beautiful place to write in the summer and stay in the winter when I'm skiing the most spectacular slopes of Vail, Colorado.

And speaking of Vail, thank you to the great people at Unity of the Mountains, including Don Bissett and Robert Bump; and to all of the Unity churches I've had the privilege to speak at. It has always been a pleasure.

To our spirit family—Anna and Charles Salvaggio, Ron Klingler, Rudy Staurbringer, Earl Taylor, Chris Cary, Flo Bolton, Flo Becker, Adam and Mary Staurbringer, Tony, Raphael, Jude, and of course the Divine Consciousness that lives in all things and loves in all ways.

Finally, I want to thank all of you who have shared your beautiful energy and support in so many ways—from your kind thoughts to your incredible e-mails. I can't express how much your loving connections have meant to me. It is my hope that we can all share a caring intention with and for each other, joining together to expand the consciousness of love, compassion, and *real* success throughout the world.

SUGGESTED READING

The Attention Revolution, B. Alan Wallace, Ph.D. Somerville, MA: Wisdom Publications, 2006.

Beyond the Quantum, Michael Talbot. New York, NY: Bantam, 1988.

The Biology of Belief, Bruce Lipton, Ph.D. Santa Rosa, CA: Mountain of Love/ Elite Books, 2005.

Chakra Meditation Kit, Monte Farber and Amy Zerner. New York, NY: The Enchanted World, 2006.

The Divine Matrix, Gregg Braden. Carlsbad, CA: Hay House, 2007.

Elemental Mind, Nick Herbert. New York, NY: Penguin, 1993.

Energy Medicine, Donna Eden. New York, NY: Putnam, 1998.

Everything You Need to Know to Feel Go(o)d, Candace B. Pert, Ph.D., with Nancy Marriott. Carlsbad, CA: Hay House, 2006.

Feel Happy Now!, Michael Neill. Carlsbad, CA: Hay House, 2008.

The Field, Lynne McTaggart. New York, NY: HarperCollins, 2002.

The Genie in Your Genes, Dawson Church, Ph.D. Santa Rosa, CA: Elite Books, 2007.

The God Theory, Bernard Haisch. San Francisco, CA: Weiser Books, 2006.

The Heartmath Solution, Doc Childre and Howard Martin, with Donna Beech. New York, NY: HarperCollins, 1999.

The Holographic Paradigm, Ed. Ken Wilber. Boston, MA: New Science Library, 1985.

The Holographic Universe, Michael Talbot. New York, NY: HarperCollins, 1991.

The Intelligent Heart, David McArthur and Bruce McArthur. Virginia Beach, VA: A.R.E. Press, 1997.

Intuition & Beyond, Sharon A. Klingler. London, England: Random House UK, 2002.

Journey Through the Chakras, Colette Baron-Reid. Carlsbad, CA: Hay House, 2007 (audio CD).

Mind into Matter, Fred Alan Wolf, Ph.D. Needham, MA: Moment Point Press, 2001.

Molecules of Emotion, Candace B. Pert, Ph.D. New York, NY: Scribner, 1997.

Mysticism and the New Physics, Michael Talbot. New York, NY: Penguin, 1981.

The Power of Intention, Dr. Wayne W. Dyer. Carlsbad, CA: Hay House, 2004.

Power of the Soul, John Holland. Carlsbad, CA: Hay House, 2007.

Psychic Navigator, John Holland. Carlsbad, CA: Hay House, 2004.

Psychosomatic Wellness, Candace B. Pert, Ph.D. New York, NY: Magic Bullets, 2004 (audio CD).

Quantum Reality, Nick Herbert. New York, NY: Anchor, 1985.

The Quantum Self, Danah Zohar. New York, NY: Quill, 1990.

Remembering the Future, Colette Baron-Reid. Carlsbad, CA: Hay House, 2006.

The Six Pillars of Self-Esteem, Nathaniel Branden. New York, NY: Bantam, 1994.

The Spiritual Universe, Fred Alan Wolf. Portsmouth, NH: Moment Point Press, 1999.

Taking the Quantum Leap, Fred Alan Wolf. New York, NY: Harper & Row, 1989.

Ten Days to Self-Esteem, David D. Burns, M.D. New York, NY: HarperCollins, 1993.

Train Your Mind, Change Your Brain, Sharon Begley. New York, NY: Ballantine Books, 2007.

The Vibrational Universe, Kenneth James Michael MacLean. Ann Arbor, MI: Loving Healing Press, 2006.

Your Destiny Switch, Peggy McColl. Carlsbad, CA: Hay House, 2007.

ABOUT THE AUTHORS

Sandra Anne Taylor is an international speaker, counselor, and corporate consultant who lectures throughout the world on the power of consciousness and personal energy. Her *New York Times* best-selling book *Quantum Success* is receiving worldwide acclaim for its enlightening approach to the field of attraction and achievement. Rich in practical application and easy to understand principles, *Quantum Success* has been called "the real science of consciousness creation."

In 2001, Sandra's first book for Hay House, *Secrets of Attraction,* applied the Universal Laws to the pursuit of love. Her in-depth nine-CD audio seminar, *Act to Attract,* is the first comprehensive audio program relating the principles of modern science to the experience of romantic attraction.

For more than 25 years, Sandra was a counselor in a private psychology practice working with individuals and couples in the treatment of anxiety, depression, addiction, and relationship issues. She teaches the principles of quantum psychology—the powerful connection between mind and manifestation—bringing exceptional clarity and practicality to the science of personal attraction. She has been interviewed on television and radio all over the world and in many national magazines, including *Cosmopolitan, Woman's World, Family Circle, Today's Black Woman, Redbook,* and *Success,* as well as *New Idea* in Australia. Her books are available in 17 languages and dozens of countries around the globe.

Website: **www.sandrataylor.net**

Sharon A. Klingler was originally inspired to investigate greater consciousness as a result of her extraordinary experiences as an identical twin. She lectures all over the world on such subjects as reincarnation, spiritual mastery, intuitive development, spirit communication, and public mediumship for professionals. A member of the International Mediums League and Lily Dale Mediums League, Sharon has demonstrated her skill in spirit communication on three continents, from Europe to the South Pacific.

Her first book was *Intuition & Beyond,* published by Random House in London. Her other titles include *Travel into Your Past Lives, Drawing on Your Intuition, Life with Spirit,* and *Divine Connections.* Her acclaimed program *Speaking to Spirit* is a complete home-study seminar for intuitive and mediumship development.

Her articles and reviews have been featured in publications around the world including *Daily Express* (London), *Now* magazine (Sydney), *Eve* magazine (London), and *Creations* magazine (New York). Sharon's appearances include ITV England, Vision TV Canada, NBC, ABC, CBS, and the BBC.

Sharon is a leading international intuitive who has run a successful private practice for more than 25 years with high-profile clients around the world. It's her desire that all people know the great presence of spirit—both the spirit within them and the guides beyond the veil who seek to share their knowledge and assistance.

Website: **www.sharonklingler.com**

★★★

Together, Sharon and Sandra cofounded Starbringer Associates, a speaker and consultant agency that produces audio seminars for personal and business enhancement. For more information—or to schedule lectures, seminars, or private consultations with Sandra or Sharon—call: (440) 871-5448, or contact them at:

Starbringer Associates
871 Canterbury Rd., Unit B
Westlake, OH 44145
www.starbringerassociates.com

Sandra Anne Taylor
P.O. Box 362
Avon, OH 44011

Hay House Titles of Related Interest

YOU CAN HEAL YOUR LIFE, the movie, starring Louise L. Hay & Friends
(available as a 1-DVD program and an expanded 2-DVD set)
Watch the trailer at: **www.LouiseHayMovie.com**

ASK YOUR GUIDES: *Connecting to Your Divine Support System,*
by Sonia Choquette

THE DIVINE MATRIX: *Bridging Time, Space, Miracles, and Belief,*
by Gregg Braden

GETTING IN THE GAP: *Making Conscious Contact with God
Through Meditation,* by Dr. Wayne W. Dyer

HOW TO HEAR YOUR ANGELS, by Doreen Virtue

INTERPERSONAL EDGE: *Breakthrough Tools for Talking to Anyone,
Anywhere, about Anything,* by Daneen Skube, Ph.D.

THE LAW OF ATTRACTION: *The Basics of the Teachings of Abraham®,*
by Esther and Jerry Hicks

THE POWER OF INTENTION: *Learning to Co-create Your World Your Way,*
by Dr. Wayne W. Dyer

POWER vs. FORCE: *The Hidden Determinants of Human Behavior,*
by David R. Hawkins, M.D., Ph.D.

YOUR DESTINY SWITCH: *Master Your Key Emotions,
and Attract the Life of Your Dreams!* by Peggy McColl

All of the above are available at your local bookstore,
or may be ordered by contacting Hay House (see last page).